TONY NORTHRUP'S DSLR BOOK

HOW
TO
CREATE

STUNNING DIGITAL
PHOTOGRAPHY

Mason Press, Inc.

ACKNOWLEDGEMENTS

First, I'd like to thank the readers that have sent me feedback, allowing me to improve the book even after the first release. Thank you, Paul Reiser, Erkki Alvenmod, Jeff Bissonnette, Evan Bobbit, Yannick Ciancanelli, Brendon Code, Nick Dahlke, Fedor Duhrmann, Britton Graefensteiner, Yannick Ciancanelli (yes, I'm thanking him twice), Tamera Hamblin Shibuya, Craig Pettigrew, John-Paul Cosentino, Greg Prince, Luis Hurtado, Lucky Fonseka, Jake Taylor, John Monju, Tom Jones, Debbie Robinson, Kay Stimer, Gisele Duprez, Gary Thurman, Billy Gray, Cindy Ellstrom, Ali Hasan, Moniek Grootenhuis, Martin Cardoza, Jon Howard, Catherine Jones, Mike Cooper, Jared Frazin, Edward Van Deventer, Tony James, Evgeny Garanin, Mark C. Thomas, Martin Silvestre, and A. Shields!

I've spent five years writing this book, and in that time, I learned to rely on many of my family and friends. I have to thank my models: Tyler Rheaume; Summer, Lily, and J.P. Antonino; Megan McSweeny; Justin and Jessica Eckert; Frankie Occhionero; Aja Filardi; Jamie O'Shea and Liz Filardi; and Madelyn Knowles.

I'd also like to thank my reviewers: Kevin Girard, Jose B. Gonzales, Brendon Code, and Kurt Dillard. Not only do I owe you thanks, but every one of my readers does, too.

Most importantly, I have to thank Chelsea, who was my publisher, co-photographer, editor, designer, shoot planner, location scout, principal model, and who eventually became my wife. I love you, Chelsea.

Published by:

Mason Press, Inc.
139 Oswegatchie Rd.
Waterford, CT 06385

Second printing

ISBN: 978-0-9882634-0-6

Printed and bound in the United States of America by Signature Book Printing, www.sbpbooks.com

Editor: Chelsea Northrup
Video Editors: Justin Eckert, Siobhan Midgett
Copyeditors: Jose B. Gonzales, Chelsea Northrup
Designer: Chelsea Northrup
Technical Reviewers: Kevin Girard, Kurt Dillard
Illustrators: Charlie Schaltz, Katie Mamula
Proofreader: Tanya Egan Gibson

For my daughter, Madelyn

Table of Contents

Introduction

Please read this! I'll tell you how to get free stuff and how to use this book. First, to receive the free updates and access the Facebook group, register your purchase at *sdp.io/signup*. Registration is optional, of course, and you don't have to register to see the videos. If you have a problem with anything, send me a message at *tony@northrup.org*.

This book includes many unique benefits:

- **Video training**. This book includes more than 14 hours of fast-paced, hands-on photography training videos.

- **Mentoring**. Optionally, join our private Facebook group by registering at *sdp.io/signup*. Post your questions or photos for help and feedback from Tony, Chelsea, and other readers. Please post only one picture per day!

- **Lifetime updates**. I plan to update this book as long as I'm alive so that it will stay current with the latest camera and software technologies. You'll get those lifetime updates for free when you register.

- **It provides hands-on lessons and quizzes**. Most chapters include an optional online quiz and hands-on practices to help you apply and remember the lessons.

- **It uses no stock photography**. Chelsea and I took every photo in this book, so you know we can teach you how to take them. Most photo books use stock photography.

- **Free ebook**. We'll send you a link to download your ebook when we process your registration. Keep it on your tablet or smartphone for quick reference while out shooting.

Throughout this book, you'll see links to the book's videos. In fact, there's one directly above this paragraph. Type the URL into any

To watch a video **introduction,** scan the QR code or visit:

sdp.io/Intro

web browser to watch the video. You can also scan the QR code using your smartphone or tablet. If you haven't used QR codes before, they're just an easier way to type a link to a website. You can find a free app by searching your mobile device's app store for "QR."

It's particularly important that you watch the introduction video on this page, because in it Chelsea and I will provide detailed information about how to use this book and how to get all the benefits that come with this book.

Chelsea and I have a weekly live show on YouTube about photography that includes our reviews of actual reader photos. To watch it, and new tutorial videos when we release them, visit *sdp.io/yt* and subscribe to our YouTube channel.

If you want to see new photos that we make, like our Facebook page at *fb.com/NorthrupPhotography*. You can find my personal Facebook page at *fb.com/tony.northrup* or follow me on Twitter at *@TonyNorthrup*. If you have a photography question, post it in the private Facebook group at *sdp.io/fb*. If you have a problem with the book, email me at *tony@northrup.org*.

One request: when someone compliments your pictures, tell them you learned from *Tony Northrup's Stunning Digital Photography*. We've spent six years creating this book, and we hope to spend the rest of our lives improving it and supporting readers. Making photos and helping people is what we love to do. If we're going to make this work, however, we need your help spreading the word.

QUICK TIPS

Let's get started with some quick tips that can drastically improve your photography in about 20 minutes. If you feel you've already mastered the basics, you can skip ahead to Chapter 2.

TAKE LOTS OF PICTURES (AND DELETE MOST OF THEM)

I would never condone thoughtless photography, but taking multiple pictures will produce better results in some situations.

The more a scene is changing, the more pictures you should take. If a soccer player is making a drive for the goal, hold down the shutter and keep shooting until she's done celebrating. It's much easier to delete all but one of those pictures than it is to recreate the action to capture the perfect moment.

In particular, take multiple pictures of people. Even if you're just snapping a shot of your friends at a party, take four or five shots. Later, you can flip through your pictures and delete all but the best shot.

For example, in the sequence of photos in Figure 1-1, holding down the shutter paid off. I took about 50 pictures of that moment; the more important a photo, the more shots you should take.

TRY DIFFERENT VIEWPOINTS

Most people hold the camera at eye-level to take a picture. This provides a realistic depiction of what you see, but it doesn't always show a subject's most interesting angle.

For smaller subjects, including kids, dogs, and cats, kneel down to see them eye-to-eye. For flowers, lie on the ground and shoot up to show the sun or the sky in the background. If you have a tilt screen, use it.

You can also go even higher than normal. For people, stand on stairs or a chair and have them look up at you. High perspectives and wide-angle lenses create an almost cartoonish distortion by making the person's head look larger than the rest of his or her body.

Chances are good that the perfect angle isn't the way you walked up to the subject. Walk around your subject and think about:

- How the subject appears from that angle.
- How the light falls on the subject. Especially when the sun is low on the horizon, changing your viewpoint can dramatically change the lighting.
- What you see in the background. Most beginning photographers spend all their time looking at the subject and never think about background distractions. Sometimes, walking a few feet to the side, or stepping back and zooming in, will give you a much more pleasing background.

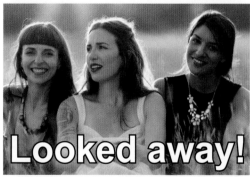

Figure 1-1: Digital film is free. Take lots of pictures and keep only the best!

To watch a video with **6 quick tips,** scan the QR code or visit:

sdp.io/SixTips

Figure 1-2 shows a handful of different viewpoints of the same subject—the Eiffel Tower. Which perspective you prefer is entirely subjective, but they're all very different because I varied my angle and distance.

You don't have to get the perfect angle with one shot. For best results, combine this with the "take lots of pictures" technique. Turn the camera sideways. Zoom in. Say something funny to make people laugh. Crouch down to get a low angle, or hold the camera above your head to get a high angle. Then, delete all but the best shot.

DITCH THE LENS CAP, CAMERA BAG

You're going to think I'm crazy, but I never, ever use a lens cap or camera bag when I'm out shooting.

I did use a camera bag and a lens cap the first couple of years I used a camera; I was very careful about it because everyone had warned me that if I didn't, I'd surely get scratches on my lens that would ruin the all-important sharpness of my photos. Every time I'd want to take a photo, I'd unzip my camera bag, pull my camera out, remove the lens cap, and finally take the picture. Then, I would reverse the whole process to put the camera away.

The bag and lens cap made me miss too many great pictures and slowed down my learning. It was simply too time-consuming to get the

Figure 1-2: Changing your viewpoint can create drastically different pictures of the same subject.

camera ready to take a picture. Any fleeting moment (kids, wildlife, street photography) would be lost by the time I removed all my camera protection, and I was more reluctant to take still-life photos because it took me so long to grab a shot.

Now, I use a shoulder strap to carry my camera and protect the lens using only a lens hood. It takes me about a second to take a picture. Some of my lenses have a decade of hard use, and they're completely scratch-free.

Some people will tell you to use a UV filter to protect your lens. Filters reduce the image quality by requiring light to pass through an unnecessary layer, and they can also introduce *flaring* (discussed in Chapter 5, "Problem Solving") and vignetting. The cheap filter *will* scratch, which might make you think it's saving your lens, but your lens (typically made of glass) is actually pretty scratch-resistant. For those reasons, I don't recommend using a UV filter.

If you do get some damage that a bag or lens cap would have protected you from, all the extra shots you got will make it worthwhile. Plus, you won't ever notice the effect of minor scratches in your pictures.

LEARN YOUR CAMERA

You'll be surprised how much your photography can improve just by knowing how to use your camera. Don't panic; I'm not going to make you read your entire manual. For now, just read the pages that tell you how to:

- Turn the flash on and off.
- Select continuous shooting.
- Set the camera's timer.
- Select aperture priority and shutter priority.
- View the histogram.

Because readers have so many different cameras, this book can't always tell you exactly which buttons to push on your camera. However, I have created free video tutorials

To see our free video tutorials for popular camera models, visit:

sdp.io/tutorials

that show you how to do everything you need for this book using many popular cameras. You can see them at *sdp.io/tutorials*. If you don't see your camera, choose a similar model.

LEARN TO USE FILL FLASH AND BOUNCE FLASH

Flash isn't just for dark spaces. Use fill flash outdoors when your subject is backlit to fill in shadows and create catch lights in your model's eyes. Use bounce flash indoors to softly light both the foreground and the background.

Figure 1-3 (on the next page) shows two outdoor snapshots. Because the sun was behind Chelsea (my wife, co-photographer, and editor), her face is in shadow. Turning the flash on balanced the foreground light with the sun. The second shot shows my favorite tip for outdoor portraits: Have the model stand with his or her back to the sun and turn on flash. The sunlight will cause the hair to glow, and the flash will light your model's face.

USE YOUR PICTURES

Don't wait until your pictures are a distant memory before looking at them. There are many different ways you can use your pictures, and the more you do, the better you'll get:

- Make prints from sites like *Shutterfly.com* and *MPix.com*, frame them, and hang them on your walls.
- Post your pictures on Facebook and tag people.
- Put a digital picture frame in a prominent location in your house.
- Create a photo book (available at *Shutterfly. com* and *MPix.com*) using pictures from a trip or party.

To watch a video comparing **online print services,** visit:

sdp.io/Prints

Once you're feeling confident with your camera, start participating in online photo communities. As a reader of this book, I invite you to visit the Stunning Digital Photography Reader's group on Facebook and post your pictures on our wall. Chelsea and I visit the page almost every day to answer questions and give feedback, and thousands of other readers will help, too. Even if you don't feel like sharing a picture or asking a question, you can learn a lot just by looking at other people's pictures.

To watch a video on **Creating an Online Portfolio,** visit:

sdp.io/Showoff

Other photo communities include Flickr, Photo.net, and DeviantArt. If you're feeling competitive, enter pictures in one of the *DPReview.com* free challenges. The best photographers at each of these sites are truly inspirational, so do your best to learn from them, rather than be intimidated by them. You can also get feedback from other photography enthusiasts. Generally, people are very supportive, so if you'd like criticism, ask for it!

Once you get a few pictures you like, you should create an online portfolio. A portfolio showcases your best 10-15 photos. It's a great way to show the world what an amazing photographer you've become, but even more importantly, it's the best way to keep track of your progress as you learn photography.

KNOW YOUR FINAL FORMAT

Think about how you're going to use your pictures when you press the shutter. For example, if you have a wall space that would be perfect for a vertical 8x10" print, shoot the

Figure 1-3: Use flash even in bright light to remove shadows.

picture vertically, and leave a little room at the top and bottom so you can crop the edges to 8x10" (because most cameras create pictures that would need to be printed at 8x12").

On the other hand, if your favorite place to display pictures is a horizontal digital picture frame in your kitchen, be sure to take horizontal pictures so you can use the entire space. If you must display a small version of the picture (such as in a small picture frame or the web), zoom in close to your subject and compose the picture as simply as possible. If you plan to display a large version of the picture, zoom out to show more detail.

If you're not sure how you'll use a picture, take both horizontal and vertical pictures, and leave room for cropping.

MAKE A GREAT THUMBNAIL

Pictures on the Internet, including Facebook, Twitter, and other social media sites, always start with a very challenging format: the thumbnail. Thumbnails are tiny versions of photos that you see when you browse, and if a thumbnail catches your eye, you'll click on it to see the full-sized version of a picture. Therefore, if you're sharing photos on the web, you need to make great thumbnails, or nobody will see the full-sized picture. Like all small-format pictures, thumbnails should have simple subjects that fill the frame and no distractions.

For example, consider the popular photography site, 500px. All the most popular photos on the site have simple subjects that are clearly visible when the image is scaled down to a 280x280 pixel thumbnail. If the thumbnail doesn't grab a viewer's attention, they won't click on it to see the full-size picture. This simple fact means many artistic but complex photos go unseen.

Even if you have a 50 megapixel camera, you need to think about each photo's 0.08 megapixel thumbnail. Consider the eight thumbnails in Figure 1-4: which catches your eye first? For most people, it's the picture of the duck (the third picture on the bottom row). The thumbnail is bright and colorful, and it's easy to see the subject. When people see the prints in the real world, however, they prefer the second photo on the top row. The complexity of that cityscape works great in a large format, but its lousy thumbnail means it'll never get many clicks on the web.

GET ANOTHER OPINION

My favorite pictures are rarely other people's favorites. Sometimes a photographer's emotions or focus on the technical details of a picture, like sharpness and contrast, can hinder his or her ability to judge the aesthetics that most non-photographers can just feel. Outside opinions, no matter who they're from, are valuable.

Figure 1-4: Only pictures that make great thumbnails get seen on the web.

For an overview of a free editing tool, scan the QR code or visit:

sdp.io/Picasa

 To watch a video about the more powerful (but not free) Adobe Lightroom, scan the QR code or visit:

sdp.io/LightroomIntro

For example, I snapped the picture of the coyote in Figure 1-5 at a zoo using an old film camera and a consumer lens. It's not especially sharp or interesting, but it's one of my bestselling stock photos of all time.

I spent hours in the woods, including standing in the rain, to get close enough to get the picture in Figure 1-5 of a robin feeding her babies. I love it because I remember the energy that I put into it. Nobody else seems to think

Figure 1-5: Though I prefer the picture of the robins, others prefer the picture of the coyote.

much of the picture, and the stock photo agencies didn't even accept it.

I stubbornly keep the robin picture in my portfolio, but I have to acknowledge that it's not as good a picture as the coyote picture—because I trust other people's opinions before my own.

EDIT YOUR PICTURES

Editing your pictures isn't cheating. Today, it's expected; every single photo you see in the media has been edited. There's no excuse for crooked or washed-out pictures anymore, because free image editing applications, such as Picasa, allow you to quickly fix just about any problem.

Editing your pictures is also a great way to learn—if you discover that your family photos are better when you crop them down, the next time you take pictures you'll remember to zoom in closer. If all your pictures are orange, you can adjust the white balance in your image editing app—and you'll know to fix the white balance setting on your camera the next time.

Once you discover the importance of post-processing, you'll spend more and more of your time editing your pictures. At that point, it makes sense to upgrade to Adobe Lightroom. Lightroom provides more powerful editing capabilities than Picasa or any other image management software, but most importantly, it makes your workflow more efficient. For that reason, every single professional and serious amateur I know uses Lightroom.

MAKE PICTURES, DON'T TAKE PICTURES

Here's the process of *taking* a picture:

1. See something you want to remember.
2. Hold the camera up.
3. Press the shutter.

Here's the process of *making* a picture:

1. Envision a photograph.
2. Find the best location.
3. Find the best viewpoint.
4. Find the best time.
5. Determine how the natural light needs to be modified.
6. Hold the camera up.
7. Identify the camera settings you need to get the right exposure, perspective, background blur, and depth-of-field.
8. Press the shutter.
9. Edit the picture to complete your vision.

The first photo in Figure 1-6 shows a snapshot I took of Chelsea at a park. A few minutes later, I found better natural lighting and a nicer background, and we made the second picture. Making pictures doesn't have to take much time—just be deliberate about your composition, lighting, posing, and camera settings.

EVALUATE YOUR PHOTOGRAPHY

People are too biased to judge the quality of their own photos. If you ever want to objectively determine how good one of your pictures is, consider the experience, planning, and camera equipment:

■ **Experience.** Many people buy a camera, take a few pictures, and then give up when the results aren't professional. People seem to think that photography is not a skill, but a gift that you're born with. Yet, every great photographer's first shots are throwaways. Photography, like just about everything else in life, requires experience. With experience, you'll learn how to set up your camera, choose the right lens and composition, and adapt to the lighting.

■ **Planning**. Ansel Adams, like all great photographers, planned every great shot. For his camera, he carefully chose a view point, a lens, film, and camera settings. He also chose a time of the year, time of the day, and weather conditions when the sunlight perfectly illuminated his subject. You can take good pictures spontaneously, but if you want to take great pictures, you need to plan them.

■ **Camera**. The last factor in the photo quality equation is equipment. No photographer should be held back by poor-quality equipment. However, don't spend money on high-end equipment before you gain the experience and learn to plan a shot.

The most experienced photographers can't take a great picture on-the-spot; they need to plan it out. Even with great camera equipment, inexperienced photographers who don't plan their shots out will produce lousy pictures. To make great pictures, build up experience by studying and practicing for years, plan your shots out, and use good-quality camera equipment.

Figure 1-6: We took the first picture and made the second.

DON'T WORRY SO MUCH ABOUT THE EQUIPMENT AND SETTINGS

The single most common mistake I see people making is being preoccupied with equipment and settings. Of course, we constantly get the question that I consider to be the highest compliment from a non-photographer: "What camera do you use?" Usually (especially when sharing pictures on Facebook), it doesn't much matter.

Settings such as the shutter speed and aperture usually don't matter as much as people think, either. Recently, Chelsea posted her photo of our daughter (Figure 1-7) to our Facebook page and a reader asked, "What was your shutter speed?"

Of course, she answered politely (it was 1/1500th), but the real answer is that the shutter speed didn't matter; Chelsea used the camera's aperture priority mode (Av or A), which automatically chooses a shutter speed to match your f/stop number.

Here's what we did to make that picture, none of which is quite as simple as buying expensive equipment, pressing a button, or flipping a switch:

- We were at the beach with our daughter.
- We went an hour before sunset so the lighting would be nice.
- We picked a day with clear skies, which creates a nice, hard light from the sun.
- There was no wind, and thus no waves, creating glassy reflections on the water and allowing you to see the ripples.
- Chelsea moved to a spot where the sun was behind Madelyn to create the silhouette.
- Chelsea composed the photo carefully, zooming in to eliminate distractions and positioning Madelyn according to the rule of thirds.
- Chelsea patiently watched Madelyn for several minutes, snapping dozens of photos.
- Back at home, Chelsea picked the single best of all of her photos and edited it to level the horizon.

Figure 1-7: With the camera in aperture priority mode, Chelsea was able to focus on the mood, composition, and her subject instead of technical details.

When asked about his photographic techniques, Arthur "Weegee" Fellig, a photojournalist from the 30s and 40s, answered, "f/8 and be there." Of course, he used a completely manual camera; with today's automatic cameras, the f/8 part is no longer especially important.

My advice to beginning photographers is simply, "Be there and think."

And when I say "think," I want you to think about the subject, the location, the perspective, the lighting, the timing, the weather, the mood, the pose, the clothes, the expression, the composition, and yes, the camera settings.

That's a lot to absorb, and I'll teach you every bit of it as you read this book, watch our videos, and share your photos on our Facebook page. But I'd rather you leave your camera in automatic mode than become preoccupied with any one aspect of making a picture, especially the equipment and settings.

CARRY EXTRAS

Nothing is more frustrating than missing a shot because you ran out of batteries or space on your memory card. Buy an extra battery and keep it ready on your charger. When you go out, grab both batteries.

Carry extra memory cards with you. Buy a handful of the cheapest memory cards you can find, even if they're small, and stash them in your bag, purse, car, suitcase, and wallet. The next time you fill up your memory card, or forget your card at home, your extra will save the day.

NEVER CLOSE AN EMPTY DOOR

When you take a memory card or battery out of your camera, leave the camera door open until you replace it. The next time you pick up your camera, the open door will remind you that your camera's not yet ready.

Photography Projects

Try these projects if you need inspiration!

Make an artistic still life photo using household items:

sdp.io/StillLife

 Take pictures at a car show:

sdp.io/CarShow

Learn to levitate:

sdp.io/Levitation

 Tell a story by overlapping multiple pictures:

sdp.io/Multiple

Create impressionist-style art with your camera:

sdp.io/Impressionist

 Create cool catchlights with custom LED lighting:

sdp.io/RingLight

PRE-SHOT CHECKLIST

Even if you learn everything in this book, you're bound to forget something important in the field. I've made a pre-shot checklist that you can print and keep with you. Better yet, copy it to your smartphone so you never leave it at home. If you don't understand everything in the list yet, don't worry—you will when you're done reading the book. You can download and print the checklist from *sdp.io/checklist*.

2
CHAPTER

COMPOSITION

Composition is the placement of subjects and the background in a photo, and it's one of the most critical parts of photography. Good composition doesn't require an expensive camera or an understanding of the technical details of photography—but it can take years of practice before it becomes second nature.

In this chapter, I'll cover basic compositional techniques that artists have been developing for hundreds of years.

THE RULE OF THIRDS

Instead of centering your subject in the frame, place your subject one-third of the way through the frame. For example, here's the same picture at two different crops: framed in the center of the photo, and framed using the rule of thirds. As you can see in Figure 2-1, the photo with the subject centered looks like a common snapshot. Following the *rule of thirds* in the second photo by placing the eye of the eagle in the upper-right third gives it a more artistic feel.

The first picture in Figure 2-2 shows what most people do naturally—place the subject in the center of the picture. The second picture reframes the same shot to follow the rule of thirds. As the diagram demonstrates, the second photo follows the rule of thirds in several different ways:

- The temple is aligned roughly with the right third of the frame.
- The sky is aligned roughly with the top third of the frame.
- The water is aligned roughly with the bottom third of the frame.

The rule of thirds is so pervasive that many cameras can display similar gridlines when framing a picture to help you follow the rule of thirds. Photo editing applications such as Adobe Lightroom display a rule of thirds grid when cropping photos, too.

Figures 2-1 and 2-2: The rule of thirds makes pictures more interesting by creating negative space.

The rule of thirds was first discovered by Greek artists, and it has withstood the test of time. Look for the rule of thirds in the world around you in magazines, paintings, movies, and television shows. You'll discover that it's used by all the masters.

The rule of thirds is a very oversimplified guideline. The most important element to remember is not to place your subject in the middle of the picture, nor just slightly off-center. One-third of the way towards the edge is really just the beginning of where composition begins to look deliberate; many compositions look great at four-fifths or even nine-tenths.

THE RULE OF SPACE

Both of the examples in the rule of thirds also demonstrate a second rule—give your subject room for movement. If the subject is moving, or looking in a direction other than the camera,

leave room in front of them to prevent the picture from feeling crowded.

Figure 2-3 shows two pictures that are cropped from the same photo. The first picture feels crowded because the deer is about to run into the left side of the frame. The second picture simply moves the deer towards the right edge of the frame, giving him room to run.

THE FOCAL POINT

Pictures must have a focal point. Often, the focal point is obvious. If you're taking a picture of your daughter, she's the focal point. If you're a bird photographer, the focal point will always be a bird.

Finding the focal point is more difficult with landscape, nature, and architectural photography. For example, you might see a gorgeous landscape around you, but the picture

Figure 2-3: Leave room in front of your subject to avoid making the picture feel crowded.

Figure 2-4: Landscapes, in particular, are more interesting with a focal point.

you take comes out boring. Without a focal point, the eye simply disregards the scene as background.

Focal points can be flowers, animals, people, or anything that draws the eye. If you can't find a focal point by changing your position or perspective, don't be afraid to add one. For example, Lake Lucerne in Switzerland (Figure 2-4) is an amazing sight—swans swimming across the glassy water with the snow-capped Swiss Alps as the backdrop. Regardless, most people would quickly flip past my first photo. Waiting a few minutes for the ferry to arrive vastly improved the photo. If you can't find a focal point, use the sun in the photo, ask a friend to pose, or include yourself in the picture. For more information about taking self-portraits, refer to Chapter 6.

The subject does not simply need to be a person or object. If you're taking pictures at your son's baseball game, the subject might be the speed of the swing, the excitement of the crowd, or the happiness of the winning team. With practice, you will be able to capture these more complex subjects.

SIMPLIFYING

Once you determine your focal point, eliminate distracting elements from the picture. The easiest ways to do this are to move around the subject to find a non-distracting background, move closer, zoom in, or crop the picture. Attempt to fill the frame with your subject without crowding the subject by placing it too close to the edge of the frame.

With portraiture, the subject is often simply their expression. For example, the portrait shown in Figure 2-5 crops deeply into the model's hair and shoulders, filling more of the frame with the subject: her eyes and smile. When you look at the picture, you don't wonder whether the top of her head is on fire or if she's actually a minotaur; your imagination fills in the missing details.

Consider the flower in Figure 2-6. The first picture is sharp and centered, but quite boring. The second photo fills the frame with the subject's key elements: the yellow eye, white petals, and water droplets. No viewer would see the second picture and want to see the rest of the flower; your brain fills in the gaps.

Figure 2-5: The subject of a portrait is rarely the entire person. Usually, the subject is the expression, and you should crop tight around the face.

Figure 2-6: Capture your subject in the simplest way possible.

16

To watch a video on **portrait backgrounds,** scan the QR code or visit:

sdp.io/PortraitBackground

Another way to simplify pictures is to blur the background using a short *depth-of-field*. For more information about aperture and depth-of-field, read Chapter 4, "Controlling your Camera."

ANGLE OF VIEW

One of the easiest ways to simplify your composition is to zoom in. Zooming in does more than move you closer—it narrows your angle of view. If you zoom out to a wide angle, you'll see more of the background. If you take a few steps back and zoom in, you'll see less of the background.

This difference in perspective gives you control over the background in your pictures. If you want to see more of the background, step closer and zoom out. If you want to focus on your subject, step back and zoom in.

Figure 2-7 shows Chelsea photographed with the Boston skyline in the background using a wide-angle (25mm), normal (50mm), and telephoto (200mm) lens. I stepped farther away from Chelsea for each shot to keep her the same

Figure 2-7: Zooming in shows less of the background, but brings it closer. Zooming out shows more of the background and makes it seem farther away.

size in the picture. Because wide-angle lenses have a large field of view, they include a great deal of background in the picture. Step back a few feet and zoom in so that your subject takes the same space in the frame, and you'll see much less of the background. Step back farther from the model and zoom in all the way, paparazzi-style, and the telephoto lens will hide most of the background. This shows you fewer buildings, but each building appears much larger and seems to be closer to the model.

Unless you have a beautiful (and simple) background, the telephoto (zoomed in) picture will probably be the prettiest of the three pictures. Telephoto lenses blur the background, which makes the subject seem to pop off the background. Telephoto lenses also make facial features appear smaller—in other words, a wide-angle lens can make your nose look big, even if it's not.

SHOWING SCALE

One of the drawbacks of simplifying your composition is losing scale. Particularly when the subject's size is important—such as with babies, puppies, monster trucks, and giant redwoods—you need to include something of a known size in the frame. That's why you see so many portraits of newborn babies being held in the father's hand; the hand, for scale, immediately gives you a sense of the size of the subject.

The same applies for large subjects, such as waterfalls and Great Danes. If you want them to look large in the picture, include something small in the frame, as close to the large subject as possible. Figure 2-8 shows two pictures of the American Niagara Falls. Without the ferries in the picture, you don't get a sense of its massive size.

To watch a video on **finding the angle**, scan the QR code or visit:

sdp.io/FindingAngle

LINES

Your eyes are naturally drawn to lines in a photograph. You can use lines to draw the viewer's eyes to key elements, create patterns, and divide a picture. Lines can be architectural elements such as railings or walls, geographical elements such as shorelines or horizons, or organic elements such as trees or people.

Lines have different qualities, depending on their shape and direction:

- Converging parallel lines create a vanishing point (a concept created by Renaissance artists)—the point at which the lines converge in the distance—creating depth and perspective.

Figure 2-8: Without the boats in the foreground, you don't get a sense of the massive scale of Niagara Falls.

- Horizontal lines give a sense of quiet and peace.

- Vertical lines feel powerful, solid, and permanent.

- Diagonal lines are more dynamic, conveying movement and change.

- Straight lines feel formal, deliberate, and manmade.

- Curved lines, especially an S-shape, feel casual and add sophistication, nature, and grace.

In the photo of the New York City skyline (Figure 2-9), the diagonal line of the Brooklyn Bridge provides a dynamic contrast to the vertical lines of the buildings and leads the eye through the frame from left to right. Also note the use of the rule of thirds, dividing the photo between water, building, and sky.

Leading lines draw your eye through the picture. For that reason, it's important to have a focal point where the lines converge. For the pictures in Figure 2-10, I found a location with interesting lines and moved sideways until I found a viewpoint that caused the lines to converge on a subject. The cityscape of Stockholm, Sweden, would be much less interesting if the lines of the railways didn't lead your eye to the most prominent of the buildings. The photo of the train tracks would be boring if my daughter weren't at the focal point.

Any time a picture has prominent lines, including the ocean's perfectly flat horizon or the vertical lines of a building, you must take care to make sure your camera is level. If you process your picture and discover that it isn't perfectly level, just rotate the picture in post-processing so that it's straight. Rotating pictures requires you to crop the edges slightly, so it helps to shoot slightly more wide-angle than you need.

When you include angled lines, choose a perspective that allows the angles to be at least 20 degrees off-level. Anything less doesn't look deliberate and isn't as appealing. To control the angle of lines, change your perspective. For example, in a landscape with a straight fence through it, you could hold your camera perpendicular to the fence so that it was perfectly straight across your picture. Or, you could move close to the fence and turn left or right so that the fence drew an attractive 20 to 30 degree angled line through the landscape.

Figure 2-10: Position your subject where lines naturally converge.

Figure 2-9: Use bridges to break up the vertical lines of a skyline.

However, you wouldn't want to be somewhere in-between; a 5 degree angle would look careless and unattractive.

PATTERNS

In the case of the travel photos in Figure 2-11, the pattern of red torii gates in Kyoto, Japan, seems to disappear into the distance, implying that there are thousands of the gates. Indeed, there are thousands of the gates, but it would be impossible to show them all in the photo. By using a pattern without a definite ending, the viewer gets the feel for the quantity without having to show it explicitly.

Figure 2-11: Patterns that lead off the frame show quantity.

To watch a video on **buildings and architecture,** scan the QR code or visit:

sdp.io/ArchitectureTravel

FRAMES

You can add depth to a picture by using a natural frame. Frames can be trees, doorways, window frames, or anything that surrounds your subject.

The photo of the author watching the Boston skyline, Figure 2-12, is framed by a lighted shelter in the foreground. The photo of a flower has depth because the flower is growing outside of its frame.

SYMMETRY

Symmetry creates pictures where one half could be a mirror image of the other (Figure 2-13). Symmetry shows geometric precision and simple beauty.

Figure 2-12: Framing adds depth and context.

When showing symmetry, alignment is critical. The picture must be perfectly centered, vertical lines must be straight, and the horizon must be completely flat. Often, you will need to disregard the rule of thirds and perfectly center the subject in the frame. When you see a reflective surface, such as still water, use symmetry.

SHOWING DEPTH

When many beginning photographers first begin thoughtfully composing their shots, they have a tendency to line up shots perfectly straight, square, and flat. Moving off-center and showing a subject at an angle shows more depth and provides a more lively, dynamic, and casual composition. Compare the photos of the Nyhavn district in Copenhagen, Denmark, in

Figure 2-13: Using symmetry requires perfectly balancing a photo's composition.

Figure 2-14: Shooting straight on made the buildings look flat (top). To show more depth, shoot the subject at an angle and/or place a focal point in the foreground (bottom).

Figure 2-14. The lively scene and fun colors aren't well suited to the square framing; the compositions that include depth simply suit the subject better.

There's value to square composition; it conveys a stately, formal, and professional attitude. If that suits your subject, then a straight composition is a good choice. Wes Anderson often uses square composition to subtly set a mood in his films, especially in *Moonrise Kingdom*. In architecture, square compositions are perfect when you want to convey formality. Square compositions are often required when using symmetry.

Figure 2-15 shows two angles of the Muckross House in Killarney, Ireland. The square composition compliments its classic, stately architecture.

To watch a video on **depth in composition,** scan the QR code or visit:
sdp.io/Depth

DUTCH ANGLE

The Dutch angle adds a deliberate twist to a photo to convey action, spontaneity, and candidness. While you should do your best to keep your camera level for most photos, you can intentionally rotate your camera left or right to add a touch of lively fun.

Figure 2-16 shows Chelsea modeling a shirt she designed. Though she was posing in a location we chose for the light and background, I wanted it to seem like an unplanned snapshot, so I twisted my camera left about 15 degrees. The fun mood of the Dutch angle fit well with her happy expression and candid pose.

If you use the Dutch angle, do so deliberately, but don't overdo it. A twist of 15 to 30 degrees is good; any less will seem accidental, and any more will look strange. Use the Dutch angle with appropriate subject matter, too. While it's great for casual shots at parties and other fun events, it's not a good choice for serious portraits and landscapes.

Figure 2-15: Shooting the Muckross House straight-on captured its beauty the way the architects intended it to be seen.

Figure 2-16: Twist your camera a bit to make photos seem more fun, casual, and spontaneous.

PANORAMAS

Panoramas create a very wide-angle perspective by stitching multiple photos together. Panoramas are easy, fun, and free. Panoramas can capture an entire environment, up to a 360 degree view around you. Not too many places in the world are beautiful in a full 360 degrees, but it's comforting to know that a photo never has to be limited by the widest angle of your zoom lens.

Panoramas are practical, too. By creating a panorama, you can create a photo with the same angle-of-view as a super-wide angle lens, or even go wider than the widest lens in the world. Because panoramas stitch together multiple pictures, they effectively increase your camera's megapixels, allowing you to take sharper pictures and create much larger prints.

Let's look at a simple example. Figure 2-17 shows a beautifully lit hotel in Copenhagen, Denmark. The streets were extremely crowded, so I couldn't step back far enough to fit the entire hotel in. So, I created a panorama by taking three overlapping photos. Back at my computer, I used free software to combine them into a single photo. The whole process took less than a minute.

To create the panorama shown in Figure 2-18, I combined four 42-megapixel photos taken at 36mm. The final result is 82 megapixels and 17mm because the photos were overlapped and cropped. Using panorama techniques allowed me to create a bigger, sharper print than would have been possible with a single shot.

Your camera might have a panoramic mode built in; feel free to follow the instructions in your manual. Here's the process I recommend for manually creating a panorama:

1. Set your camera's focusing to AF-S or One-Shot, or just use manual focusing.

2. Imagine the boundaries of your panorama.

If you're not doing a 360 degree panorama, it helps to have a focal point, just as you should when composing a traditional photo. Without taking a shot, pan your camera from left to right. You don't have to hold your camera horizontally—if you hold it vertically, you will need to take more photos to create the same panorama, but the final picture will have more than twice the detail. Adjust the zoom so that there is plenty of room to crop both above and below all parts of your subject. You won't be able to zoom while creating the panorama.

3. Focus on the most important subject of the photo by pressing your shutter button halfway. Keep the shutter depressed halfway without taking a photo.

4. Start from the left side of your panorama, and be sure to leave room to crop from the left. Frame your first shot, and press your camera's auto-exposure lock (AE Lock) button. The AE Lock button keeps your exposure the same throughout the entire shot, which makes it easier to stitch the photos together. If you don't remember how to set AE Lock, don't worry about it.

5. Make a mental note of where the right edge of your picture will be, and take your first picture. Keep the shutter depressed halfway to prevent your camera from

Figure 2-17: Three photos combined to create the panorama of the beautiful Denmark hotel.

refocusing. While keeping the camera as level as possible, pan to the right so that your second picture overlaps your first by about one-third. Continue this process until you've reached the right side of your panorama (and left some room to crop).

6. Now, copy your pictures to your computer. Download and install Microsoft Image Composite Editor (ICE) from *sdp.io/ice.* Run the app and drag your pictures into it. ICE does all the hard work, though you might need to crop the picture a bit to eliminate any black borders that result. Save the result.

When creating a panorama using a tripod with a panning head, make sure the tripod is completely level. Otherwise, the horizon will drift upwards or downwards, requiring you to crop it heavily.

There are a couple of things to avoid when composing a panorama:

- Using a polarizing filter.

- Including subjects very close to the camera.

- Composing a picture with trees and bushes in the foreground. They won't stitch together well.

- Photographing moving subjects. A moving subject that spans more than one photo might appear in multiple photos or not at all. If this can't be avoided (for example, if

To watch a video on **panoramas,** scan the QR code or visit:

sdp.io/Panorama

you're in a crowded area), try to keep the moving subjects in the middle of a single frame.

Microsoft ICE is my favorite panorama stitching application, but it only works on Windows. If you have a Mac or use Linux (or you use Windows and just don't like Microsoft ICE), download Hugin from *hugin.sourceforge.net.* Lightroom and Photoshop are also quite capable of making panoramas, and you can download panorama software for your smartphone.

Wide panoramas consisting of one row of pictures are the most common because that most closely resembles how humans see the world. However, you can also create vertical panoramas by following the same process. If you want to create a really high megapixel picture, you can create structured panoramas with multiple rows and columns of pictures in a two-dimensional grid. Microsoft ICE can automatically combine your photos, regardless of how you arrange them.

If you look for information about creating panoramas on the Internet, you might think panoramas are far too complicated to create. You'll find many people recommending

Figure 2-18: Four photos digitally combined to make a panorama of Machu Picchu, Peru.

using a tripod with a special head designed for panoramas and going through a great deal of trouble to avoid parallax errors. While specialized hardware does allow you to make more perfect panoramas, and might be required when creating panoramas with nearby subjects, today's panorama software does such a great job that you can hand-hold shots with stunning results.

If you don't believe me, take a second look at the three individual shots used to create the panorama in Figure 2-17, and you'll see that I did a terrible job of keeping the camera level while panning. The software corrected this for me automatically, and there's no evidence of my poor hand-holding even upon close inspection of the final image.

BALANCE AND VISUAL WEIGHT

Just like two kids on a seesaw have balance, the subjects in a photo have balance. Rather than balancing based on physical weight, subjects in a photo balance based on visual weight.

Five elements determine a subject's visual weight:

- **Size.** The bigger something is in the picture, the more visual weight it has.

- **Brightness.** Brighter subjects have more visual weight than darker subjects.

- **Color.** Brightly colored subjects have more visual weight than dull subjects.

- **Sharpness.** Subjects that are in focus have more visual weight than out-of-focus subjects.

- **Direction.** An object that's moving, looking, or facing to one side carries its visual weight forward. It's this factor that makes the Rule of Space work.

Figure 2-19: In this photo, the visual weight of the bright balloon is enough to balance massive buildings.

Figure 2-20: Moving the balloon unbalances the photo, creating a much less pleasing composition.

To understand an image's balance, deconstruct it into the most basic components. For example, consider the picture of Stockholm, Sweden, in Figure 2-19, and the deconstructed version of the image. If you were to place the deconstructed image on a balance, it wouldn't tip to one side or the other. Note that the circle representing the deconstructed balloon is larger than the balloon itself; the balloon's bright color and contrast with the background gives it more visual weight.

Moving the balloon to the heavy side of the picture creates a very unbalanced composition, as shown in Figure 2-20. The subjects in the photo are the same, but a balanced arrangement creates a much more pleasing image.

Most of us can feel whether a composition is balanced or unbalanced without deconstructing it. If you like the subject in a photo, but the overall composition feels uncomfortable, you might be able to fix it by changing the balance.

FRAME EDGES AND NEGATIVE SPACE

Watch the edges of the frame as you compose your picture. Too often, photographers have a beautifully composed picture with either an uncomfortable crop or something sticking in near the edge of the frame.

This is an easy problem to solve. Before pressing the shutter button, simply look around the edges of the frame for any distractions. You might be able to fix the problem by moving to the side, crouching, or stepping back and zooming in.

You also need to provide a bit of negative space around the edges of your frame. Negative space is the area in your photo that's not filled by the main subject. Though I often urge photographers to fill the frame with the subject, I never mean it literally—every photo needs a subject and negative space around the subject.

Strive to provide a similar amount of negative space around all edges of a subject. Specifically, if you choose to include both the head and feet of a person or animal in a photo, be sure to leave a similar amount of room below the feet and above the head. Too often, people leave room above the head, but crop too closely to the feet, as Figure 2-21 demonstrates.

Please don't think this means that you need to zoom back and take only full-body photos so you can leave room around the entire person. As I discussed in the Simplifying section earlier in this chapter, when taking pictures of people, your subject is rarely the entire body, hair, clothes, and shoes. You should, however, carefully control the negative space around the real subject: their face and expression.

BLACK AND WHITE

Black-and-white photography is a tribute to photography's history, when we used films coated in chemicals to capture light. Today, black and white photography is an artistic choice rather than a practical one.

Compositionally, converting a picture to black and white changes the visual weight of objects to de-emphasize colorful subjects. If you love your child's expression in a photo, but

Figure 2-21: Provide a balanced amount of room around your subject at the edges of the frame.

26

 To watch a video about using **Black and White,** scan the QR code or visit:

sdp.io/BandW

they're wearing an obnoxiously bright shirt that distracts from the subject (their face), try converting the picture to black and white. If you make a cityscape of Boston but the orange Citgo sign annoys you, black and white will almost make it disappear without requiring you to alter the truthfulness of the photo.

Shooting in black and white can be as simple as selecting an option in your camera. However, if you're a serious black and white photographer, you should capture images in color and then convert them to black-and-white so that you can more carefully control the brightness of different colors. Film photographers do this, too, by using different colored filters. Chelsea tells you more about black and white photography in the video above.

STORYTELLING

Pictures of people, wildlife, and landscapes are all relatively simple: you're taking a picture of a person, place, or thing, and that's your subject. The most amazing photos, however, tell a story. During those moments, you become more than a photographer; you become a storyteller.

For example, you're a storyteller when you're taking pictures at a child's birthday party. Your job isn't simply to document what the attendees look like; your job is to tell a story. If you were to tell part of the story in words, you might say, "She blew out the candles on her birthday cake while everyone cheered." Making a picture of that moment would require including all the elements in the sentence:

- **She blew out the candles.** Not only do you need to capture the birthday girl and the candles, but you need to capture the action of her blowing them out. This means that a photo with puffed cheeks and pursed lips tells the story better than a picture with just a smile. Similarly, it's not enough to capture the candles, but you need to capture them going out. You could do this by capturing a moment when the flame is bent from her breath, or when there's smoke from extinguished candles. This is the most important element of the story, so it should have the most visual weight

Figure 2-22: Event photography, such as birthdays, requires storytelling.

Figure 2-23: In sports, storytelling requires not just the player, but the ball and the opponents.

■ **On her birthday cake.** Obviously, you need to show the cake, because it's an important part of the story. It's not as important as the girl or the candles, however.

■ **While everyone cheered.** While you should show people cheering, this element should carry the least visual weight.

Figure 2-22 shows an example from my daughter's 9th birthday. While it's not a posed picture, I didn't *take* it, I *made* it. I zoomed in to fill the frame with the most important elements, and chose an angle that included just enough of the people in the background to tell that part of the story. Madelyn and the candles have the most visual weight because they're in focus and brightly lit. To be sure I caught a moment with Madelyn blowing out the candles and people clapping, I followed the first tip in this book: I took lots of pictures and deleted most of them.

Sports require storytelling composition, too. The photos in Figure 2-23 were taken within seconds of each other, but they tell very different stories. If you were to look at the first picture, you might guess that a girl was running to practice, but you wouldn't even know what the sport was. The second photo does a much better job of storytelling because it includes key elements of the story: the soccer ball, the opponents, and the fans.

When telling a story with pictures, remember that you as the photographer witnessed it unfolding, and seeing the photo causes you to remember story elements that don't have enough visual weight to be conveyed. Therefore, if you want to know if your photo successfully tells a story, show someone else the photo and ask them to guess the story.

Besides event photography, storytelling is an important part of fine art, commercial,

and conceptual photography. Consider the three photos in Figure 2-24. They all have most of the same storytelling elements: a woman, a fancy red dress, heels, and a suitcase. Yet, they tell different stories.

In the top picture, the story seems to be about a woman eager to travel, but tired of waiting. She seems to be thinking, "I can't wait to leave." When we asked people to tell the story behind the first picture, most people didn't mention the rain; the photo simply didn't capture that important element of the story. It's raining heavily, but people viewing the photo on the web couldn't easily see the rain in the background. Storytelling elements need to be prominent and obvious.

Figure 2-24: Pose, expression, and movement change a story.

We added the umbrella to the second picture to help convey the rain. When you see the umbrella, you also notice that her hair and dress are wet, even though you might have missed those elements in the first picture. The suitcase conveys more about the story in this picture, too, because the contrast with the bright background allows you to better see the shape. As the model, Chelsea changed the story completely by standing instead of sitting. The story in the second photo is, "It's about time you got here. Let's go!"

Take a moment to look at the third picture and imagine the story that it tells. How do the elements of the heels, red dress, and suitcase shape the story? If Chelsea wore jeans, sneakers, and a t-shirt, how would the story change? What if she were holding a beach ball instead? What if the setting changed, and she were going into a building instead of passing through a gate? Everything in the picture becomes part of the story, so plan every element carefully.

Whether you're capturing an event or creating fiction, storytelling requires composing photos to prominently show the key elements of your story. You've only succeeded as a storyteller when the image tells a story to others. If you're creating art, you've succeeded if you engage the viewers' imagination, even if the story means something different to them than it does to you.

MOOD

Like people, every photo has a mood: happy, serious, sad, mysterious, scary, or anything else you might imagine. The best photos have a cohesive mood created by the lighting, expression, pose, location, clothing, and post-processing. If you don't think about the mood when you take a picture, the different elements in your photo might clash, creating a mixed mood.

Using the photo on the cover of this book as an example, Chelsea and I wanted to create an ethereal mood. To achieve the appearance of floating, we chose a pool as the location. Compositionally, I dove beneath Chelsea so the sun would be in the frame behind her, creating the bright background and God rays. Chelsea, as a model, supported this mood by choosing a white dress, spreading her hair through the water, stretching out her arms, and showing a peaceful expression. For more information about how we made this picture, refer to Chapter 13, "Underwater Photography".

If you flip forward to the second picture in Figure 10-6, you'll see a very different mood. Every aspect of the photo was deliberately chosen: we went to an abandoned asylum after dark. I, as the model, created a costume using a doctor's coat, a mask, and an axe. Chelsea used flashlights to illuminate me, creating a blurry, ghostly effect. Finally, I adjusted the color and contrast of the image in post-processing to support the horror theme.

If you examine the photos technically, they're both awful. Shooting through water and lighting people with flashlights creates unsharp photos and unrealistic colors. Both photos are too noisy and contrasty. Yet, nobody has ever complained because both photos have a deliberate, consistent mood. Mood always trumps detail.

Mood isn't only about composition; your location, lighting, posing, and processing must all support your photo's mood. For that reason, I'll bring up mood many different times throughout this book. However, I wanted to introduce the concept early so that you could begin to think about the mood of your photos.

DELIBERATELY BREAKING THE RULES

These rules of composition have existed for hundreds of years, and we've all seen thousands of paintings and photos that followed them perfectly. Any photo that follows these rules will feel comfortable to the viewer, and every photographer must master creating comfortable compositions. At some point, following the rules becomes boring, though, and at that point, I encourage you to defy them.

When you choose to break the rules, do so deliberately. Don't place a subject just slightly off the rule of thirds; place it in the center of the frame or completely at the edge. Don't make your horizon just slightly off-level; tilt it at least 15 degrees. Don't take a slightly unbalanced picture; make a strikingly unbalanced photo.

When you break the rules, it's important that every other aspect of your photo be technically perfect. This lets the viewer know that the composition isn't just an accident by an inexperienced photographer, but a deliberate artistic choice by an expert.

PRACTICE

Now that you understand the theory of photographic composition, perform these practices:

- Watch Chelsea and I review and edit other reader photos on YouTube at *sdp.io/readerreview*. In particular, note how many photos have their composition improved by cropping.

- Visit an art museum and note which of these techniques your favorite pieces use.

- Go through your existing pictures and see which of your pictures used each of the compositional techniques described in this chapter.

Practice and test yourself!

sdp.io/Quiz2

- Every time you take a picture, make a point of following at least one of these compositional techniques. Often, you will use two or more techniques in the same picture.

- If there is a technique you've never intentionally used, find a subject you can use the technique on.

- Take both square and off-center pictures of a person, a house, and a car. Which do you prefer?

- Create a horizontal panorama using at least three photos and process it using Microsoft ICE. Next, create a second panorama by holding your camera vertically.

- Using Lightroom or Picasa (as described in Chapter 1), browse through your pictures and find at least one photo that looks better in black and white.

- Think of a story, and attempt to capture it in a picture. You don't need models, props, and outfits—you can use toys. Show the picture to someone without describing it first, and ask what they think the story is.

- In abstract photography, composition itself is the subject of the photo. Create abstract photographs by composing lines, shapes, colors, and shadows using the techniques described in this chapter.

- Create a still life photo using objects around your house and natural light. For detailed instructions, watch Chelsea's video.

3 Lighting&Flash

No matter what you're shooting, your subject is the same: light. The most amazing subject will be boring when the lighting is bad, and even dull subjects come alive with great lighting.

You always have some control over the lighting. When you're close to a subject, you can add direct flash to increase the light on the subject or bounce flash off the ceiling to increase the lighting in the room. For landscape photography, you control lighting by planning your pictures when the sun and clouds will give you the desired effect.

Once you develop an appreciation for lighting, the world around you takes on a new dimension. Cloudy days won't seem dull. Instead, you'll appreciate how the soft top lighting creates smooth shadows and hides texture. You'll smile when the sun is at the back of your loved ones, because you'll see the sunlight create a glowing halo through their hair. You'll appreciate sunsets not just for the colors in the sky, but for the warm side lighting they cast on the world around you.

This chapter explains how you can make the best use of natural lighting and how you can improve it with flash. You'll study highlights and shadows, hard and soft light, and directional lighting. You'll learn how to use timing and positioning to control sunlight when working outdoors. You'll learn the basics of lighting people for portrait work, and how to use flash to add many different types of light to your picture. Finally, you'll learn why some of your pictures have an orange or green tint to them.

HARD AND SOFT LIGHTING

Every scene has highlights, shadows, and the transitions between them. Soft lighting creates long, smooth transitions between highlights and shadows, while hard lighting creates sharp transitions.

Look at the room around you and notice the highlights and shadows. Notice that smooth, reflective surfaces create bright highlights with sharp, distinct lines. Soft textures and gently curving shapes create highlights with a gradual gradient into shadow. Direct sunlight or a bare bulb creates hard lighting, while reflected and diffused light creates soft lighting.

Between highlights and shadows are the mid-tones. In soft lighting, most of a picture is mid-tones. Photographers cherish soft lighting because cameras capture mid-tones the best. In hard lighting, pictures can consist entirely of highlights and shadows with almost nothing in-between. Only the most skilled photographers are able to take great pictures in hard lighting.

Consider the pictures of an orange in Figure 3-1. The first uses hard side lighting to show both form and texture. The shadow on the left of the orange clearly shows the orange's spherical shape and reveals the direction of the light. The high contrast lighting creates a highlight on the side of the orange closest to the bulb, and a shadow on the far side. This

Figure 3-1: Hard lighting shows form and texture, while soft lighting shows shape.

To watch a video on **lighting and shadows,** scan the QR code or visit:

sdp.io/Shadows

accentuates the three-dimensional shape of the orange. Hard lighting also accentuates texture; every pore in the orange has its own highlight and shadow. If the orange were a person's face, this lighting would be extremely unflattering.

Soft lighting minimizes highlights and shadows. By looking at the second picture of the orange, you can tell that the orange has a round shape, but you don't get a sense of its three-dimensional form or its texture; it looks flat. This low contrast lighting would be much more flattering for portrait photography because the pores and dimples are mostly hidden by the lighting.

Hard lighting is created by small or far-away light sources, while soft lighting is created by large, nearby light sources. Because the sun is so far away, direct sunlight creates hard lighting with distinct shadows. On an overcast day, however, the clouds become their own light source, diffusing the harsh sunlight. Indoors, uncovered bulbs create hard lighting while light reflected off ceilings and walls creates soft lighting.

DIRECTIONAL LIGHTING

Whether hard or soft, all light has a direction. The side of your subject closest to the light will have highlights and the far side will be cast in shadow.

The direction the *main light* (also called the *key light*) shines from can completely change the look of your subject. The highlights draw attention to features, making them seem larger. Shadows diminish and hide features. Therefore, whether photographing a person or a landscape,

choose lighting that highlights the focal point of a picture.

Top lighting gives a natural appearance, but it casts unattractive shadows on faces. Front lighting is better for faces, but it removes texture and depth. Side lighting highlights texture and depth and casts long shadows. Back lighting creates the most dramatic effect but can be challenging to work with.

As you progress through these pictures, notice how the main light's direction shows different shadows on the faces and varying amounts of texture in the tree bark.

TOP LIGHTING

Top lighting (Figure 3-2) is the most common type of lighting. When you're outdoors and the sun is high in the sky, you're in top lighting. When you're indoors with the lights on, they're shining down on you.

Depending on the subject, the downward-pointing shadows created by top lighting can convey depth and form. Soft top lighting, such as that created outside on overcast days, can be ideal for flowers and wildlife. Though lighting from above is common, it's quite unflattering for people. Top lighting casts deep shadows over the eyes and a long shadow below the nose—and hard top lighting is even more unflattering. Avoid top lighting by moving people into the shade or by using your flash to add front lighting.

FRONT LIGHTING

When a subject faces the main light, it's called front lighting (Figure 3-3). Front lighting automatically hides most shadows because they are cast behind your subject. Shadows create texture and depth in a picture, however, causing front-lit pictures to appear very two-dimensional.

For people, front lighting can be very flattering because it makes the nose appear smaller and hides bumps in the skin. To restore some of the depth that front lighting removes, position the main light slightly off to the left or right of the camera. For architecture and landscape, front lighting is less than ideal because it removes depth. For wildlife photography, front lighting hides important texture in fur and feathers.

When you use your camera's built-in flash, you're always using front lighting. To minimize the negative effects of front lighting, use an external flash and move it to one side and up, at about a 30 degree angle to your subject. The sun provides front lighting near sunrise and sunset when the sun is low on the horizon; simply shoot with the sun at your back.

SIDE LIGHTING

Side lighting (Figure 3-4) is the best way to show texture, form, and depth. Just as the

Figure 3-2: Top lighting.

Figure 3-3: Front lighting.

setting sun casts the longest shadows, side lighting creates tiny highlights and shadows for every bump and crease in your subject. Curved shapes, such as faces and bodies, become gradual gradients from highlight to shadow. Shadows are necessary for form—if lighting is perfectly even, objects lose their three-dimensional quality and appear flat.

Side lighting is notoriously unflattering for people. Pores and blemishes across the front of the face are exaggerated. One eye is highlighted while the other is in shadow. The nose casts a long shadow across the cheek. For those reasons, front lighting is a better choice for people.

BACKLIGHTING

The most challenging type of light to work with, backlighting (Figure 3-5) can also make the most dramatic photos. Backlit pictures tend to be all highlights and shadows with few mid-tones. Even worse, the background tends to be

Figure 3-4: Side lighting.

Figure 3-5: Backlighting.

highlighted, while the foreground is in shadow. Because of the shadows, foreground colors also tend to look dull.

For people, backlighting creates a ring of light around the face that can be very flattering. For flowers, backlighting passes through petals, making them glow. For animals, backlighting filters through the fur, creating a halo. Each of these effects helps to separate the subject from the background.

By creating a great deal of contrast between the foreground and background, backlighting highlights a subject's shape. When the only source of lighting is backlighting, the subject becomes a silhouette, which forces the viewer to concentrate on shape by eliminating texture, color, and form.

As discussed later in this chapter, you can use fill flash to remove the foreground shadows that backlighting creates. Fill flash adds light to the foreground, allowing both the foreground and background to be properly exposed.

Backlighting is one of the rare scenarios that require a good quality lens. Less expensive lenses, especially those with plastic elements, diffract light when the light is pointed directly into the camera. As a result, backlit shots can appear hazy if taken with a lower quality lens.

HOW YOUR ENVIRONMENT CHANGES LIGHT

You'll almost always have a main light, and its direction will be some combination of front, side, back, or top lighting. It's never that simple, though. Even a single light source, such as the sun or a flash, reflects, bends, and changes color.

Everything around you interacts with light. Water absorbs light, but also reflects it, creating highlights at the top of every ripple. Dark colors absorb light, but a black car still creates intense highlights reflecting from creases in the metal. Walls, floors, and ceilings reflect and diffuse light, creating a new light source with the same color as the surface. The sky itself reflects and diffuses light, giving a cool blue color to outdoor shade.

Translucent subjects allow light to pass through them, changing it on the way. Backlighting through a person's hair, an animal's fur, or petals on a flower causes them to glow pleasantly. Thin sheers in front of a window diffuse light, making it softer. A red lamp shade diffuses the light from the bulb, but also changes its color, creating a warm color cast on the surroundings.

Shade is a great example of reflected light; without reflected light, shade would be complete darkness. Instead, shade is filled with soft light reflected off the ground, nearby buildings, and moisture in the air. In fact, it's reflected light bouncing off the moisture in the air that gives skies a hazy look on humid days.

Indoors, you can open the blinds on a single window and sunlight will fill the entire room. The main light, the sun, might not even be shining directly through the window. The light that does make it through the window will reflect off the floor, walls, and ceilings before finally reaching your eye or the camera.

Reflected light is the reason white walls and light carpet make for a bright room—it's not simply an illusion; there's actually more light. Step into a log cabin made of light-absorbing natural wood, and the room will be dark no matter how many windows are open. Photograph a person in the snow, and the cool light reflected from the ground will fill in shadows from underneath.

All light is hard when it leaves its source; your environment softens and diffuses it. Later in this chapter, you will learn how to turn hard sunlight into soft light perfect for portraits by finding spots where the light is diffused by fabric and reflected off walls. Once you understand the qualities of the ambient light around you, you can learn to supplement natural light by using flash and how to change the light from your flash by reflecting it off walls.

Tip: If you ever want to reduce the amount of reflected light, put a polarizing filter on your lens.

THE GOLDEN HOUR

Light is usually the most beautiful an hour after sunrise and an hour before sunset. Photographers call these times *the golden hours*. The golden hours are special for several reasons:

- The rising or setting sun casts a warm light across your surroundings, giving everything a golden glow.
- The sky is less hazy (especially in the morning), making your pictures sharper and showing more contrast.
- The sky, and shadows the sky illuminates, take on a deep blue color that complements the warm sunlight.
- The sun is low on the horizon, providing side lighting that adds depth.
- Light is softer than in the middle of the day, so the shadows are not as harsh.
- The crowds are smaller (especially in the morning), making photography easier.

Tip: Depending on where you are, the golden hour might be longer or shorter than an hour. The closer you are to the equator, the shorter the golden "hour" is.

The two unretouched pictures in Figure 3-6 of Salzburg, Austria, were taken from about the same place, but at different times of day. Can you tell which was taken during the golden hour, and which was taken mid-day?

The golden hour is especially important when photographing fall colors. Figure 3-7 shows two unretouched photos of the same spot on a pond during the fall in New England. The first picture was taken just minutes before the sun began to set. The second was taken as the sun approached the horizon to the left of the frame. Both are pretty, but the warm setting sun made the fall colors pop off the picture in the second photo. In this example, I didn't even have a full hour to get the picture—the best lighting disappeared after just a couple of minutes.

Figure 3-8 is a shot of the Wasserturm (water tower) and Kapellbrücke (Chapel Bridge) in Lucerne, Switzerland. The only shot that worked was taken during the sunset golden hour. The sun, low on the horizon to the right of the frame, cast a warm light across all west-facing walls. More importantly, it cast shadows against the other facets of the octagonal water tower, highlighting its interesting form.

Figure 3-6: The golden hour provides clearer views, warmer colors, and more interesting lighting.

I know I'm pushing the golden hours hard, but it demands the extra salesmanship. I am *not* a morning person, but it's worth it to get up early and get those golden hour photos. Photographers who are truly committed to making the best outdoor pictures possible plan their day around the golden hours. You can look up sunrise and sunset times for any location with a quick Internet search.

> **Tip:** Cruise ships usually dock after sunrise and leave before sunset—making them less than ideal for photographers, who need to be out-and-about at those times.

CONTROLLING THE SUN

When shooting outdoors during the day, the sun is always your main light. You're still in control, however:

- Get top lighting by shooting mid-day.
- Get side lighting, front lighting, or back lighting by shooting in the morning or evening when the sun is low in the sky.

- Move between side lighting, front lighting, and back lighting by shooting your subject from different angles.
- If you can't shoot your subject from a different angle, plan the picture for a time of year when the sun is in the right place in the sky.
- Use flashes, reflectors, or other light sources to overpower the sun.

To determine exactly where in the sky the sun will be at any time of day, and any day of the year, use the Photographer's Ephemeris (a free download for Mac, PC, and Linux from *sdp.io/tpe*, and also available as an iPhone app). It will show you which side of buildings will be illuminated and where shadows will be cast, which is important, because every subject has exactly one ideal time for lighting. Usually it's during the sunrise or sunset golden hour, but it's never both.

To make it more complex, the sun rises and sets in very different places at different times of the year. For example, the next two screenshots from The Photographer's Ephemeris show the sunset direction in orange for the water tower in Luzern, shown in Figure 3-9. During the summer, you'd need to be on the south side of the river to catch the light from the setting sun. During the winter, you'd need to be on the north side of the river.

Figure 3-7: The warm colors of the rising and setting sun brighten fall colors.

Figure 3-8: The side lighting cast by the setting sun highlights the form of this interesting building.

Another amazing free tool is Google Earth, shown in Figure 3-10. You can pan around a subject, such as a cityscape (displayed in 3D for many cities), to find the best viewpoints. Google Earth accurately represents hills and valleys, allowing you to accurately anticipate obstructions. To tilt your viewpoint down to ground level, hold down the shift key and drag downward with the mouse.

> **Tip:** Twice a year—near the end of May and the middle of July—the setting sun is aligned perfectly with the east-west streets of Manhattan. Known as Manhattanhenge, it's a perfect example of the importance of planning your shots around the movement of the sun.

Once you find a viewpoint, click the View menu and then click Sun. Adjust the time on the slider, and watch the sun, moon, and stars move across the sky. This allows you to see exactly how buildings and hills will be illuminated and where the sun will be for the time you're visiting a location.

SILHOUETTES & SHOOTING INTO THE SUN

As a general rule, photographers tend to keep their back to the sun when taking photos and let their subject bask in the sunlight. Like many rules, there's a time for this rule to be broken. Shooting into the sun isn't the best way to get a highly detailed subject, but it produces an ethereal mood by creating soft, warm, monochrome lighting and deep silhouettes such as that in the cover and Figure 3-11.

Shoot during the golden hour while facing into the sun to create the ethereal mood. If you use autofocus, you may find your camera has a hard time focusing due to the strong sunlight eliminating contrast from the frame, so be prepared to manually focus.

Grass and reeds are a good choice for subjects; not only will they wait patiently while you compose your shot, but the sun will shine through them. Next, play with the location of the sun. Sometimes it looks nice directly behind your subject. At other times, you might prefer it slightly outside the frame.

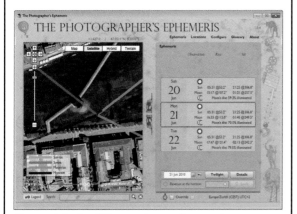

Figure 3-9: At different times of year, the sun can rise and set in very different places on the horizon.

Figure 3-10: Use Google Earth to determine where the sun will shine at different times of day.

Be sure to examine your pictures as you go. If your photos look too bright or washed-out, try setting your exposure compensation down a stop. By lowering your exposure compensation, you'll create more contrast and will likely silhouette your subject like in the photo in Figure 3-12.

You can get bright orbs known as flares in your photos any time you have a light shining into your lens. Flares have been a popular photography trend lately, and many people intentionally add flares in post-processing, so you don't necessarily need to avoid them. Professional-quality lenses typically have less flaring than consumer-quality lenses. In other words, the cheaper your lens, the more flare you're likely to get.

If you're shooting into the sun and don't want to create silhouettes, bracket your shots and use HDR techniques to combine the photos. For more information about HDR, refer to Chapter 11.

USING FLASH

Flash has a deservedly bad reputation for blinding people, overexposing faces, casting ugly shadows, and making eyes glow like demons. You might think flash is evil, but once you learn to properly use flash, you'll consider it your most important camera feature. First, I'll show you the difference between on-camera and external flash. Then, I'll describe how to use fill flash to reduce shadows when your subject is in bright light. Next, I'll describe two ways to prevent hard lighting and redeye: bounce flash and flash modifiers. Finally, I'll wrap up the

To watch a video on **buying a flash,** scan the QR code or visit:

sdp.io/BuyingFlash

flash lesson with a fun section on using high-speed flash.

Tip: For information about off-camera flash, using multiple light sources, and using external strobes, refer to Chapter 6, "Portraits."

Figure 3-11: Shooting into the sun creates an ethereal, nearly monochrome, style.

Figure 3-12: To create more contrast and silhouette your subject, lower your exposure compensation.

DIRECT FLASH

The series of pictures in Figure 3-13 shows a model in a typical office environment: multiple sources of light but still too dim to shoot without flash. The first picture was taken without flash, leaving the backlit model underexposed. The second picture was taken using the built-in flash, and the final picture was taken with a an external flash mounted to the hot shoe on top of the camera. Notice that using an external flash creates more shadow below the chin because it's farther above the lens, but this extra distance eliminates red-eye and adds more depth to the picture.

As these pictures show, external flash is better than built-in flash, and built-in flash is better than no flash (when the face is in shadow). Many cameras automatically remove red-eye, but the result is never as nice as using an external flash.

Figure 3-13: Pictures without flash, with built-in flash, and with an external flash.

Figure 3-14: Use fill flash to reduce the negative effects of top lighting.

FILL FLASH

Flash is not just for indoors—you can use it anytime you want front lighting. If you use the flash in daylight, a technique called fill flash, the flash will fill in ugly shadows and create a catch light in the model's eyes. I almost always use fill flash when photographing people, but it's especially important when the sun is to a subject's back or directly overhead.

When shooting outdoors, an overcast sky is considered ideal for portrait photography because it casts a soft, even light. The light is still top lighting, however, which casts shadows below the eyes and highlights lines in the face.

The two pictures in Figure 3-14 show the power of adding fill flash with soft lighting from an overcast sky; the difference is even more extreme with direct sunlight. As you can see by looking at the background, the exposure didn't change between shots. Adding the front lighting reduced the appearance of lines, removed the shadows from the eyes, and added catch lights to the eyes. If the fill flash feels too powerful, you can reduce the flash output.

To use fill flash, switch your camera to Aperture Priority or Shutter Priority mode and then turn on the flash. Take a sample picture with the flash at the default output: if the subject looks washed out or the background is dark, reduce the flash; if your model still has harsh shadows or the background is overexposed, increase the flash.

Control the flash output using Flash Exposure Compensation (FEC). Most external flashes have buttons on the back to allow you to control the flash output directly. If your flash lacks these buttons, or if you're using the on-camera flash, adjust the FEC directly from your camera. Refer to your camera's manual, or one of the tutorials at *sdp.io/tutorials*, for detailed instructions.

To watch a video on **fill flash & FEC,** scan the QR code or visit:

sdp.io/FillFlash

Tip: When using flash, be careful not to shoot faster than the flash can recharge (also known as recycling). If you find that your flash takes too long to recharge, increase your ISO setting, replace your batteries, or buy an external battery pack for your flash.

BOUNCE FLASH

While flashes are perfect for front lighting, the small size of flash heads always creates hard lighting. To soften the light, external flashes often give you the ability to change the angle of the flash head to point up or to the side. This technique, known as bounce flash, reflects the light off the ceiling or a wall before it reaches your subject. Naturally, it only works indoors.

Bouncing flash dramatically changes the lighting in a picture. By tilting the flash upward, you make the light reflect from the ceiling. Essentially, the ceiling becomes a massive reflector, greatly increasing the surface area transmitting the light. This larger surface area softens the light as it falls on the model's face.

Figure 3-15 shows a model lit by direct flash and then lit by bounce flash pointed directly at the ceiling. The light from the direct flash is much harsher, washes out the model's skin, makes the skin and hair seem oily, and casts a dark shadow under the chin. By simply pointing the flash head at the ceiling, you will make the skin appear smoother, soften the shadows, and make the background look more natural.

You can rotate some flash heads to the left or right, as well as up or down. When possible, try to bounce the flash off a corner of the room behind you. The first of the two pictures in Figure 3-16 shows the flash bounced off the left corner of the room, creating *short lighting*

To watch a video on **bounce flash,** scan the QR code or visit:

sdp.io/Bounce

by lighting the side of the model's face farthest from the camera. The second picture shows the flash bounced off the right corner of the room, creating *broad lighting* by lighting the side of the model's face closest to the camera. Changing the direction of the light gives the model a very different look; broad lighting tends to make the face seem wider. For more information, refer to Chapter 6, "Portraits."

In a portrait studio, the photographer would need to move lights around the room to achieve the different looks that you can create by simply changing the angle of your flash head. Because bounce flash uses walls and ceilings to reflect light, every room is different. Experiment with different bounce flash angles to find the best angles for the room you're in. If you're moving around a room (like a wedding photographer does at a reception), your best bet is to angle

the flash almost straight up, but rotate it slightly forward (towards your subject) and to one side.

You should be aware of several things when using bounce flash:

- Because the light is distributed over a greater area, the flash will use much more power. This will cause the flash to take longer to recharge and will wear down your flash's batteries faster. Pack an extra set of batteries.

- If the ceiling or wall you reflect the light from is anything other than white, it will change the color of the light. For example, bouncing flash off a red ceiling will give the model a red cast.

- Bounce flash won't work outdoors, in places with very high ceilings, or in rooms with dark ceilings (such as natural wood). However, you can bounce your flash off a reflector.

Figure 3-15: Direct flash vs. bounce flash.

Figure 3-16: Flash bounced from camera left and camera right.

Beware of products that fit over a pop-up flash to bounce it upward. Pop-up flashes aren't powerful enough to fill a room with light. Save your money and buy a higher-powered, external flash.

To watch a video on **flash modifiers,** scan the QR code or visit:

sdp.io/Mods

FLASH MODIFIERS

Bounce flash is convenient when using an external flash, but it only works indoors and requires low, white ceilings. To improve your flash when you can't use bounce flash, you can attach a modifier to your flash. The three pictures in Figure 3-17 show the effects of the three external flash modifiers shown in the upper left hand corner: a diffuser (a small plastic cap that fits over your flash head), a small soft box, and a large soft box. Because the diffuser bounces light in all directions, it creates the softest light while still creating a catch light. It also uses the most power, however. The small and large soft boxes create softer, more flattering light than a bare flash bulb, use less power than a diffuser, and function when bounce flash will not.

In practice, the only flash modifier I use is the small soft box. The additional surface area significantly improves direct flash without being as unwieldy as a large soft box.

Another popular modifier is a bracket, a favorite of wedding photographers. Brackets connect to your camera's tripod mount and hold the flash farther away from the lens, increasing shadows but decreasing the risk of red-eye. More importantly, the bracket allows you to hold your camera vertically while keeping the flash above the camera. Without a bracket, vertical shots require the flash to be off to the left of the camera, creating ugly side lighting. Because the lighting is still direct, rather than bounced, the flash does not use excessive battery power.

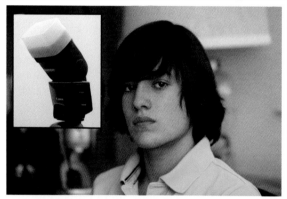

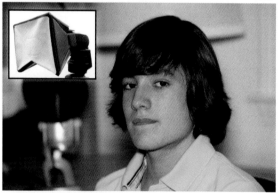

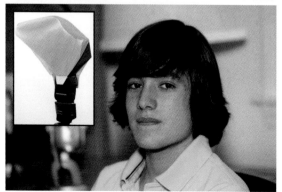

Figure 3-17: Pictures taken with a diffuser, a small soft box, and a large soft box.

STOPPING MOTION

Flash is also good for stopping motion in wildlife or sports photography. If you find that your pictures are blurry because the subject is moving too fast, turn the flash on. The camera will freeze the action the moment it fires the flash.

On most cameras, you will need to enable high-speed sync before your flash will work properly with faster shutter speeds (usually over 1/250th or 1/500th, which will be displayed as "250" or "500" on your camera). Not all camera bodies or flashes support high-speed sync, however. Specifically, many entry-level Nikon cameras (including the D3x00 and D5x00 series) do not support high-speed sync. While most name-brand flashes support high-speed sync, most generic flashes do not.

Fortunately, you don't need to understand the mechanics of flash and high-speed shutters—just read your flash's manual and know how to turn on high-speed sync when you use faster shutter speeds. Usually, it's as easy as pushing a button or flipping a switch. Then, set your camera to shutter priority mode and choose a high shutter speed. If you do want to understand how high-speed sync works, refer to "Flash Sync Problems" in Chapter 5.

To effectively stop water droplets, as shown in Figure 3-18, choose 1/4000th or 1/8000th and the highest f/stop number possible without underexposing your pictures.

To take the pictures of water droplets, I added red food coloring to a bag of water. I hung the bag of water over a glass dish and poked a hole in it so the bag would drip every few seconds. I then put a blue gel over my flash, pointed the flash directly at the dish, and set the flash to high-speed sync. I put my camera on a tripod and manually focused. I set the camera to Manual mode, set the aperture to f/8, and set the shutter speed to 1/2000th. I tried to snap a picture as each droplet hit the dish. Timing is critical, of course—I had to take hundreds of pictures to get a couple of usable pictures.

For the strawberry picture, I once again set my flash to high-speed sync. I connected the flash to an off-camera flash sync cord (about $20 for a generic cord) so I could light the strawberry from the side, and used a reflector to fill in the shadows. Otherwise, my camera settings were the same as for the water droplets. Figure 3-19 shows the setup.

USING OFF-CAMERA FLASH

Once you're comfortable working with on-camera flash, you should take control of your light by moving your flash off-camera. It's not as difficult, or expensive, as it sounds: you can use a $45 Neewer TT560 manual flash and $22

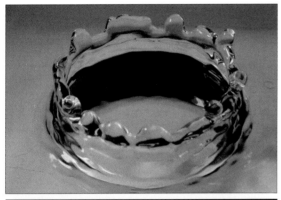

Figure 3-18: High-speed flash sync can stop the motion of water droplets.

CowboyStudio NPT-04 trigger to achieve any single light effect you can imagine (with any camera that has a flash shoe).

Even if you plan to focus on natural light photography, mastering a single off-camera flash will help you understand and master light. In this chapter, I've discussed different types of light and the effects of directional lighting, but there's no substitute for hands-on experience. Every photographer should, at the very least, experiment with an off-camera light and different subjects. You don't even need a light stand; simply hold the flash in your hand, as I demonstrate in the off-camera flash video.

Before you buy an off-camera flash setup, practice controlling off-camera light by using a flashlight to illuminate a model (or mannequin head) in a dark room. First, study how moving the light changes the catch light in your model's eyes. Start with the flash near the camera and move it higher and higher. Watch how the light's position impacts the catch light.

To watch a video on **directional lighting,** scan the QR code or visit:

sdp.io/DirLighting

To watch a video on **off-camera flash,** scan the QR code or visit:

sdp.io/Flash

Make note of how high you can raise the flash before the brow casts a shadow across the eyes, blocking the catch light. Move the light gradually to one side, watching as the catch lights move. Where are you when the nose blocks the catch light from the far eye?

Next, study the shadow under the nose. Start with the light directly at eye level, and slowly move it higher, watching as the shadow under the nose grows longer. Move the light to one side, and watch as the shadow under the nose grows larger and moves away from you. Where are you when the shadow is the most pleasing?

You should also study how the location of your light changes the shadow under the chin. Start with the light below the chin, illuminating the neck. This under lighting isn't flattering for anyone, because it makes the neck seem fat and the chin seem weak. As you raise your flash to eye level, notice that the shadow under the chin hides the neck. As you raise the light higher, the neck becomes completely dark. Where should your light be to best hide a double chin?

Now, study how the light changes the appearance of the cheekbones. Start with the light at eye level, and raise it higher. With the light at eye level, the cheekbones will completely disappear, flattening the face. With the light higher, gentle shadows will appear below the cheekbones, accentuating the facial structure.

Finally, watch how moving the light changes the appearance of hair. With the light pointed

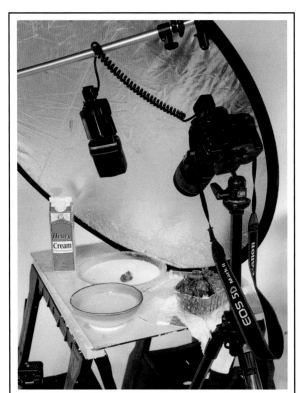

Figure 3-19: I used an off-camera flash sync cord to enable high-speed flash sync.

away from your model's hair, the hair will seem flat, and might disappear completely in shadow. When you point the light directly at your model's hair, it will shine. Move the light behind your model, and shine it through his or her hair, and notice how the hair glows. Which conditions were the most flattering for the hair?

After separately studying how light placement affected the appearance of each of your model's features, find the single most flattering light placement. Now, consider whether adding a second light source from another direction to add some light to the shadows might be even more flattering. Would adding a third light to the hair improve the picture further?

Off-camera lighting isn't limited to portraiture; you should perform this same exercise with different objects. Create a still life scene with fruit, and try lighting the reflective surface of a tablet or smartphone. Watch your light on your home as the sun moves across the sky from sunrise to sunset. Watch the shadows cast by car headlights as they drive past. Watch your

own shadows as you walk past streetlights at night. As long as your eyes are open, you can be studying light and shadow.

White Balance

It's morning, and you're reading a book on your patio while eating your breakfast. The pages are white in the morning light, just as they always are. At lunchtime, in your office, the pages look the same under the fluorescent lights. Before bed, you use your LED book light to read a few more pages from the (still very white) pages.

White is white, right? Wrong. Your brain is lying to you.

Different light sources have different color temperatures. Your brain tries its best to hide this from you by adjusting the signals from your eye so that white looks white, regardless of the light. If you don't believe me, go for a drive at night. If your car has conventional headlights, the newer high-intensity discharge (HID) or LED headlights look blue. If you have

Light Source	Color Temperatures
Candles	*1800 K*
Incandescent Bulb	*3000 K*
Fluorescent Bulb	*3000 K*
Sunrise Daylight	*3000 K*
Moonlight	*4000 K*
LED Bulb	*5000 K*
Daylight	*6000 K*
Flash	*6000 K*
Overcast Daylight	*6500 K*

Figure 3-20: Common color temperatures, measured in Kelvin.

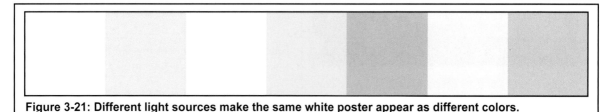

Figure 3-21: Different light sources make the same white poster appear as different colors.

HID or LED headlights, everyone else seems to have orange headlights. Your headlights always look white, though. Conventional headlights and HID headlights are both white; they just have different color temperatures.

Some common color temperatures, measured in Kelvin, are shown in the table in Figure 3-20. Unfortunately, these measurements are not as precise as they seem, because light bulbs of the same type can have widely varying color temperatures.

Lower color temperatures are considered "warm," meaning they cast an orange light. Higher color temperatures are considered "cool," meaning they cast a bluish cast. I know it's confusing, but you'll figure it out with the practices at the end of this chapter. Figure 3-21 shows a section of the same white poster photographed under different types of light with the camera's white balance set to daylight. From left to right, the light sources are: perfect daylight, daylight on a snowy day, fluorescent office lights, a compact fluorescent bulb, incandescent light, halogen lights, and LED lights.

Flash and daylight have the same color temperature, so you can take flash pictures in the sun without worries. If you take a flash picture under warm artificial light, the foreground (lit by the flash) will be cooler than the background. For best results, bounce your flash off the ceiling so that the light from the flash overwhelms the warm artificial lights.

Your brain automatically adjusts to different color temperatures, but it gets confused when there are multiple light sources with different color temperatures. Digital cameras work the same way by applying a feature called *auto white balance*. Auto white balance is sometimes completely wrong, though, so it's important to understand how to set it manually.

Auto white balance, your camera's default setting, works most of the time. For those times it doesn't, it's generally easy to adjust color

To watch a video on **gels with flash**, scan the QR code or visit:

sdp.io/FlashGels

temperature in post-processing. If you shoot raw (as described in Chapter 4, "Controlling Your Camera"), don't even worry about it— while your camera will display the picture using the color temperature it sensed, once you get it into your computer you can adjust it however you see fit. Otherwise, adjusting the white balance is still simple in any image editing application.

Higher-end cameras allow you to set a custom white balance by reading the actual color temperature from a white or gray card, or any other neutral object.

If there are multiple light sources with different color temperatures (such as daylight and incandescent lights) or if you use artificial light and your flash, part of your picture will definitely be off—regardless of how you set the white balance. Allow your camera to select a white balance and then selectively adjust the color temperate in post-processing. If you're really determined to match the color temperature of your flash to artificial lighting, place a color-correcting gel over the flash head. Then, set the white balance on your camera to match the artificial lights. Usually, you'll be taping an orange gel over your flash head to warm the flash to match incandescent lights, or a green gel to match fluorescent lights. Bulbs vary so much that getting a perfect match might take some experimentation.

SUMMARY

You need shadow to show texture. Because hard lighting gives more distinct shadows, hard lighting also emphasizes texture, while soft lighting hides texture. Front lighting, such as on-camera flash, also hides texture by minimizing the shadows cast by uneven surfaces.

Take a quiz!

sdp.io/quiz3

Therefore, if you want to show texture, use hard top or side lighting. If you want to hide texture, as you would when photographing someone's face, use soft front lighting from the same direction as the camera. To add depth by casting some shadows, move the light source up and to one side.

If you want to show three-dimensional form, use top or side lighting that's hard enough to cast shadows. If you want to show shape, use front or back lighting to create contrast between the subject and background.

The most important lesson in the chapter is this: to take a great picture, you must take control of the lighting. For landscape and architectural photography, wait until the golden hours. For wildlife, find a viewpoint where the sun is behind you so that your subject is nicely illuminated. For portraits, move your models out of hard light and into the shade, and use flash to add front-lighting. When indoors, bounce your flash to add more depth.

PRACTICE

This chapter's practices help you understand the different qualities of light and master white balance.

- **Natural light:** For the next week, wherever you go, study the light around you. Is there a single source of light or multiple sources? Are there light-colored surfaces such as walls and ceilings that softly reflect the light? Is the light diffused by lampshades, curtains, or clouds? How big is the light source, and how far away is it? What color is the light, and how does that change the color of the surfaces it strikes?

- **Understanding lighting in photographs:** Look through older pictures of yours and examine the lighting. Can you identify the light sources? What could you have done differently to improve the light?

- **Hard and soft light:** On a sunny day, take a picture of someone standing in full sunlight. Then, have him or her move into the shade. Which picture turned out better?

- **Fill flash:** On a sunny day, take pictures with and without fill flash by having a person face into the sun, with the sun to his or her side, and with the sun to his or her back. Then, have the person move into the shade, and take another pair of pictures with and without fill flash. Which pictures turned out best? Did having the sun in the model's face affect his or her expression?

- **The golden hour:** Starting at an hour before sunrise, take pictures of your home or another building every hour throughout the day until the sun has set. Which picture turned out best, and why?

- **White balance:** Override automatic white balance by setting your camera's white balance to daylight. Photograph white paper in sunlight. Then, after dark (or in a room with no sunlight), take a picture of the same paper indoors without flash. For bonus points, use different light sources to light the paper. Compare the different photos and notice that the paper appears to be different colors depending on the light source.

- **Art:** Research the paintings of impressionist Claude Monet. His paintings completely disregard the sharpness and detail we've come to cherish with digital photography, but his understanding of light is unparalleled. In particular, look up his Haystacks series of paintings, which depict the same subject from the same viewpoint in varying light conditions.

- **Outdoor light:** Pick a convenient outdoor subject. Over the course of several weeks (or even seasons), photograph it at different times of day and in different weather conditions. Take each picture from the same spot with the same camera settings.

CONCEPTUAL PHOTOGRAPHY

BY ERKKI ALVENMOD, *HTTP://ALVENMOD.SE/*

The subject of most photographs is a person, place, or animal. My passion, however, is conceptual photography. In conceptual photography, the subject is an abstract idea, feeling, or thought.

For example, I created the Sleepwalker series in Figure 3-22. You can see the story at *sdp.io/sleepwalker*. My vision of the Sleepwalker series was a man who dreams he is floating over a lake and can sense a presence that is trying to drown and kill him. He does die in the dream, but the presence turns out not to be a dark evil force. Rather, the presence is soothing, loving, and warm. Sleepwalker is about death, and that death can be a peaceful relief for the suffering.

I use five steps to create my photos:

- **Create the concept**. What idea you want to communicate? What feelings do you want to awaken within the viewer? To create truly unique conceptual photos, you need to have an open mind and to think outside of the box. I get my ideas from everyday life, on the subway, during my son's football practice, in the middle of a business meeting, while fishing, while walking, or just before I fall asleep.

- **Sketch the photo**. Sketch the idea on paper. This simple exercise will help you envision the final result, add or remove details, and change the overall composition of the shot.

- **Test the sketch**. If it is important to you that your audience understands your message, simply ask people around you to guess your sketch's concept. If you find that most people don't get it, you might want to consider being more obvious by adding more elements or making existing elements more prominent. In the case of Sleepwalker, the idea is to provoke thoughts and feelings, and not simply to send a message.

- **Prepare the shot**. Identify everything you might need for the shot, including the location, the time of day, weather, season, props, camera gear, lighting equipment, assistants, and models. Visit the location at different times of day and take test shots from different angles and with different compositions. Make note of the camera settings you will need for your shot. Make a list of all the equipment that you need, including extra batteries and memory cards. If you are planning a self-portrait, as I did with the Sleepwalker series, bring a remote shutter release.

- **Make the photo**. Plan to begin your shoot several hours early, when you know you will have plenty of sunlight to work with, so you won't find yourself rushing because the sun is setting. If you did all the preparation steps above, you'll come home with a great conceptual shot to show off to your friends and on your favorite website.

Figure 3-22: The Sleepwalker series.

4 CHAPTER Controlling your Camera

This chapter teaches you how to control your camera, including how to:

- Choose the right focus mode for still or moving subjects.

- Troubleshoot autofocus problems.

- Control depth-of-field with aperture, distance, and focal length.

- Control motion blur and camera shake with shutter speed.

- Set ISO to get good image quality with the shutter speed you need.

- Use histograms to understand exposure.

- Use raw files to improve image quality.

This chapter gets technical at times, but don't let it discourage you. If you don't understand a section right now, skip it, and come back to it once you've gotten some more practice.

FOCUS

Like the human eye, cameras focus on a two-dimensional plane parallel to the sensor known as the focal plane. Anything in front of or behind the focal plane will be out of focus. Depending on your camera settings, subjects behind or in front of the focal plane might be completely blurred or sharp enough to seem in focus.

The videos in this chapter will help you understand the focal plane, so if it doesn't yet make sense, just keep reading.

FOCUS MODES

Cameras can lock focus onto a still subject or continually track moving subjects. Typically, you have two or three choices:

- **Single focus (known as AF-S, S-AF, One-shot, or Single)**. Best for still subjects. Depress the shutter button slightly, and the camera will find the focus point, and hold it until you shoot (even if you recompose). If the subject moves forward or backwards, it will be out of focus. Typically, cameras select this focus mode in landscape and portrait shooting modes.

- **Continuous focus (known as AF-C, C-AF, AI Servo, Monitor, or Tracking)**. Best for moving subjects. Depress the shutter button slightly, and the camera will find the focus point. If the subject moves forward or backwards, keep the focus point on the subject, and the camera will do its best to keep the subject in focus. Continuous focusing does not allow for focus-recompose, discussed in the next section. No camera tracks moving subjects perfectly, so use continuous shooting and take dozens of pictures. Typically, cameras select this focus mode in sports mode.

- **Automatic focus (known as AF-A, A-AF, or AI Focus)**. Designed to be one mode for any situation, this mode is only the right choice when you don't know how to set the focus mode. This mode initially behaves like single focusing, but if it detects the subject moving in or out of focus, it switches to continuous. Some cameras do not have a third focusing mode.

Tech details: Sometimes you'll hear from old-school camera users who insist on focusing manually. Modern cameras don't include the special focusing screens that manual-focus-only cameras had, which allowed the human eye to focus precisely. Therefore, autofocusing is more precise unless you follow the steps in the "Precise Focusing" section later in this chapter.

USING MULTIPLE FOCUS POINTS

All modern cameras have multiple focus points. By default, most cameras have all focus points enabled simultaneously, and the camera will arbitrarily focus using any of the focus points. This doesn't mean that everything in the picture will be in focus; there is still only a single focal plane. Using multiple focus points simply means the camera is choosing where to focus. Unfortunately, cameras often choose the wrong focus point, leading to pictures that seem to be out of focus.

For this reason, I recommend using a single focusing point and selecting the focusing point closest to where you want to focus in the frame. Because all cameras are different, you will need to refer to your camera's manual (or a tutorial at *sdp.io/tutorials*) for specific steps that allow you to select a single focus point.

HOW TO FOCUS-RECOMPOSE

Much of the time, the best composition requires you to place your subject off-center. The easiest way to do this is to select an off-center focusing point. However, most DSLRs have focusing points clustered around the center of the frame, preventing you from using the Rule of Thirds.

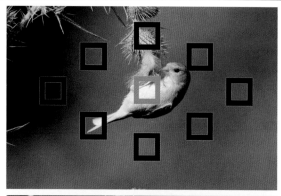

Figure 4-1: To achieve the off-center focus in the second picture, focus on the subject in the middle of the frame and then recompose.

Mirrorless cameras, on the other hand, typically allow you to autofocus anywhere in the frame.

If you are using a DSLR and need to focus away from a focusing point, follow these steps:

1. Select Single focus mode and select the focus point closest to where you want to focus. If you're having trouble focusing, or changing the focus point is difficult, simply choose the center focus point—it's the fastest.

2. Place the selected focus point over your subject, as shown in the first picture in Figure 4-1, and depress the shutter button halfway. This causes the camera to focus on your subject.

3. While keeping the shutter button partially depressed, recompose the picture, as shown in the second picture in Figure 4-1. The subject will stay in focus even though it is no longer in the center of the frame.

4. Press the shutter all the way down to take the picture.

Focus-recompose works with almost every camera, so it's a useful technique for making an off-center composition using an unfamiliar camera—like when a tourist asks you to take a picture of him or her. With mirrorless cameras, you can focus anywhere in the frame, making focus-recompose unnecessary.

Note: Focus-recompose is not a precise way of focusing because the focal plane is flat, but you move the camera in a circular motion when you recompose. Also, both you and your subject might move slightly during the time it takes you to focus-recompose. This isn't a problem with most kit lenses, but recomposing can throw your subject noticeably out of focus if you have a very shallow depth-of-field. If you find your subject is out of focus after using focus-recompose, don't use focus-recompose. Instead, select the focusing point closest to where you want to focus and then crop the image in your image editing software to get the composition you want. Remember to step back or zoom back to leave room to crop later.

HOW TO FOCUS ON MOVING SUBJECTS

Focus-recompose won't work with moving subjects; by the time you recompose, they'll already be out of focus. For moving subjects, set your camera to continuous focusing and select the focus point closest to where you want the subject to appear in the frame.

To focus on off-center moving subjects, select a focus point closest to where you want the subject to be.

For example, if you want to compose a picture using the rule of thirds, you might put the subject in the right third of the frame. By selecting the right-most focus point, as shown in Figure 4-2, you can be sure your camera has your off-center subject in focus.

When using telephoto lenses with small moving subjects, such as when photographing flying birds, it can be almost impossible to keep a single focus point on your subject. In these cases, you should select multiple focus points to allow your camera to choose the best point automatically. For more information, refer to Chapter 8.

Having an expensive camera body and a fast lens makes it much easier to focus on moving

To watch a video about **autofocus,** scan the QR code or visit:

sdp.io/Autofocusing

subjects. A "fast" lens is a lens with a low minimum f/stop number, such as f/1.8 or f/2.8. Focusing on moving subjects is inaccurate no matter what type of camera you have, however. For that reason, set your camera to continuous shooting and take as many pictures as possible. Many of your shots will be out of focus, but a few should be in focus. The faster the subject is moving towards or away from you, the more shots will be out of focus.

TROUBLESHOOTING AUTOFOCUS

If it's dark, or you are focusing on a single color subject like a shirt, autofocus might not work. You'll see the autofocus "hunt," which means it moves to the closest focus point, all the way out to infinity, and then perhaps back in. This can take a couple of seconds—long enough to annoy both the photographer and the subject.

This happens because cameras autofocus by focusing farther and closer until they find maximum contrast. For example, if you're focusing on a black-and-white checkerboard, the edges will appear blurred and gray when out of focus. The camera will adjust the focus until the edges are sharp and black-and-white.

If you're attempting to focus on a solid color, the autofocus system won't be able to find any contrast, regardless of the amount of light you have. The easiest thing to do is to focus on an area of high contrast near

Figure 4-2: Manually select a focus point for off-center moving subjects.

your subject and then recompose. So, move the focus point to an area of high contrast about the same distance as the subject, focus the picture, and then re-frame it.

In dark situations, try using flash—if only during the focusing period. Most flashes assist focusing in dim light by emitting an infrared beam or flickering the flash. If your camera does not have a flash built in, try attaching an external flash. When a camera focuses by adding light to a scene, it's called *active focusing*.

You can switch to manual focus, but manual focus is highly overrated on DSLRs. First, if it's dark enough that autofocus isn't working, it's also going to be difficult to see well enough to manually focus. Also, autofocus is more precise than the human eye—you just can't see sharply enough through your little viewfinder to focus that precisely. Many mirrorless cameras offer focus magnification and focus peaking, which makes manual focusing more practical.

Here's an expensive way to troubleshoot autofocus problems: buy a fast lens with a low minimum f/stop number. During focusing, the camera keeps the aperture wide open so the maximum amount of light hits the autofocus sensor. If your current lens has a maximum aperture of f/5.6, an f/4.0 lens will allow twice the amount of light to reach the sensor, and an f/2.8 lens will allow four times as much light. That's another reason why lenses with big apertures are worthwhile—even if you select a higher f/stop number, they make focusing faster and more reliable.

> **Tip:** I keep a small but bright flashlight in my camera bag. Not only is it useful for lighting up your camera controls in total darkness, but you can shine the flashlight on the subject and use the light to focus.

If your camera is focusing correctly, but you want more of your picture to be in focus or you want the background to be thrown out of focus,

read the "Aperture" and "Depth-of-Field" sections later in this chapter.

ADVANCED FOCUSING TECHNIQUES

At this point, you know all you need to know about focusing. On rare occasions, however, you might benefit from one of the following three advanced focusing techniques: back-button focus, focus traps, and precise focusing using live view. If you are a casual shooter, skip forward to the Exposure section.

BACK-BUTTON FOCUS

By default, all cameras autofocus when you depress the shutter halfway. Many DSLRs and some mirrorless cameras also have a separate button for focusing, usually labeled AF-On or AEL. It takes several sessions to get used to pressing a separate button for autofocus, but once you learn the technique, you'll never go back, because back-button focusing allows you to keep your camera set to continuous focus mode to track moving subjects, while still allowing you to use focus-recompose or even manually focus without changing your camera's focusing mode.

To use back-button focus, refer to your camera's manual or a tutorial at *sdp.io/tutorials*, and change two or three camera settings:

- **Select continuous autofocusing**. This is the last time you'll ever have to change your focusing mode.

- **Turn off autofocusing when you depress the shutter.** After you change this setting, depressing your shutter halfway will start metering but not focusing.

- **Enable back-button autofocus.** Some camera bodies have an AF-On button that autofocuses by default. If your camera has that button and it causes the camera to autofocus, you don't need to adjust any other settings. If you don't have that button, or it has been assigned a different function, refer to your camera's manual to redefine a button's function to start autofocusing.

For stationary subjects, just press-and-release the AF-On button to achieve single focus, allowing you to focus-recompose. For moving subjects, hold down AF-On to use continuous. To manually focus, or to keep the same focus point as your previous shot, just don't press AF-On.

To understand the usefulness of this, imagine that you're watching a heron standing in a pond. While the bird is stationary, you can focus on the eye and then recompose the picture to use the rule of thirds. When the bird takes off, simply keep your focus point on the bird and hold down the AF-On button. If you weren't using back-button focus, you would have to switch your camera from single to continuous focus, a process that would waste several seconds and make you miss the shot.

Back-button autofocus is useful for other types of photography where you might not want to autofocus between shots, especially when using a tripod. For example, with landscape or night photography, you might want to carefully autofocus and then recompose. If you want to take multiple pictures without refocusing, you would need to switch your lens to manual focus, a process that often moves the camera. With back-button focus, your camera never refocuses unless you press the AF-On button.

FOCUS TRAPS

Sometimes the subject is moving too quickly for you to be able to focus, even when using continuous focusing. Get the shot by using a focus trap. Focus on an area where you know your subject will be in the future, switch your lens to manual focus, and wait. When the subject crosses the plane of focus, snap the shot.

To watch a video about **back-button focus,** scan the QR code or visit:

sdp.io/BackButton

PRECISE FOCUSING USING LIVE VIEW

When taking still-life pictures with extremely shallow depth-of-field and a tripod, you might need to be extremely precise with your focusing. In those circumstances, you can use live view to choose the exact focus point:

1. If you have a DSLR, switch your camera to live view mode.

2. Zoom live view (not the lens) in as far as possible to view the focal point.

3. Focus the camera in one of two ways:

   - Manually focus your lens.

   - Use the *contrast-based focus* of live view mode.

Zooming with live view allows you to see individual pixels and verify that the picture will be in focus when viewed at full size, which is impossible when looking through the viewfinder. Additionally, live view's contrast-based focusing eliminates the possibility that the camera's standard *phase detection focusing* is miscalibrated.

Don't bother if you're not using a tripod or if your subject is moving, because the movement will be too great for you to benefit.

SHUTTER MODES

Cameras include at least three or four different shutter modes:

- **Single shot.** When you press the shutter button, the camera takes one picture.

- **Continuous.** When you press the shutter button, the camera takes pictures as fast as it can until you release the shutter.

- **Delayed or timed.** When you press the shutter button, the camera waits a few seconds to take the picture.

- **Quiet or silent.** Some newer cameras have a mode that reduces the noise of the shutter, which is useful during weddings and when photographing wildlife at close range.

I almost always use continuous shooting. Even if I'm photographing a still subject, I like to take a few pictures to be sure I get one that's not shaky.

Delaying the shutter is useful in two situations, both of which require a tripod:

- **Self-portraits.** Choose delayed shutter, press the shutter button, and run into the frame.

- **Eliminating camera shake.** Even if your camera is on a tripod, the act of pushing the shutter button can shake the camera and reduce the sharpness. You won't ever notice this minor amount of shake unless you're taking a picture at night with a shutter speed between a 1/4th and 10 seconds.

CAMERA MODES

Most cameras have four different modes (among others you won't typically need):

- **Program Mode (P).** The camera chooses your settings. Choose this mode when you don't have time to think about your camera settings.

- **Aperture Priority Mode (A or Av).** You control the aperture (discussed in the next section) with your camera's main dial.

Your camera determines the shutter speed required to expose your picture. Choose this mode when you want to control background blur.

- **Shutter Priority Mode (S or Tv).** You control the shutter speed (discussed later in this chapter) with the main dial. Your camera determines the aperture required to expose your picture. Choose this mode when capturing action and movement.

- **Manual Mode (M).** You control the shutter speed with the main dial, and you control the aperture by turning a secondary dial or by holding the exposure compensation button and turning the main dial. If you also choose to control the ISO, you will have complete control over your camera's exposure. Choose this mode when you need to control both the background blur and freeze movement.

The sections that follow will describe aperture, shutter speed, and ISO in more detail.

APERTURE

A lens' aperture works exactly like the pupil of an eye. The wider it is, the more light it lets in. The more light it lets in, the shorter the shutter speed needs to stay open to properly expose a picture. Figure 4-3 shows approximate relative sizes of the most commonly used apertures.

Aperture is measured in f/stops, such as f/2.8, f/8, and f/16. It seems counterintuitive, but the smaller the f/stop number, the wider the aperture. Therefore, f/2.8 is a much wider aperture than f/8 and f/16.

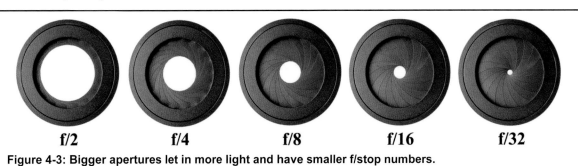

| f/2 | f/4 | f/8 | f/16 | f/32 |

Figure 4-3: Bigger apertures let in more light and have smaller f/stop numbers.

Tech details: If you're interested in the math, f/stops are a factor of the square root of 2—about 1.4. Each f/stop is 1.4 times the previous f/stop. Two stops higher always has an f/stop number two times higher.

To watch a video about **aperture and DoF,** scan the QR code or visit:

sdp.io/Aperture

Besides controlling the amount of light that enters the lens, aperture is the easiest way to control *depth-of-field*. With a short depth-of-field, out-of-focus subjects are very blurry. With a long depth-of-field, out-of-focus subjects can appear to be in focus.

Figure 4-4 shows the same picture at three different apertures: f/2.8, f/8, and f/16. In each picture, the lens is focused on the green apple in the foreground. Because f/2.8 is a very

wide aperture, the depth-of-field is very short, making the orange blurry and throwing the bananas in the background very out of focus. At f/8—shutting down the aperture three stops—the smaller aperture reduces the amount of blur in the bananas. At f/16—shutting down the aperture another two stops and five full stops down from f/2.8—the bananas are almost in focus. Shooting at f/16 requires a shutter speed 32 times longer than shooting at f/2.8.

Figure 4-4: Focused on the green apple and shot at f/2.8, f/8, and f/16.

Figure 4-5: Depth-of-field at f/1.8, f/8, and f/22.

Small f/stop numbers, such as f/1.8 or f/2.8, are especially useful for portrait photography. Figure 4-5 shows three photos taken with an 85mm f/1.8 portrait lens. With the camera in aperture priority mode, I took the first picture wide open at f/1.8—enough to completely blur the background, making the model stand out. I turned the main dial to increase the f/stop three stops to f/8, making the background in the second picture clear enough that you can tell the model is standing in an alley, but still reducing distractions. I then turned the main dial to increase the f/stop number three stops to f/22, showing the buildings and cars in the background of the third picture clearly.

The only way to really understand aperture and depth-of-field is practice. To remember which way to adjust the aperture, remember this: low f/stop number, low background sharpness; high f/stop number, high background sharpness.

> **Tip:** When you look through an SLR's viewfinder, you're always seeing the lens' lowest f/stop, because having the aperture wide open allows the most light to the viewfinder. Though most SLRs have a depth-of-field preview button that shuts the aperture down to the setting you have selected, this makes the viewfinder very dark. The easiest way to see the depth-of-field you'll get with a photo is simply to take a picture and review it on your camera's display.

Figuratively speaking, depth-of-field is not black-and-white, but shades of gray. While your camera always focuses on a single focal plane, subjects directly in front of and behind the focal plane will be *almost* in focus. Move a bit closer to or farther away from the camera, and subjects will be slightly less in focus. The farther something is from the focal plane, the more out of focus it will be.

In Figure 4-6, everything in the cone will be in the picture. The model will be perfectly in focus, because the camera is focused at 10 feet. As the cone fades from white to black, subjects will be less in focus.

Figure 4-6 demonstrates that depth-of-field is deeper behind a subject than in front of it. In this example, a subject could be 5 feet in front of the focal plane to be sharp enough to be considered part of the depth-of-field. A subject 10 feet behind the focal plane would be similarly sharp. Neither would be as in focus as the subject in the focal plane, however.

If you want to get as much of a scene in focus as possible, try this:

■ Choose aperture priority mode and adjust the main dial (shown in Figure 4-7) to select the highest f/stop number possible, such as f/22 or f/32.

■ Zoom out or use a wide-angle lens.

■ Focus about 1/3 of the way through the scene.

If you want a nicely blurred background, try this:

■ Choose aperture priority mode and adjust the main dial to select the lowest f/stop number possible.

■ Zoom all the way in or use a telephoto lens.

■ Get as close to the subject as your camera will focus.

■ Choose a location with a distant background.

> **Note**: I use aperture priority mode almost all the time, because it allows me to quickly change the aperture to control depth-of-field.

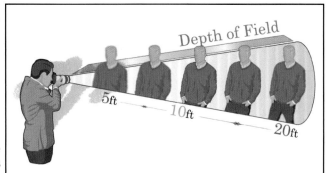

Figure 4-6: Depth-of-field is always shallower in front of the subject and deeper behind the subject.

If you still can't get enough background blur, consider buying a telephoto lens with a minimum f/stop number of f/2.8 or lower. All major lens manufacturers make 70-200 f/2.8 lenses that provide beautiful background blur when used at 200mm and f/2.8. A less expensive option is to use an 85mm f/1.8 lens.

The apertures you can choose from are defined by your lens. The lowest f/stop number is so important that they put it right into the lens' name. For example, my favorite standard zoom is commonly referred to as "24-105mm f/4.0." The f/4.0 is the smallest f/stop number I can use with the lens. Some zoom lenses have variable apertures, such as the "18-55mm f/3.5-5.6." When zoomed out to 18mm, the smallest f/stop number is f/3.5. When zoomed in to 55mm, the smallest f/stop number is f/5.6.

CONTROLLING DEPTH-OF-FIELD

The easiest way to control depth-of-field is to change the aperture. There are actually two other ways you can control depth-of-field: distance and focal length.

To shorten your depth-of-field and blur your background more, move closer to the subject and zoom in as much as possible. To increase your depth-of-field and sharpen the background, move farther from your subject and zoom out as much as possible.

Note: Sensor size impacts depth-of-field for a given f/stop, and all the examples in this book are shown in full-frame 35mm terms. Most cameras have smaller sensors, however.

To compare the depth-of-field you'll get with that of a full-frame sensor, multiply the f/stop by your camera's crop factor. If you don't know it, search for "<camera model> crop factor".

If I show an example at 200mm f/5.6 and your camera has a 1.5X crop factor, you would get similar results using 133mm f/3.7, because 200/1.5=133, and 5.6/1.5=3.7. If your camera has a 2X crop factor, you would need to use 100mm f/2.8 to get the same perspective and depth-of-field.

CHANGING DISTANCE

The three pictures in Figure 4-7 were taken with the same camera (a full-frame DSLR), lens (a 150mm macro lens), and aperture (f/8). The first picture is taken the farthest away. Notice that the bananas are slightly blurry in the background.

For the next picture in Figure 4-7, I moved the camera closer. Notice that the bananas got much blurrier, because moving the camera closer to the subject decreased the depth-of-field.

Figure 4-7: Moving closer to a subject reduces the depth-of-field.

To watch a video about **blurring the background,** scan the QR code or visit:

sdp.io/Blur

For the final picture in Figure 4-7, I moved very close to the apple. Notice that even the bottom of the stem isn't in focus and the bananas have been completely blurred. An extreme close-up creates an extremely shallow depth-of-field, completely blurring anything more than half-an-inch from the plane of focus.

For more information about distance and depth-of-field, refer to Chapter 12, "Macro."

CHANGING FOCAL LENGTH

Depth-of-field gets shorter as you zoom in. In other words, if you want to throw the background out of focus, zoom in. If you want to make the background clearer, zoom out.

The three pictures in Figure 4-8 show the same set of fruit at three different zoom levels: 28mm, 50mm, and 100mm. All photos are focused on the apple stem, but you should pay attention to the bananas in the background. As the photos progress and the photos zoom in more and more to the apple, the bananas get more and more out of focus—even though the aperture stayed at f/8.0 throughout.

In the first photo in Figure 4-8, taken at 28mm, the bananas appear to be perfectly in focus. 28mm is very wide-angle, and wide-angle photos always have a very deep depth-of-field.

In the next photo, taken at 50mm, the bananas are noticeably blurry, but the orange still looks mostly in-focus.

In the last photo, taken at 100mm, the bananas and the orange are completely blurry. As you might imagine, depth-of-field gets extremely shallow with super-telephoto lenses at 200mm, 400mm, and 800mm.

SHUTTER SPEED

We think of pictures as capturing an instant. In truth, pictures capture everything that happens within the short length of time that the shutter stays open. If the camera or the subject moves at all while the shutter is open, the camera will record that movement with motion blur or camera shake.

The shutter rests between the lens and the sensor and blocks light until you take a picture. When you press the shutter button, the shutter opens for the exact amount of time needed to get enough light to properly expose your picture, and then closes again.

Figure 4-8: Zoom in to reduce depth-of-field.

Typical shutter speeds range from 1/60th of a second (for a picture taken outdoors in the shade) to 1/1250th (for a picture taken in full sunlight). However, many cameras can take pictures at 1/8000th, and night photography often requires exposures taking more than 30 seconds.

When taking pictures, you often don't need to think about shutter speed. However, the picture will be blurry if either the camera or the subject moves while the shutter is open.

Figure 4-9 shows three pictures, taken at 1/125th, 1/30th, and 1/8th, that demonstrate the effect of varying shutter speed with a moving subject. My daughter and I were spinning at the same speed in all three pictures. As the shutter speed slowed, the background became more blurred. Because both my daughter and I held still on the spinning ride, she did not become blurry. If you move with your subject, or follow their motion with your camera, you can keep the subject sharp while blurring the background—the best way to convey motion in a picture. In these sample pictures, only the third photo (taken at 1/8th) has enough motion blur to really convey spinning.

The longer the shutter speed, the more motion blur the picture captures. Therefore, if you take a picture and the subject is blurry because it's moving, increase your shutter speed by selecting Sports mode on your camera, using a smaller f/stop number, increasing your ISO speed, or adding flash.

AVOIDING CAMERA SHAKE

If you've ever had a picture come out shaky (like Figure 4-10), you've discovered the limitations of your hand-holding ability. Even if you feel like you're holding a camera steady, your hand is moving very slightly. With a quick shutter speed, such as 1/1500th, you won't be able to see the movements in the picture. With

To watch a video about **shutter speed,** scan the QR code or visit:

sdp.io/ShutterSpeed

a slow shutter speed, the movements will be visible.

Many cameras warn you if your shutter speed is too slow by displaying a shaking hand icon or by simply turning on the built-in flash. If this happens, you can avoid camera shake by doing

Figure 4-9: Pan your camera and use a slow shutter speed to blur the background (1/125th, 1/30th, and 1/8th).

one of these things (in order of preference, but not necessarily convenience):

- Attach your camera to a tripod.
- Use image stabilization.
- Use continuous shooting and take multiple shots.
- Use flash.
- Increase your ISO speed (as described in the next section).
- Zoom out to a wider angle.

Your posture and the way you hold the camera can also reduce shakiness. Always hold your camera gently and with both hands. If camera shake is a problem, keep your elbows against your torso. If possible, sit down or lean against a wall. Set your camera to continuous shooting mode, exhale smoothly, and hold the shutter down for multiple shots.

RECIPROCAL RULE

Before I get into the mathematics, here's what you need to understand about photos taken while hand-holding the camera: the more you zoom in, the faster the shutter speed you need to prevent camera shake. With a wide-angle picture, you can hand-hold photos at very slow shutter speeds. With a telephoto picture, you need a shutter speed four to eight times faster. Therefore, if a telephoto picture comes out blurry, a wide-angle picture of the same subject might be fine.

To determine the slowest shutter speed you can use to hand-hold a camera, follow the

Figure 4-10: Hand-holding a camera with a slow shutter speed can result in camera shake.

Reciprocal Rule: Keep your shutter speed faster than your focal length. If you're using a 100mm lens, use a shutter speed faster than 1/100th. If you're using a 400mm lens, use a shutter speed faster than 1/400th. The more you zoom in, the faster your shutter speed needs to be.

Notice that the reciprocal rule uses the 35mm-equivalent focal length. If you're using anything other than a very expensive full-frame digital camera, you'll have to multiply your focal length by your camera's crop factor. For example, if you're using an APS-C camera with a 1.5x crop factor and a 100mm lens, your effective focal length is 150mm. Therefore, you would need a shutter speed faster than 1/150th to hand-hold a camera while taking a picture.

The Reciprocal Rule is just a guideline. Many people (especially kids) can follow the Reciprocal Rule and still produce a shaky picture. They should use a shutter speed twice the 35mm-equivalent focal length. If you have steady hands, and you exhale evenly while taking the shot, you might be able to use a shutter speed half the 35mm-equivalent focal length. Use continuous shooting and take lots of shots to improve your chances of getting a sharp picture.

IMAGE STABILIZATION

Camera shake is such a common problem that camera and lens designers often incorporate image stabilization. Image stabilization is a technology that moves camera or lens elements to compensate for your shaking hands. Image stabilization can allow you to break the reciprocal rule by two, three, or even four stops.

That's a huge difference—a four stop difference allows you to hand-hold in 1/16th the light you normally would. Being able to use a slower shutter speed allows you to use a higher f/ stop number to get more depth-of-field. It also allows you to use a lower ISO, reducing the noise in the picture.

The sequence of hand-held frog pictures in Figure 4-11 was taken at 200mm with an image stabilized lens that advertises 4-stops improved hand-holding. All pictures were cropped to show detail.

Without image stabilization, the reciprocal rule says that I need a shutter speed of 1/200th to get a clear picture. The first picture in Figure 4-11 was taken at 1/90th—about one stop slower than I should be able to hand-hold. The second picture was taken at 1/10th—about four stops slower, and right at the limit of the advertised hand-holding capability. It's not quite as sharp as the first picture, but it's usable, and without image stabilization, it would have been completely blurry. The final picture was taken at ¼—almost six stops below the reciprocal rule. Because it exceeds the lens' image stabilization capability, it's shaky and unusable.

The table at the bottom of this page shows common focal lengths and the shutter speeds at which you should be able to hand-hold pictures without noticeable camera blur. The focal lengths are 35mm equivalents, so you should multiply your camera's crop factor by the focal length. You might need faster shutter speeds to get pixel-sharp images with high-megapixel cameras, such as those with 36 or more megapixels.

Image stabilization lets you hand-hold photos at slower shutter speeds, but it doesn't slow your subject down. Even if you can hand-hold a still-life shot at 1/10th, if your subject is moving (or even breathing), it will end up blurry.

To control the shutter speed, select shutter priority (S or Tv) mode. Then, move the main dial (the small dial next to the shutter button) to select the desired shutter speed. Note that as you choose faster shutter speeds to freeze motion, your camera will decrease the f/stop number or increase the ISO. As you choose slower shutter speeds to create more motion blur, your camera will increase the f/stop number or decrease the ISO.

> **Note**: Try using shutter priority when shooting moving subjects. If they're blurry, increase the shutter speed. Set your ISO to automatic for more flexibility.

ISO

ISO controls your camera's sensitivity to light. Every time you double the ISO (from, say, 100 to 200), you double the camera's sensitivity. So your camera requires half as much light to properly expose a picture at ISO 200 as it does at ISO 100.

To watch a video about **tripods,** scan the QR code or visit:

sdp.io/Tripods

Figure 4-11: Image stabilization worked up to four stops slower than the reciprocal rule.

Focal Length	Min. Shutter Speed	2 Stop IS	4 Stop IS
24mm	1/25th	1/8th	1/2
100mm	1/125th	1/30th	1/8th
200mm	1/250th	1/60th	1/15th
400mm	1/500th	1/125th	1/30th

To watch a video about **ISO,** scan the QR code or visit:

sdp.io/ISOIntro

Low ISOs (like ISO 100 or 200) decrease your shutter speed but increase image quality. Higher ISOs (like ISO 1600 or 3200) increase your shutter speed but decrease image quality. Therefore, you should always use the lowest ISO that will allow you to get the shutter speed you need to stop motion blur and camera shake.

If you take a picture and it's shaky, double your ISO and try again.

In aperture priority mode, every time you double the ISO, your camera will also double the shutter speed, because the higher ISO setting means it requires half as much light. The table at the bottom of this page shows how your shutter speed would change as you changed the ISO, assuming you kept the aperture constant. If you were using a 100mm lens, you would need a shutter speed of 1/125th to hand-hold the camera, requiring you to use ISO 800 or faster.

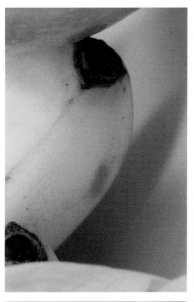
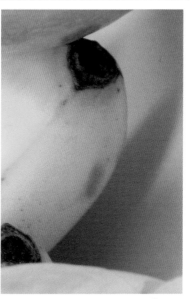

Every camera has different amounts of noise, so you should experiment with your own camera at different ISO speeds. Take pictures of the same subject at 100, 200, 400, 800, 1600, 3200, and any higher ISO speeds your camera offers. Then, copy your pictures to your computer and zoom in so you can see individual pixels. Especially in shadows, you'll notice more noise in the higher ISO pictures.

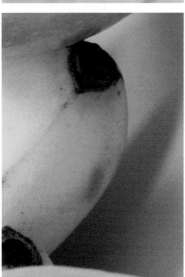
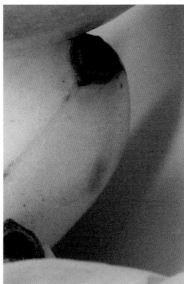
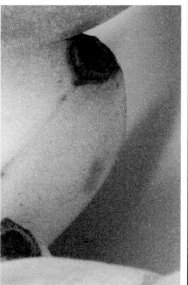

Figure 4-12: Close-ups of a picture taken at ISO 100, 400, 1600, 6400, and 25,600.

Figure 4-12 shows a crop of a fruit close-up at two-stop intervals: ISO 100, 400, 1600, 6400, and 25,600. At ISO 100, the shadow is very smooth—there is virtually no noise. With digital pictures, shadows always have the most noise. Moving up two stops to ISO 400 would allow me to use a shutter speed four times faster, making it much easier to freeze motion or hand-hold the camera. However, as you can see, there's a bit more noise in the shadow. The picture still looks good, though.

> **Note**: ISO is pronounced "eye-so" in the US and "EEE-so" in much of the rest of the world.
>
> ISO is not an acronym, however, so it's not correct to spell out the letters as I-S-O. ISO is the nickname for the organization that created the film sensitivity standards: the International Organization for Standardization. The name ISO is based on the Greek word isos (ἴσος), meaning equal. The organization specifically chose not to use an acronym because it would be different in different languages. However, many people understandably (but incorrectly) assume that ISO is an acronym because the name has the same letters as the organization's initials (though not in the same order in English) and ISO is always written in capital letters.

Increasing the ISO another two stops to ISO 1600 dramatically increases the noise. I regularly use ISO 1600 when photographing hand-held indoors without flash. Depending on your camera, ISO 1600 might produce very noisy, unattractive pictures. I'm often forced to use ISO 6400 (shown in the fourth picture), two stops faster than ISO 1600, when hand-holding pictures in dark rooms such as restaurants and bars. The noise definitely impacts the picture quality. The last picture was taken at an extremely high ISO 25,600. You can improve noisy pictures by using noise reduction software such as Adobe Lightroom

(the easiest), Topaz DeNoise, Neat Image, or Noiseware.

> **Tip:** In the human eye, the iris functions like a camera's aperture, opening and closing to allow more or less light in. The human eye can also adjust the ISO, in a way. If you spend more than 15 seconds in a dark environment, your body will increase the rhodopsin levels in your retina, allowing your eyes to get more sensitive to light over about the following half hour. You'll notice, however, that you won't be able to see color and your resolution will drop significantly. Like cameras, our eyes aren't as good at high ISOs. Studies have shown that our eyes can get about 600 times more sensitive to light at night. For a camera, that would equate to an ISO range of 50-30,000.

Until you fully understand ISO, set your camera to use auto ISO. Auto ISO allows the camera to choose the ISO setting that will allow it to properly expose a picture. In manual mode, auto ISO allows your camera to auto expose pictures while still giving you complete control over shutter speed, aperture, and light.

EXPOSURE COMPENSATION

Even though your camera automatically chooses the correct exposure, parts of a picture can be *overexposed* or *underexposed*. Overexposed means that part of the picture is too bright and underexposed means that part of the picture is too dark. The examples in the Fill Flash section in Chapter 3, "Lighting and Flash," show this well; if you take a picture of someone outdoors with the sun behind him or her, two things can happen:

- The person will be exposed properly, but the sky will be overexposed.

- The sky will be exposed properly, but the person will be underexposed.

ISO	Shutter Speed
100	1/15th
200	1/30th
400	1/60th
1600	1/250th
3200	1/500th
6400	1/1000th

Figure 4-13 illustrates this problem. In the first photo, the camera's autoexposure system measured both the bright outside with the dark interior. In this case, the exposure left the faces dark. In the second photo, I added two stops of exposure compensation by moving exposure compensation towards the + sign. The faces are now better exposed; however, the background outside is overexposed. Adding exposure compensation definitely improved the picture (because at least you can see the faces), but it's still not great.

Other scenarios where you will need to use exposure compensation are when shooting a dark subject on a light background or a light subject on a dark background. For example, Figure 4-14 shows a young red-tailed hawk with a fresh squirrel. Because most of the frame is snow (the picture is a crop of a wider-angle shot), the camera exposed the picture so that the snow would be *middle gray* (also known as *18% gray*). Middle gray is halfway between black-and-white.

That exposure would be fine if the snow were the subject of the picture. However, the subject of the picture is the dark-colored hawk. Because the camera calculated the exposure based on the bright snow, the hawk is underexposed, hiding the detail in his feathers. To resolve that problem, I used exposure compensation to increase the exposure one stop (moving the exposure compensation towards the + sign). The snow is now bright (as the human eye expects it to be) and the bird is properly exposed. Another way to solve the problem would have been to use *spot-metering*, as described later in this chapter.

Compared to your own eyes, cameras have a very limited *dynamic range*. The dynamic range is the difference between the darkest part of a picture and the brightest part of a picture. Even if you haven't heard the term dynamic range, you already know how it works, because your eyes have a limited dynamic range, too.

Figure 4-13: Use exposure compensation when your camera's autoexposure system makes the wrong choice.

Figure 4-14: Increase exposure when shooting light subjects such as snow.

Most cameras have a dynamic range of 8-12 stops, with professional cameras having a higher dynamic range than consumer cameras. If your camera has a dynamic range of 10 stops, that means you'll be able to see subjects in the shadows and highlights of a picture as long as the brightest part of the picture isn't more than 1,000 times brighter than the darkest part of the picture. 10 stops, or a contrast ratio of about 1:1,000, sounds like an extreme difference, but the human eye can see about 20 stops of dynamic range, for a contrast ratio of about 1:1,000,000. That's why exposure is such a challenge—your eye sees your friend's face and the blue sky behind them and they both look fine, because the sky isn't more than 1,000,000 times brighter than your friend's face. However, the sky is more than 1,000 times brighter than your friend's face, so if the face is properly exposed, the sky will be overexposed in a photo.

All but the most basic cameras provide exposure compensation, but they do it in different ways. Refer to your camera's manual for more information. Typically, however, you simply move the thumb dial on the back of cameras clockwise to increase exposure and counter-clockwise to decrease exposure—every two clicks is one stop. On cameras without a thumb dial, hold the exposure compensation button (+/-), and then either turn the main dial or press the directional buttons on the back of the camera with your thumb.

> **Tip:** Make a habit of returning exposure compensation to neutral, so that you don't under- or overexpose later pictures.

BLINKIES

Use blinkies, more formally known as exposure highlight warnings or highlight alerts, to know when part of your picture is overexposed. Blinkies flash overexposed portions of your picture on your camera's LCD, allowing you to immediately reduce the exposure (by moving

the exposure compensation towards the - sign) and then re-shoot. However, if your model's face is blinking, you'd better reduce the exposure.

Refer to your camera's manual for instructions on how to enable blinkies.

HISTOGRAM

A histogram is a chart of how bright or dark your picture is. You can show a picture's histogram on your camera so you can tell whether you need to adjust the exposure and shoot again. Cameras do not typically display a histogram by default; refer to your camera's manual for instructions on how to display histograms.

The left of a histogram represents dark parts of the picture, while the right represents bright parts. Therefore, if your histogram has high bars on the left, the picture might be too dark. You might want to use exposure compensation to brighten the picture. If the histogram has high bars on the right, the picture might be too bright, and you might want to use exposure compensation to darken the picture.

Figure 4-15 shows a dark picture with its histogram—notice that the graph peaks on the far left, indicating that parts of the picture are completely black. If you're intentionally creating a silhouette, that's fine. If you're trying to record as much of the scene as possible, having the histogram touching the left edge means that the shadows are too dark, and you should increase the exposure or add flash. The sky in this picture is properly exposed, as indicated by the center portion of the histogram.

A bright, high-key picture has a histogram that peaks on the right, as shown in Figure 4-16. That's fine if you want the picture to look bright. If you wanted a more classically exposed picture, you would use exposure compensation to reduce the exposure by one or two stops and then shoot again.

A properly exposed picture, such as Figure 4-17, has a histogram that peaks in the center and does not touch either the left or right side. This type of exposure is ideal for editing on your computer. If you want it to be brighter or darker, you can always adjust a well-exposed picture using photo editing software. If portions of a picture are under- or overexposed (as indicated by having histograms peaking on the left or right sides), those areas will always be completely black or white and can never be recovered in photo editing software.

Some scenes, such as the sunset shown in Figure 4-18, are both too dark and too bright.

In this case, the dynamic range of the scene is greater than the camera is capable of capturing. If you were to use exposure compensation to brighten the picture, you'd be able to see the detail in the palm leaves. However, the sun and sky would be completely blown-out. To brighten the shadows and allow for a correct exposure, add flash. To capture both the highlights and shadows using natural light, use HDR techniques as described in Chapter 11, "HDR."

These photos show color histograms, illustrating the levels of the individual red, green, and blue channels that go into making a full-color digital picture. Many histograms show only the total brightness, however.

Note: If you're shooting raw, your histogram shows your picture after it's been converted

Figure 4-15: Dark photos show peaks on the left portion of the histogram.

Figure 4-17: Well exposed pictures have a histogram that peaks in the center and does not touch the left or right sides.

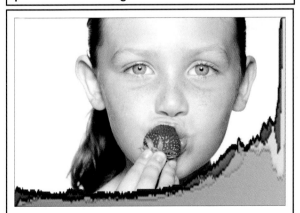

Figure 4-16: Bright photos show peaks on the right portion of the histogram.

Figure 4-18: If the histogram peaks on both the right and left, the scene may have too much contrast.

to JPEG. So, make sure you haven't set your camera to do any crazy adjustments to the JPEG, like making it high contrast. You'll see that in the histogram, but not in your raw file.

METERING MODES

Cameras can determine how to expose a picture in several different ways, but they fall into two categories:

- **Evaluative, matrix, or center-weighted**. This metering mode chooses the exposure by averaging the brightness of the entire picture. Typically, subjects in the center or foreground are weighted more heavily. This is the best choice for almost all types of pictures.

- **Spot metering**. This metering mode chooses the exposure by using the brightness at a very small area in either the center or focus point of the picture. Spot metering ensures one small part of your subject is properly exposed, but can cause the background to be severely underexposed or overexposed.

With digital cameras, spot metering is almost never the best choice. I recommend every photographer, in all scenarios, use his or her camera's default metering system. After you take a picture, review the exposure. If your picture is under or overexposed, adjust the exposure compensation and retake the picture.

Many photographers recommend spot metering for wildlife; however, in practice, it works poorly. Imagine that you're photographing a black-and-white bird flying overhead. If the spot metering happened to meter a white part of the bird, the camera would underexpose the shot. If it metered a black part of the bird, the camera would overexpose the shot. If you didn't hold the focus point exactly over the moving bird (something that happens constantly with fast-moving subjects), the camera would meter off the background or

sky, completely changing the exposure. The result is that using spot-metering results in unpredictable exposure settings. In any series of shots, the exposure can change by several stops in subsequent pictures.

However, you don't always have the time to take a picture, make adjustments, and reshoot, especially with wildlife. Therefore, remember this guideline: adjust exposure compensation to the opposite of the subject's brightness. For white subjects, use -1 or -2 stops underexposure. For dark subjects, use +1 or +2 stops overexposure.

FIXING EXPOSURE PROBLEMS

Fortunately, you can fix the overexposure or underexposure in several different ways. If the subject is going to be underexposed, add fill flash, as described in the Fill Flash section in Chapter 3, "Lighting and Flash."

The sky is the most likely subject to be overexposed. When shooting into the sun or on overcast days, reducing the exposure enough to fix the overexposed sky can cause your subject to be severely underexposed. To get around this, add flash to balance the exposure of your subject with the sky. Alternatively, you can turn so that the sun is at your back, which will have you photographing the darkest part of the sky. Polarizing filters help to darken the sky, too. If the sky is still too bright, adjust your angle to remove as much of the sky as possible from the frame.

Use High Dynamic Range (HDR) techniques, as described in Chapter 11, "HDR," to expose both the foreground and the background properly. Newer cameras can do this

To watch a video about **metering**, scan the QR code or visit:

sdp.io/Metering

automatically. For all other cameras, you can take multiple pictures at different exposures and blend them together using software.

UNDERSTANDING EXPOSURE

Figure 4-19 shows how light, shutter speed, aperture, and ISO combine to determine your exposure. Moving any of these sliders up makes your picture brighter. Moving any of the sliders down makes your picture darker. Therefore, if you adjust one setting up, you must adjust another setting down if you don't want to change the brightness of your photo.

For example, if the sun comes out from behind a cloud (pushing the light slider up), your picture would become brighter unless you adjusted one of the other three settings down. Your camera's auto exposure system usually does this for you automatically, choosing a faster shutter speed such as 1/4000th (moving the shutter speed slider down), a higher f/stop number such as f/32 (moving the aperture slider down), or a lower ISO such as ISO 100 (moving the ISO slider down).

Here's another example: If you increased your aperture's f/stop number from f/5.6 to f/8 to increase the depth-of-field, you'd be pushing the aperture slider down. To keep your picture from getting darker, you would need to move one of the other three sliders up. You could increase the ISO from 100 to 200 (pushing the ISO slider up), decrease your shutter speed from 1/60th to 1/30th (pushing the shutter speed slider up), or turn on your flash (pushing the light slider up).

UNDERSTANDING STOPS

Photographers measure light in *stops*. Each stop is twice as much light as the previous stop. Two stops is four times as much light, because 2 x 2 = 4. Three stops is eight times as much light, because 2 x 2 x 2 = 8. If you're mathematically inclined, think of stops as exponents of two.

Let's say you take a picture outside on a sunny day at 1/60th. If the sun moves behind a cloud

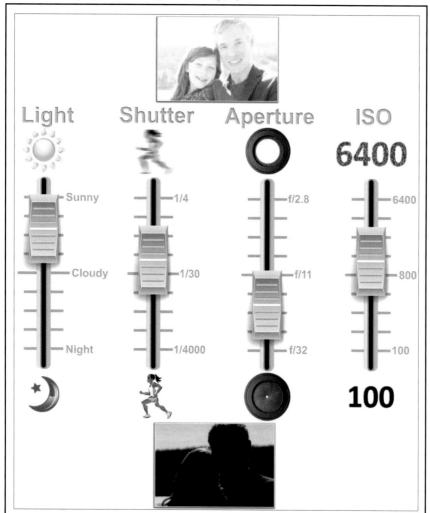

Figure 4-19: Aperture, shutter speed, ISO, and light together determine exposure.

and the cloud blocks half the light, you have one less stop of light available to you. When you take your next picture, your camera might automatically double the shutter speed to 1/30th to allow in the same amount of light.

> **Fact:** Because your eyes and brain automatically adjust to different light levels, your living room seems to be about as bright in the day (lit by sunlight) as it is at night (lit by artificial lights). As your camera will teach you, it's actually about ten times brighter during the day—more than three stops.

If you double the shutter speed from 1 second to 2 seconds, you are allowing one more stop of light—twice as much light—to reach the sensor. If you halve the shutter speed from 1/30th to 1/60th, you are allowing one less stop of light—half the light—to reach the sensor.

If a photographer adjusts the shutter speed from 1/250th to 1/1000th, she might say, "I'm adjusting the shutter speed up two stops." Even though the shutter speed is four times faster, it's only two stops, because each stop is twice the light.

ISO speed works the same way—each stop doubles or halves the light. ISO 100 is one stop slower than ISO 200, and ISO 200 is one stop slower than ISO 400. Therefore, ISO 100 is two stops slower than ISO 400, even though it will require four times as much light.

If you take a picture with a shutter speed of 1/60th at ISO 100, you can get the same exposure by using a shutter speed of 1/125th and ISO 200.

> **Tip:** Shutter speeds are often rounded a bit—1/125th is considered one stop faster than 1/60th.

Imagine this real-life scenario: You take a picture of your daughter playing soccer. The camera sets a shutter speed of 1/60th and f/2.8 at an ISO of 100. The picture is well exposed, but your daughter runs so fast that her legs are blurred. You need to increase the shutter

To watch a video about **exposure settings,** scan the QR code or visit:

sdp.io/Exposure

speed to freeze the motion, so you increase it to 1/120th. If you left the ISO and aperture the same, the picture would be one stop underexposed. If f/2.8 was your lens' smallest f/stop number, you would not be able to decrease it one stop. Therefore, you would need to adjust the ISO speed up one stop to ISO 200.

Let's review: you can control the amount of light reaching your camera's sensor by adjusting the aperture, shutter speed, ISO speed, and flash. If you open up the aperture one stop by choosing a lower f/stop number, you'll need to adjust either the shutter speed or the ISO down one stop to get the same exposure. Increase the shutter speed one stop, and you'll need to adjust the aperture or ISO by one stop.

All of these settings (typical for a dimly lit room) have exactly the same exposure:

- f/2.8, 1/60th, ISO 1600
- f/2.8, 1/30th, ISO 800
- f/4.0, 1/15th, ISO 800
- f/4.0, 1/60th, ISO 3200
- f/5.6, 1/8th, ISO 800
- f/5.6, 1/60th, ISO 6400

Similarly, these settings (for a sunny day) are all equivalent:

- f/5.6, 1/500th, ISO 100
- f/5.6, 1/1000th, ISO 200
- f/8.0, 1/250th, ISO 100
- f/8.0, 1/500th, ISO 200
- f/11, 1/125th, ISO 100
- f/11, 1/250th, ISO 200

USING MANUAL MODE

First, let's clear up a few common myths:

- **Manual mode doesn't use autoexposure.** This isn't always true, because you can use manual mode to set the shutter speed and aperture, while still using auto ISO to control the exposure. Also, most cameras will use the exposure compensation display to show the photographer the proper exposure based on the camera's meter. However, you can use manual mode and manual ISO to take control of exposure.

- **When you get to a scene, you should set the exposure with manual mode and then leave it.** The theory behind this myth is that the light at a scene is constant, whether you're at a wedding reception or a mountain range. So, you should meter the scene once, lock the settings in with manual mode, and then do all your shooting with those settings. That can work, but it's not very reliable. Even indoors, a person standing near a light can be several stops brighter than a person standing a few feet away. Outdoors, a bird flying from sunlight to shadow will change exposure by 2-6 stops.

- **Manual mode is the choice of professionals**. This isn't true; most professionals use autoexposure. Lighting conditions can change instantly (for example, if the sun goes behind a cloud) and a working professional has more important things to worry about than changing the ISO. However, manual mode is the only choice for studio work (as described in Chapter 6).

To watch a video about **using manual mode,** scan the QR code or visit:

sdp.io/Manual

Manual mode is incredibly useful, however, especially when used with auto ISO, because you can control the shutter speed to stop motion and the aperture to blur the background. Follow this process to choose the right settings:

1. Choose the slowest shutter speed that prevents camera shake and freezes motion.

2. Choose the lowest f/stop number that gets your entire subject sharp and within the depth-of-field.

3. Select the ISO you need (if you're not using auto ISO) to control how bright or dark your picture is. Verify that you're using the right side of the histogram.

Choosing the slowest shutter speed and the lowest f/stop number configures your camera to gather as much light as possible without ruining the picture. This ensures you'll be using the lowest ISO possible, minimizing the noise in your image.

This process is similar to the process your camera uses in automatic modes, but your camera doesn't know as much about the scene as you do. For example, your camera might not know that you need more depth-of-field to get everyone's face in a group photo sharp. It also won't know when you're resting your arms against a table, allowing you to use a slower shutter speed without camera shake (and thus use a lower ISO to get cleaner images).

In Shutter Priority mode, your camera will almost always choose to use the lowest f/stop number. It will only choose higher f/stop numbers when there is plenty of light, such as when shooting in directly sunlight.

In Aperture Priority mode, most cameras will choose the slowest shutter speed that will cancel camera shake without going below about 1/60th. Only in bright light will it choose a faster shutter speed. Each camera is different, however.

USING RAW

Most digital cameras save JPG files by default. To create a JPG, your camera takes all the raw data captured by its sensor, makes some guesses about the brightness, color temperature, and saturation, and throws away data that it doesn't think you need. If you're not a perfectionist, the JPG is fine.

If you're the type who wants as much detail as possible from your shots, or if you tend to edit pictures on your computer, you should save the raw files. Raw files store every bit of data captured by the camera. With a raw file, you can adjust the exposure and color of a picture on your computer much better than you could with a JPG. Raw files also tend to have more detail, especially in the shadows.

While you can do these tasks with a JPEG, using raw gives you more power to:

- Brighten or darken the picture
- Recover highlights or shadows
- Adjust the color temperature
- Remove noise
- Customize sharpening settings

Raw files have some disadvantages, though. First, they're huge. A 20 megapixel camera produces JPGs that are about 3MB each or raw files that are about 20MB each. Obviously, you're going to need a bigger memory card and disk drive to save the raw files. Raw files also take longer to open on your computer. Before you share them, you have to convert them to a JPG file—but at least you have the chance to edit the raw file first.

Finally, you'll need to use software that supports working with raw files to take advantage of the benefits. If your camera supports raw files, it probably came with the software you need, but I recommend using third-party raw processing software instead.

To watch a video about **raw files**, scan the QR code or visit:

sdp.io/Raw

Personally, I use Adobe Lightroom ($140 to purchase, or $10/month with Photoshop at *sdp.io/adobedeal*) to convert them to digital negative (DNG) format. DNG is like raw, but it's not camera specific. Other software that allows you to work with raw include:

- Picasa (Free)
- iPhoto ($15)
- BreezeBrowser Pro ($70)
- DXO Optics Pro Standard Edition ($170)
- Capture One Pro ($300)

RAW FILES FOR TECHIES

JPEG pictures have 8-bits per channel, which allows up to 256 gradients for red, green, and blue. That's generally enough to make the gradual change in the color of a sky smooth; however, it is possible to see the color changes in a sky.

Most cameras capture raw data using 12- or 14-bits per channel. That means that there can be up to 4,096 (for 12-bit) or 16,384 (for 14-bit) gradients. Your camera might not have that level of precision, but the extra bits allow the camera to record the light more precisely. This allows gradients in the sky, for example, to be perfectly smooth, whereas they might appear jagged in 8-bit JPG.

Figure 4-20 (on the next page) shows 4-bit color vs. 8-bit color because you wouldn't see the difference between 8-bits and 12-bits in this book. However, you can definitely tell the difference in prints or on your monitor.

To take an interactive video quiz, scan the QR code or visit:

sdp.io/VirtualTony

Raw can make a difference even if you plan to export your pictures to JPEG. First, your computer can do a better job of converting raw files to JPEG files than your camera. Second, if you adjust the exposure of a JPEG file, you're losing a portion of those 256 gradients. If you adjust the exposure of a raw file, the lost gradients make a much less noticeable difference.

PRACTICE

This chapter's practices help you understand how to control your camera.

- **Focus Practice**: Try to use autofocus in a dark room. Did your camera successfully focus? Did it use active focusing by flickering the flash or by transmitting red light?

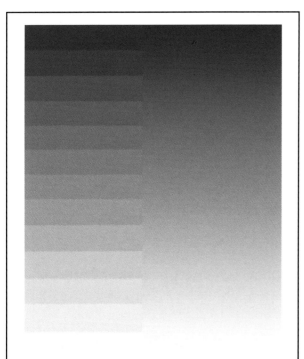

Figure 4-20: Higher bit depth provides smoother gradients.

- **Manual Focus Practice**: Use autofocus to focus on a well-lit subject. Now, focus elsewhere, and then switch your lens to manual focus mode and focus it back on the subject. Which was quicker?

- **Focus-recompose Practice**: Set your camera to AF-S/One-shot/Single focus mode. Place a subject in the middle of the frame; push the shutter button halfway to focus, and then position the subject one-third of the way to the left or right of the frame. Note that the focus stays locked in. Push the shutter all the way to take a picture.

- **Continuous Focus Practice**: Set your camera to continuous focusing mode. Push the shutter button halfway to focus, and then point the camera at different subjects. Note that each time you move, the camera automatically refocuses on the new subject.

- **Moving Subject Practice:** Find someone willing to run for you—kids and dogs work well. Set your camera to continuous focusing mode with the shutter set to continuous shooting (or set your camera to Sports mode). Have the subject run from left to right, and get as many pictures as possible in focus. Next, have the subject run towards you, and see how many shots you can get sharp.

- **Basic Exposure Practice:** Take a picture outdoors during the day. Then, take a second shot indoors. If the flash fires, turn it off and then shoot a third shot. Review the pictures and configure your camera to display the shutter speed and aperture. Notice how the camera adjusted the shutter speed and/or aperture to properly expose pictures in different lighting conditions.

- **Advanced Exposure Practice:** Take a picture using your camera's automatic settings, and then examine the shutter speed, aperture, and ISO. Switch your camera to manual, set the exact same settings, and then take another picture with the same exposure. Now, adjust the shutter speed up one stop.

The pictures will be twice as bright. Return to the original settings, and repeat for aperture and shutter speed.

- **Shutter Speed Practice:** Put your camera into shutter priority mode (S or Tv) with auto ISO and turn the flash off. Set the shutter to 1/10th, and take a picture of a moving subject, such as a fan. Next, adjust the main dial to set the shutter to 1/100th and take a picture, and then set it to 1/1000th and take a picture. Note how the motion blur changed in the different pictures, and whether your camera adjusted the aperture, ISO, or both.

- **Handholding Practice.** Put your camera into shutter priority mode (S or Tv) with auto ISO and turn the flash off. Set the shutter to 1/125th and zoom all the way in. Set your shutter to continuous shooting, and take ten consecutive pictures of a still subject (such as this book). Now, set your shutter speed to 1/60th, and take ten more pictures. Repeat the process at 1/30th, 1/16th, 1/8th, and ¼. Copy the pictures to your computer and examine them close-up. Out of each set of ten photos, how many were sharp? What was the slowest shutter speed that still gave you at least one sharp picture? Repeat the experiment with different focal lengths and different zooms so you know exactly how many pictures you need to take to get a single sharp picture in different conditions.

- **Raw Practice:** Set your camera to shoot raw files. Take pictures both indoors and outdoors. Be sure to take a few high contrast pictures, such as a picture of someone outdoors with the sun behind him or her. Now, process the raw files on your computer using software provided by your camera manufacturer or a free trial of Adobe Lightroom. Make adjustments on your computer to the raw files, such as brightening the shadows, darkening the highlights, and changing the color

 Take a quiz!
sdp.io/Quiz4

temperature. Note how much more flexibility you have with the raw files. Also compare the size of the raw pictures to the size of the JPG pictures.

- **Decoupled Metering Practice.** Prevent your camera from using auto exposure by setting your camera to manual mode. For your aperture, select the smallest f/stop number your lens supports. For your ISO, select ISO 100 if you're outdoors in full sunlight, select ISO 400 if you're in the shade, or select ISO 1600 if you're indoors. Instead of using your camera's built-in light meter (a feature of all modern cameras that estimates the amount of light and adjusts the settings for proper exposure), use an external light meter. There are a variety of free iPhone and Android apps that work perfectly—just search your app store for Light Meter. Set the ISO and aperture in the light meter app to match the settings on your camera, and then use the light meter app to determine the proper shutter speed by reading the settings from an area of mid-tones in your scene (neither the brightest nor the darkest part of your view). Manually set the shutter speed on your camera to match, and take a picture. It should be properly exposed. Do this for a week, and you'll have a perfect understanding of exposure, and you'll probably be able to guess the proper camera settings in any environment. Naturally, you're welcome to select any aperture and ISO.

- **Build your own camera.** For $35, buy the Konstruktor DIY SLR kit (available at *sdp.io/diy*), and build it in less than an hour. It's a 35mm film camera, but even if you never put a roll of film through it, the process of building it will help you master all the major parts of an SLR camera.

5

PROBLEM SOLVING

Often, pictures don't turn out the way you intended. Unfortunately, the technical aspects of photography often interfere with artistic vision.

This chapter lists the most common photographic challenges and provides suggestions for how to work around them. At the very least, you should skim this chapter and read the sections that relate to problems you've had in the past. If you run into other problems in the future, return to this chapter for detailed advice.

BLURRY PICTURES

Many different problems can cause blurry pictures. Most often, the problem is camera shake caused by hand-holding a camera at slow shutter speeds. However, focusing problems and lens quality can also cause blurry pictures.

First, identify whether the problem is your equipment or technique. If some of your pictures are sharp and others are blurry, it's your technique. If all your pictures are blurry, there might be a problem with your camera. To test this, take a picture in ideal conditions: on a bright day, take your camera outside, set it to automatic mode, and take a picture of a still subject a few feet away. If it's blurry, it's an equipment problem. Otherwise, it's technique.

DEPTH-OF-FIELD

If you want all of your picture in focus, but only part of it is in focus, your problem is caused by shallow depth-of-field. You can

Figure 5-1: The hand is in focus, rather than the bird, because the camera back-focused.

To watch a video about **blurry pictures,** scan the QR code or visit:

sdp.io/Blurry

solve the problem by choosing a higher f/stop number, stepping farther back from your subjects, and zooming out. For more information about controlling depth-of-field, refer to Chapter 4.

FOCUS PROBLEMS

Autofocus systems often choose to focus on the wrong part of the image, causing the picture to seem out of focus. The lower the f/stop number of your lens and the more you are zoomed in, the more severe focus issues will appear, because depth-of-field will be very shallow.

You can determine whether blurriness is caused by a focus problem by looking for an area of the picture that is sharp. If the grass just in front of your subject is in focus, but the subject is out of focus, it means the camera front-focused. Similarly, if something behind your subject is in focus (as is the model's hand in Figure 5-1), your camera back-focused.

Most cameras use area autofocus by default, which focuses on any of several different autofocus points. This often results in the camera choosing the wrong part of the picture to focus on; always use only a single autofocus point. In fact, most focus problems are caused by the photographer's technique. For information about how to fix focus problems, read Chapter 4, "Controlling your Camera."

It's important to realize that no camera has a perfect focusing system; they're never 100% accurate. No matter how great your gear is, and how perfect your technique is, some portion of your photos will be slightly out-of-focus. The shallower your depth-of-field, the more obvious this will be. To overcome this limitation, follow the advice I first gave in Chapter 1: take lots

To watch a video about **Testing Focus,** scan the QR code or visit:

sdp.io/TestFocus

of pictures and delete most of them. Focus, snap several pictures, refocus, and snap several more. When the depth-of-field is very shallow, such as when taking close-up or telephoto shots, I'll often take more than 100 shots just to be sure I get one that's in focus.

Very rarely, focus on a DSLR body or lens can become miscalibrated (most mirrorless cameras won't have this problem). Many DSLRs support microadjustments that can solve these focus calibration problems. I've seen dozens of photographers incorrectly blame focusing problems on their lens or body, and then attempt to solve the problem by using microadjustments. Because there wasn't a problem to begin with, the microadjustments introduce a focusing problem, making everything worse.

Before you begin applying microadjustments, it's important to test your camera in a controlled environment. To show you exactly how to test your camera to verify that it's focusing accurately, watch the video on this page.

If you use my test method and your camera focuses properly, the camera doesn't need repair or microadjustments. Instead, you can solve your focusing problems by improving your technique. Be sure to use a single focus point, take lots of pictures, regularly re-focus, and then choose the sharpest picture.

If you determine that your camera's phase detection autofocus system is consistently front- or back-focusing, you might be able to

To watch a video about **Full-frame lenses on crop bodies,** scan the QR code or visit:

sdp.io/BigGlass

solve it using microadjustment settings in your camera. Refer to your camera's manual for detailed instructions. If that's not an option, or if it doesn't solve the problem, you should contact your camera manufacturer for repairs.

If you perform the test and nothing is sharp, the optics could be misaligned (for example, by dropping the lens) or you might have fungus growing inside your lens. Either replace or repair your lens, whichever is less expensive.

The most common cause of all-over unsharp photos is pairing full-frame lenses with APS-C or smaller sensors. Even professional lenses produce unsharp results when used with smaller sensors. For detailed information, watch the video to the left.

If your lens has image stabilization, you might try repeating the test with it turned on and turned off. If the image stabilization system fails, it can actually work against you, making your pictures blurrier. If you think that might be the issue, try repeating the test while hand-holding the camera with a shutter speed of 1/30th. Take a dozen shots both with and without image stabilization. If image stabilization provided more clear shots, than it's working properly. If you got more shots clear without image stabilization, you should have your lens repaired. Some image stabilization systems must be turned off when using a tripod.

MOTION BLUR

If your shutter speed is too slow, your pictures will show either camera shake or motion blur. Camera shake results in the entire picture appearing shaky, including still objects. Motion blur, as shown in Figure 5-2, appears when the subject is moving too fast.

The easiest way to fix either problem is to increase your shutter speed. Use the smallest f/stop number possible. If your pictures are still blurry, use a higher ISO.

Finally, take more pictures. Set your camera to continuous shooting mode, and take three to five pictures instead of one. When you copy them to your computer, flip among the pictures in a set and delete all but the sharpest picture. You'll be surprised just how much difference there can be between two pictures taken only a fraction of a second apart.

USING THE IDEAL APERTURE

The primary consideration when choosing an aperture is depth-of-field. However, if the conditions give you some flexibility in the aperture you choose, select the sharpest aperture for your lens.

Lenses tend to not be their sharpest when shooting wide open (at the largest aperture, such as f/2.8) or shut-down (at the smallest apertures, such as f/22). While the sharpest aperture setting varies for different lenses, most lenses are at their sharpest two stops higher than wide open.

Therefore, a lens with a maximum aperture of f/2.8 would be at its sharpest around f/5.6. A lens with a maximum aperture of f/4.0 would be at its sharpest around f/8. A lens with a maximum aperture of f/5.6 would be at its sharpest around f/11. To identify the sharpest aperture for your specific lens, put your camera on a tripod and take test photos at each aperture—or just search the Internet for people who have already tested your lens model.

USING A TRIPOD

Even if you're using a shutter speed fast enough to allow hand-holding, you can improve the sharpness by attaching your camera to a sturdy tripod. If you can't use a tripod because you need to move the camera freely, consider using a monopod.

Once your camera is attached to a tripod, turn image stabilization off if your camera or lens

To watch a video about **hand-holding in low light,** scan the QR code or visit:

sdp.io/HandHolding

supports it (and if it does not automatically turn off when attached to a tripod). To further improve sharpness while the camera is attached to a tripod, use these techniques:

- **Timer**. All cameras feature a timer that delays taking a picture for 5-10 seconds after you press the shutter. Typically, you use this when you want to include yourself in the photo. The timer can improve sharpness by allowing the vibrations caused by you pressing the shutter release to stop.

- **Remote shutter release**. If you don't want to wait for a timer, connect a remote shutter release to your camera. Remote shutter releases can be either wired or wireless and they will eliminate the vibrations caused by pressing the shutter button.

- **Live view**. DSLRs have a mirror in front of the sensor that directs the light to the viewfinder when you're not taking a picture. Moving the mirror can make the camera shake a tiny amount. To eliminate this shake, enable live view (which moves the mirror) and then take the picture. Mirrorless cameras don't need this.

Figure 5-2: A shutter speed of 1/250th was too slow to stop the motion of this Doctor Bird (a Jamaican hummingbird).

To watch a video about **lens quality and sweet spots,** scan the QR code or visit:

sdp.io/DxOMark

- **Mirror lock-up.** If your DSLR does not support live view, you can enable mirror lock-up in your camera's settings to make the camera wait a couple of seconds after moving the mirror to take the picture. Mirrorless cameras don't need this.

- **Faster shutter speed.** Even if your camera is on a tripod, using a fast shutter speed can increase the sharpness of your pictures. Wind might be moving the leaves and blades of grass, clouds can move slightly, and the tripod might move a tiny amount. If you're troubleshooting blurry pictures, increase the shutter speed and see if that solves the problem. Unfortunately, increasing the shutter speed will require you to either use a bigger aperture (reducing depth-of-field) or use a higher ISO speed (increasing noise). Experiment to find the ideal compromise between shutter speed, depth-of-field, and noise to maximize sharpness.

LENS QUALITY

Professional lenses cost thousands of dollars, but offer extreme and consistent sharpness. Anything less than a professional lens provides slightly less sharpness. Before you upgrade your lens in search of more sharpness, be sure that the blurriness isn't caused by technique problems. Put your camera on a tripod and take a picture of a still subject with the aperture set to f/8. If that's not sharp, the problem is probably your lens.

While P&S users are stuck with their lens, DSLR users might be able to improve sharpness by choosing a sharper lens. To see exactly how sharp your lens is and whether you might benefit from a different lens, visit DxOMark, or search the web for lens tests.

AIR QUALITY

One of the most common sources of soft images isn't caused by technique or gear, but rather by air. Air isn't a perfect medium for transporting light.

Air always bends and blocks light; that's why the sky is blue or white rather than black. The sky is reflecting light passing through the atmosphere, making itself visible. If air transferred light more efficiently, we'd be able to see the stars during the day.

Humidity is the biggest cause of our air's poor optical qualities. The more humid it is, the more the air is going to randomly scatter light that's passing through it. That's why clouds appear white; they're huge collections of humidity. That's also why it's difficult to see through fog.

We see fog when the humidity is near 100%. Obviously, if you took a picture in dense fog and it wasn't sharp, you'd blame the fog for your blurry picture instead of your lens. But the light-bending effects of humidity don't start suddenly; the closer the humidity is to 100%, the more the atmosphere is diffusing your light and reducing the sharpness in your picture.

The more air between you and your subject, the more the effect of the humidity is magnified. That's why you can't get sharp pictures of faraway subjects. It's also why buying a huge telephoto lens isn't the answer to every wildlife photographer's challenge. If you want sharp pictures, you need to be close to your subject. The more humid it is, the closer you need to be.

Air quality is another good reason to shoot during the golden hour; humidity tends to be lower during sunrise and sunset.

SOFT LIGHT

As you learned in Chapter 3, hard light comes from a small light source. Soft light comes from a large light source, or from being reflected off of the atmosphere or objects around you.

Soft light produces soft pictures, whereas hard light produces sharp pictures. Even in a studio environment, if you use a huge soft box to produce soft light, your pictures won't be sharp when zoomed in. If you want to see your model's eyelashes separated, you'll need to add a source of hard light.

This relationship between hard light and sharpness is one of the reasons beauty dishes have begun to replace soft boxes in studios. Both light modifiers produce pleasing light, but beauty dishes produce a harder, direct light whereas soft boxes produce a softer, diffused light. At a glance, you might not be able to easily tell the difference between a photo taken with a beauty dish and a soft box. However, if you zoom in tight on detail such as eyelashes, you'll see that the photo taken with the hard light from the beauty dish is noticeably sharper.

LOW LIGHT

The easiest way to take pictures in low light is to use a flash—but then, technically, you're no longer taking pictures in low light. Flash changes the lighting dramatically, and often ruins what you liked about the scene in the first place.

In order of most to least preferred, use these tips and camera settings to improve your chances of successfully taking pictures in low light:

- **Use a tripod or image stabilization**. When practical, use a tripod. If you're taking pictures of people or other moving subjects, the low shutter speed will still result in motion blur, however.

- **Use less flash and bounce it.** If you use your flash at full-power, your subject will be well illuminated, but the background will be black. Turn your flash power down two or more stops and follow the other tips in this list to get the most out of the available light. Bounce your flash, if you can, to achieve more natural-looking

lighting. For more information, refer to Chapter 3, "Lighting and Flash."

- **Use a large aperture**. Set your camera to aperture priority mode (A or Av) and use the widest aperture possible, such as f/2.8, f/4, or f/5.6.

- **Get a faster lens**. Fast prime lenses gather far more light than your kit lens, and they don't have to be expensive. Most camera systems offer an inexpensive 50mm f1.8 lens that gathers about 3.3 stops more light than an f/5.6 lens. That's ten times more light!

- **Use raw**. Raw files store more data than JPEG files, and that extra data often allows you to improve the look of low-light pictures (especially in the noisy shadow areas). Raw files also allow you to set the white balance after the fact, which is helpful in environments with different types of light in a single room.

- **Take many pictures.** Put your camera into continuous shooting mode, and take five pictures for every one picture you hope will turn out. You'll end up deleting most of your pictures, but chances are good that a few will turn out.

- **Use a high ISO**. Each time you double your ISO, you can also double your shutter speed to reduce motion blur and camera shake. You'll almost always need to shoot near your camera's maximum ISO setting to take a decent picture in low light. Increasing the ISO increases noise, so use the lowest ISO setting possible.

- **Use noise reduction.** Noise reduction software can help make those noisy low light photos more appealing (but less sharp).

Most of these tips involve the primary challenge of low light photography: getting a fast enough shutter speed to stop camera shake (if you're hand-holding the camera) and stop motion blur (if your subject is moving).

Figure 5-3 shows an example of a usable (for personal purposes) low light photo taken in a room lit by only black lights. The subject's face is lit only by seven candles. I took the picture with an image stabilized lens at 100mm, f/4.0, 1/125th, and ISO 6400. Of the 20 pictures I took, only four or five were clear—but I only needed one. I later cropped the picture significantly, because I couldn't get close enough to the birthday girl. At full size, the image is very noisy, but scaled down and with a bit of noise reduction, the image was a hit on Facebook.

Figure 5-4 shows one of the many pictures that didn't turn out. Most of the candles were blown out, reducing the lighting. I had my camera in aperture priority mode, so it automatically reduced the shutter speed to 1/15th. This shutter speed provided the correct exposure, and with image stabilization it was fast enough to stop camera shake (you can see that the cake is sharp), but too slow to freeze the subject's motion (as evidenced by the blurry face).

Notre Dame in Paris, the second largest church in the world, is one of the finest examples of Gothic architecture in the world. It's also exceptionally dark inside, lit primarily by light streaming through intricate stained glass and a few artificial lights. To make it even more challenging, they don't allow flash photography or tripods. To be able to photograph the relatively bright stained glass with the statue in

the foreground (Figure 5-5), I used the widest aperture on my lens and turned on image stabilization, exhaled slowly, and took about a dozen pictures at different ISOs. I used the lowest ISO picture that was sharp. The best-quality picture was taken at 75mm, f/4.0, 1/13th, and ISO 800—about three stops slower than you can normally hand-hold a camera.

> **Tip**: Sometimes places that don't allow tripods will allow you to use a monopod. A monopod supports your camera like a tripod, but it only has a single leg—making it less likely that other people will trip over it.

For more information about hand-holding, read the "Shutter Speed" section of Chapter 4, "Controlling your Camera."

NOISY PICTURES

As described in the ISO section, the best way to decrease the noise in your pictures is to use a lower ISO. Often, however, you're forced to use a higher ISO to keep the shutter speed high. In these cases, you can often use noise reduction software to reduce the amount of visible noise.

Figure 5-6 shows a crop of a picture of fruit taken at ISO 6400. The first picture is unedited, and shows significant noise in the shadow area. The second picture shows the results after I used software to reduce the noise. First, I applied the default settings to the entire picture.

Figures 5-3 and 5-4: Use high ISO, a low f/stop number, and image stabilization, and take lots of pictures to get sharp results in low light.

Figure 5-5: Use the smallest f/stop number to make the most use of low light.

This improved the noise, but also reduced the overall sharpness. There was still significant noise visible, however, so I selected only the white background and applied a large amount of noise reduction without any sharpening. The following result is noticeably less sharp, but the visible noise has been almost eliminated.

Stock photo agencies allow zero visible noise in pictures. Even at ISO 100, you will get some visible noise in shadow areas and clear sky. Typically, I don't apply noise reduction to the entire picture. Instead, I select areas without any details (such as the sky or an out of focus background) and apply noise reduction without sharpening to that area. That reduces the visible noise while leaving all detail intact.

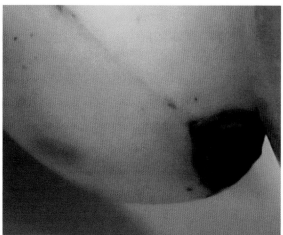

Figure 5-6: A close-up, before and after noise reduction.

To watch a video about **noise reduction,** scan the QR code or visit:

sdp.io/NoiseReduction

When shooting a picture that has deep shadows, consider using HDR techniques. With HDR, your camera will shoot several pictures in a row, including a picture that correctly exposes the shadows (but overexposes the rest of the picture). Using software, you can combine the pictures into a single, natural-looking picture with noise-free shadows. For detailed information, read Chapter 11, "HDR."

BAD COLOR

Pictures taken under artificial lights often have an unnatural tint to them, especially when there is also sunlight in the room. Typically, pictures have an orange or green tint. This tint is caused by incorrect white balance.

There are several ways you can fix this while taking pictures:

- Manually set the white balance on your camera to the correct setting.

- Turn off artificial lights.

- Turn on your flash.

Image editing software allows you to use your computer to fix bad color in pictures you have already taken. Though every program is different, most have an "Auto Color" option that will work well. Alternatively, most programs allow you to select a white portion of the picture, and then the program adjusts the color cast of the entire picture so that the white really is white. Finally, these programs allow you to manually adjust the color until it looks right.

Figure 5-7 shows a picture taken under incandescent light with the camera set to automatic white balance. The orange tint was fixed with two clicks in Adobe Lightroom—I chose the white balance selector and then clicked the paper, which I knew was true white. The software adjusted the color temperature of the photo so that the paper would be white and the rest of the picture was correctly balanced.

For more information about white balance, read Chapter 3, "Lighting and Flash."

SPOTS IN PICTURES/DUST ON SENSOR

Spots in your pictures are typically caused by dust. Dust is unavoidable—if you use your camera, you're going to get dust on it. Check the following locations on your camera for dust:

- **Lens**. Lenses will get dust on them and inside of them; however, it won't usually visibly affect the picture unless you are focused closely and using a high f/stop number (such as f/22). Nonetheless, it's good practice to use a dry lens cleaning cloth to clean the front and rear elements of your lens. Wipe from the center of the lens to the outside. Then, hold the lens up to a light and peer through it (both forwards and backwards). For most lenses, it's fine to see some dust inside. For macro lenses, however, dust will often be visible in your pictures. If dust becomes a problem, have your lens professionally cleaned.

- **Sensor**. Digital sensors tend to collect dust, and it will be visible in your pictures (especially in areas with solid colors, such as the sky). Many modern cameras include dust-reduction techniques, which repel dust using a chemical coating or vibrate the sensor to shake dust off. Neither works perfectly, so you need to clean your digital sensor regularly.

You can test whether spots are caused by the lens or the sensor. Attach your favorite lens and take a picture of a blank wall. Then, swap lenses, and take a picture of the same wall. On your computer, compare the two pictures. Any spots that appear in only one picture are caused by dust on that lens. Spots that appear in both pictures are caused by dust on the sensor.

I've used Photographic Solutions' Sensor Swab and LensPen's products to clean both lenses and the digital sensor, but there are dozens of different companies that sell cleaning products. Don't use just any cloth or tissue, especially on your delicate sensor. The wrong cloth will leave fibers behind, making the dust even worse. It might even scratch the lens, causing permanent damage.

You might see spots when looking through your viewfinder, but they won't appear in pictures. This is caused by dirt on the eyepiece, mirror, or prism. Any of these can be cleaned with a cotton swab. To access the mirror and prism, remove your lens. The mirror is directly in front of the sensor, and the prism is located directly above it.

Figure 5-7: Before and after automatic white balance correction.

looking at your camera, you're bound to tilt it off-level. So, put your camera on a tripod if you really need the horizon to be level. When hand-holding, the best you can do is to line the horizon up with the focus points visible in your viewfinder.

LOW CAMERA BATTERIES

You forgot to bring your battery charger on vacation, and now your battery meter is showing one bar. Here's how you can get the most out of your battery:

- Use the optical viewfinder instead of live view.
- Turn off automatic picture reviewing.
- Do not use the built-in flash.
- Turn down the screen brightness.
- Turn off GPS and wireless capabilities, if your camera has them.
- Turn off image stabilization if you don't need it.

Cold greatly reduces battery power. Often, you can get more life out of a cold battery by taking it out of the camera for a while and warming it in your hand or pocket for a few minutes. When you put it back in your camera, you'll be able to get ten or fifteen minutes of shooting done before the battery gets cold again.

Most cameras use lithium-ion (Li-ion) batteries. Unfortunately, Li-ion batteries lose capacity over the course of years. Depending on the conditions, batteries can lose 20-40% of their maximum capacity every year. After three or four years, even a fully charged battery won't last very long. Therefore, you should plan to buy a new battery about every two years (or whenever the shortened lifespan becomes annoying).

If you decide to buy a replacement battery, you'll discover that a typical name-brand battery costs about $60 and a generic battery costs about $15. In my experience, the generic batteries only work well for a few months before rapidly losing their maximum capacity. You'll see well-reviewed batteries, but these reviews are typically written while the battery is still new. Therefore, I recommend buying name-brand batteries, despite their being overpriced.

NO MEMORY

You took a few hundred more shots than you expected, and now your camera says you only have room for 36 more pictures. To old film photographers, that's an entire roll of film, but to a digital photographer, that's about 5 seconds of continuous shooting. Here's how you can get the most out of your memory card when you're running low:

- Shoot JPG instead of raw.
- Shoot lower quality or lower resolution JPG.
- Delete videos that you've recorded.
- Delete pictures that didn't turn out. If you shoot JPG, deleting pictures shot at high ISO or those with large areas of shadow will free up the most memory.

There are a couple of ways to prevent running out of memory. If you're the type who plans ahead, bring an extra memory card—even if it's a small one. You can buy small, cheap memory cards, and stash them in your car and bag in case of emergency. If you're traveling

Figure 5-10: Use a bubble level to get straight horizons.

on vacation, bring a computer and copy all the pictures from your camera every day. If you're concerned about losing your pictures if your computer fails, copy your pictures to your computer *and* leave a copy on the memory card—just be sure to bring enough memory.

BAD WEATHER

Bad weather doesn't have to mean a day without shooting. You can still get some great shots in fog, rain, and, cold—if you're properly equipped.

Fog adds depth to pictures by washing out the background. The farther from the camera it is, the more washed out it becomes. Fog also adds a gloomy, quiet atmosphere to pictures. As I'm looking for new locations to shoot, I make a note of places that will look good with fog, and then head back when the weather is right.

In landscape photography, use fog to show depth and distance. In portrait photography, use fog to make the model pop from the background. Fog is practically required for shooting in cemeteries.

Your camera equipment should hold up fine in fog. Check the front of your lens periodically and clean off any condensation that appears.

At some point, you're going to be surprised by rain. Underwater housings aren't generally practical above ground, so I always keep a plastic bag with me when I'm out with my camera. If it starts to rain, I can toss my camera in the bag. It's not elegant, but it's better than ruining my equipment. If you don't happen to have a bag with you, you can probably get one from a nearby store.

Plastic bags won't let you take pictures, however. Fortunately, you can buy rain sleeves for anywhere from $5 to more than $200, depending on the size and quality. You can even buy rain sleeves that work with external flashes and massive telephoto lenses.

Some photographers recommend going out to shoot in the rain. I've seen some nice shots of lightning (shot from indoors, naturally) and of rainy days through a rain-covered window. Otherwise, raindrops don't show up well in pictures. There are two things that make it hard, or even impossible, to capture rain the way you see it:

- **Movement**. With long shutters, rain and snow disappear completely. With fast shutters, they'll appear as small dots, which really isn't what you see. Experiment with different shutter speeds and you might be able to find a shutter speed that provides some movement.

- **Lighting**. When it's raining or snowing, it's also usually overcast, so all the light is really soft. Both snow and rain will look great if they're illuminated with a hard, direct light, but it's rare for it to be both sunny and raining. Flash can light it up, but the light falloff is obvious and distracting.

There are a few workarounds:

- **Use storytelling techniques**. For rain, you might show someone with an umbrella, or show a puddle on the ground, or raindrops on glass. For snow, you might show the snow piled up around a window or coming at a kid's head in the form of a snowball.

- **Use telephoto lenses**. Telephoto lenses compress the foreground and background. With a wide-angle lens, most of the raindrops and snowflakes will be so tiny they'd hardly appear in the picture. Zoom in tight, and the foreground and background magnification will be closer to that of your subject's magnification, so the rain and snow in the background will be larger than they would with a wide-angle lens. Figure 5-11 shows a tufted titmouse during a heavy rainstorm, but the rain appears to be a light drizzle.

- **Set up the shot**. For rain, you could wait for a sunny day and run a sprinkler— the rain will look great because of the hard light. For snow, do what movie studios do, and sprinkle fake snow in direct light.

- **Fake it**. Adding rain or snow is fairly straightforward with Photoshop; simply draw short white vertical lines in a picture, blur them, and lower the opacity until it looks natural. To add depth, create several layers with these lines and set the opacity different for each layer. This isn't really capturing the moment, but for conceptual photography, it's an option.

SHORT FLASH BATTERY LIFE OR LONG FLASH RECYCLE TIMES

If your flash seems to be running out of batteries too quickly, or your flash seems to take too long to recharge after just a few pictures, you might be able to solve the problem by changing your flash settings, buying better quality batteries, adjusting the ISO on your camera, or upgrading your flash.

First, check your flash settings. If you have high-speed sync set and you don't need it, turn it off because high-speed sync uses significantly more batteries than the regular flash setting. If you're using a diffuser and you don't need it, put it away. Bounce flash provides much nicer lighting than direct flash, but requires several times more power.

Next, check your batteries. I recommend using NiMH rechargeable batteries for your flash for two reasons, not just because they're far less expensive over time, but because they perform better with a flash. With good rechargeable batteries, your flash will recycle faster and last longer than with non-rechargeable batteries. Specifically, I recommend the Sanyo Eneloop AA NiMH batteries, which cost about $10 for a pack of four. In recent tests, they dramatically out-performed other batteries. An intelligent battery charger can make a difference, too, because inexpensive chargers might not charge all your batteries evenly. I recommend the La Crosse BC-700 for about $40.

You can reduce your flash recycle time and increase the number of shots you get before having to change your batteries by increasing your camera's ISO. Each time you double your ISO, you halve the output needed to light your subject. Higher ISO settings also more nicely balance flash and ambient light. However, high ISO settings also increase the noise in your pictures.

Some flash models are more efficient than others. If your flash doesn't have a zoom head, you might consider upgrading to a flash with a zoom head, because the zoom head can greatly improve your flash efficiency when using direct flash with focal lengths over 40mm. If you have an inexpensive generic flash that doesn't support TTL, it might be putting out far more power than required. Consider upgrading to a flash that does support TTL.

FLASH SYNC PROBLEMS

A flash seems to occur in an instant. However, in reality, a flash typically takes about 1/200th of a second. That's still pretty quick, but when shooting in bright daylight, your camera's shutter speed can be much faster.

Figure 5-11: A tufted titmouse in the rain.

If your shutter speed is faster than your flash sync speed, the lighting might be uneven, or part of the frame won't be illuminated at all. Figure 5-12 demonstrates this: I took a picture with the shutter set to 1/4000th using a flash that had a sync speed of 1/200th.

Some flashes have a high-speed sync mode that evenly illuminates the frame when you use faster shutter speeds. Usually, you have to remember to manually turn high-speed sync on, and I have no idea why it doesn't turn on automatically. If your flash doesn't support high-speed sync mode, or you don't turn it on, your camera usually detects this and automatically adjusts to use a slower shutter speed, equal to its X-sync speed, which is the fastest shutter speed that can be used with a conventional flash. This exposes the picture properly, and if you don't need the faster shutter speed to freeze the action, the lack of high-speed sync isn't a problem at all.

You don't need to understand how high-speed sync works to use it. Just remember these points:

- Know the sync speed of your flash and camera body.

- If your flash doesn't support high-speed sync with your camera body, don't use a shutter speed faster than your camera's X-sync speed. Most cameras will prevent this automatically.

- If your flash does support high-speed sync, turn on high-speed sync when you want to use a faster shutter speed.

If you're curious, sync problems occur because your camera has two shutter curtains: a front curtain and a rear curtain. When your shutter is slow (say, 1/60th), this is the process of taking a flash picture:

1. The front curtain moves down, revealing the entire sensor.
2. The flash fires, illuminating the scene all at once.
3. After waiting the length of the specified shutter speed, the rear curtain moves down, covering the entire sensor.

When your shutter speed is fast (say, 1/2000th), this is the process of taking a flash picture without high-speed sync:

1. The front curtain begins moving down, revealing the top part of the sensor.
2. After waiting the length of the specified shutter speed, the rear curtain begins to move down at the same rate as the front curtain. The shutter curtains block all light from hitting the sensor except for a small window between the rear curtain and front curtain. All parts of the sensor are exposed for the specified shutter speed, but only a small horizontal strip of the sensor is visible at any time.
3. The flash fires, illuminating whatever part of the sensor is currently exposed.

As shown by Figure 5-12, the result is that only part of your picture is illuminated by the flash; the remainder is dark. The bottom part is completely black. That's because it took the flash a few milliseconds to fire after the shutter had opened, and the rear shutter curtain

Figure 5-12: A flash photo without high-speed sync.

had already begun blocking the top part of the sensor. Note that the lens flips your picture upside-down, so the top part of the sensor captures the bottom part of your picture.

The flash output is not completely even; it starts out bright and then gets dimmer. The brightest part of that picture was the part that the shutter was exposing when the flash was at its peak output. As the shutter exposed the bottom of the sensor (and thus the top of the picture), the flash output was getting weaker, making the rest of the image gradually darker.

When your shutter speed is fast and your flash supports high-speed sync, this is the process of taking a flash picture:

1. The front curtain begins moving down, revealing the top part of the sensor.

2. In effect, the flash fires and stays lit. Technically, it's turning on and off very rapidly.

3. After waiting the length of the specified shutter speed, the rear curtain begins to move down at the same rate as the front curtain, exposing only a small portion of the sensor at any one time.

4. Once the rear curtain covers the entire sensor, the exposure is complete, and the flash can turn off.

Fast exposures take much longer than you would think. For example, a picture at 1/2000th of a second might actually take 1/200th of a second to completely expose because different parts of the sensor are exposed at different times. Each part of the sensor is exposed for exactly 1/2000th of a second, but the bottom 10% is exposed for roughly the first 1/2000th, the second 10% for the next 1/2000th, and so on.

Even though high-speed sync is used for faster shutter speeds, the flash stays lit for longer and puts out much more light. Continuing the

Take a quiz!

sdp.io/Quiz5

example from the previous paragraph, a flash picture taken at 1/2000th of a second might require ten times more light than a flash picture taken at 1/200th. If the shutter only exposes 10% of the entire sensor at any one point during the fast exposure, the flash must basically fire ten times to separately expose each 10% of the sensor. For that reason, you shouldn't use high-speed sync unless you absolutely need to; you'll go through batteries faster than necessary and your flash will take longer to recharge.

Tip: See a video of high-speed shutters in slow motion at *sdp.io/slowmo*.

LOST PICTURES

Your pictures are gone, but don't panic! If a memory card or hard drive with your pictures fails, or you accidentally format it or delete images, PhotoRec might be able to save them.

PhotoRec (*sdp.io/PhotoRec*) is a free tool for Windows, Mac, and Linux that scans your disk or memory card for traces of pictures that have been deleted. PhotoRec can often recover images (and almost any other type of file) when the media has been formatted, the images have been deleted, or the media is failing.

If you accidentally delete files or format media, immediately stop using the media until you can run PhotoRec. Any new files might overwrite your lost files.

The video at the bottom of this page will show you how to use PhotoRec.

To watch a video about **Recovering Lost Photos,** scan the QR code or visit:

sdp.io/Recover

Portrait photography is showing the world your loved ones through your own eyes. When you study portrait photography, you learn to capture a person's essence. Finally, your loved ones will be as beautiful in pictures as they are in person.

At its best, portrait photography captures much more than a person's likeness; it captures his or her personality, emotion, attitude, skills, and beauty. When you study portrait photography, you learn to make people comfortable rather than anxious, and to cause an outburst of laughter rather than a forced smile. You'll learn that a slight tilt of the head or turn of the shoulders drastically changes the model's appearance, and that finding the right light is often as easy as turning to the side, moving into the shade, or turning on the flash.

This chapter is about taking great pictures of people, whether they're walking through the park or posed in a studio. In the beginning of this chapter, I'll describe fundamental portrait concepts, including portrait styles, lengths, and camera equipment. Then, I'll show you how to take great, low-cost outdoor and indoor portraits. Having mastered choosing a location and working with natural lighting, you'll be ready to learn the details of posing and how to make your subject comfortable. For those more serious about portrait work, I'll describe studio lighting, corrective posing, and the basics of post-processing.

PORTRAIT STYLES

The term "portrait" conjures an image of sitting on a stool in front of a painted backdrop. While traditional portraits are still used for business, other types of portraits, such as casual, environmental, and glamour portraits, have become much more common. This section describes each of these portrait types.

To watch a video about **portrait basics,** scan the QR code or visit:

sdp.io/PortraitBasics

TRADITIONAL AND BUSINESS

Traditional portraits, as demonstrated by Figure 6-1, have their roots in painting. The subject or group sits on a stool in front of a simple backdrop (typically a neutral shade of gray) with a main light on his or her face, a fill light, a hair light, and a light on the background behind him or her. The model makes eye contact with the camera. The model's expression varies with the purpose—if it's a portrait for the CEO of a financial services firm, she'll keep a serious and thoughtful expression. If it's a high school senior portrait, he will smile pleasantly.

Traditional portraits are easy when done simply—high-volume photography studios (such as those you find in a mall) often give photographers only a week or two of training. After all, at the most basic, traditional portrait

Figure 6-1: A traditional portrait.

lighting hardly changes, and there are only a handful of poses you need to learn. Even if you are not interested in taking traditional portraits, the controlled conditions are great for mastering lighting and posing.

CASUAL

In recent years, casual portraits (as demonstrated by Figure 6-2) have become more common than traditional portraits. Casual portraits are done in natural environments. They might look as if the subject is just relaxing next to a brick wall or walking down the beach, but they should be carefully lit and posed. Because they are done on location rather than in a studio, they require you to choose a good location. At times, you might be able to use natural lighting, but typically you will get better results by adding a remote flash or reflector.

ENVIRONMENTAL

Environmental portraits, such as Figure 6-3, show the subject at work or play. Businesses often have photographers shoot their management team while sitting at a desk, and they might even want shots of employees sitting around a meeting room. Environmental shots can be personal, too. If someone loves to cook, he might want a picture of himself in the kitchen. If your grandfather has a favorite

chair that he always sits in, that's a perfect spot for a portrait. Because the surroundings are an important part of the picture, you will consider both the subject and the background as you compose and light the picture.

GLAMOUR

Glamour portraits, such as Figure 6-4, freely show an idealized version of the subject, rather than the realistic version people expect from most portraits. Glamour focuses on beauty and mystery. They resemble the fashion shots you see in magazine advertisements, but the subject is the model, rather than the clothes.

Glamour portraits are most easily done in a studio. If you shoot them in a home or bedroom environment, the room itself should be upscale and impeccably clean. As shown in the example, glamour portraits typically have heavy post-processing; instead of simply removing blemishes, you'll be smoothing skin entirely (including removing any trace of

Figure 6-2: A casual portrait.

Figure 6-3: An environmental portrait.

pores), tanning skin, removing wrinkles, and reshaping the subject's body. Glamour shots are for anyone who has ever dreamed of being a model.

PORTRAIT LENGTHS

The more of the subject you include in the photo, the more work it becomes for you as the photographer. Overall, headshots are the easiest shots to do, because posing and lighting are simpler and you don't have to worry as much about wardrobe.

- **Headshots**. Also known as head and shoulders portraits, headshots show the most detail in a person's face. You can optionally include one or both of the person's hands in the shot. Makeup, hair, and retouching are very important with headshots.

- **Waist-up Portraits**. Waist-up portraits show the person's torso and face, and tend to be cropped.

- **Three-Quarter Length Portraits**. Portraits framed so that the bottom of the frame is cropped mid-thigh or mid-calf.

- **Full-Length Portraits**. Portraits that show the subject's entire body.

To watch a video **Glamour and Fashion,** scan the QR code or visit:

sdp.io/Glamour

Always take shots of a subject at different distances. Mid-range shots that show the head, shoulders, and part of the upper body are traditional, and close-up shots can be very powerful by accentuating the eyes and other features. The difficult part is setting up the lighting and getting your subject in the studio; reframing the shot only takes a few seconds.

PORTRAIT PHOTOGRAPHY LENSES

If you plan to shoot headshots of a single person and you want a nice background blur, you'll need a good portrait lens. The ideal lens is a moderate telephoto lens in the 85-200mm range, with a minimum f/stop number of f/2.8 or lower in 35mm equivalent terms. If you're not using a full-frame camera, divide both the focal length and the f/stop number by your camera's crop factor to identify an ideal lens. For APS-C cameras, an inexpensive 50mm f/1.8 lens is a great choice for beginners.

Zoom lenses allow you to quickly switch from an upper-body shot to a headshot without moving your tripod, and they're highly recommended if you can justify the price of a zoom with a large aperture. Canon, Nikon, Sony, Tamron, and Sigma each offer 70-200 f/2.8 lenses $1,300 to $2,300—expensive, but perfect for portraits and weddings. For specific detailed recommendations for all budgets, refer to my book *Tony Northrup's Photography Buying Guide: How to Choose a Camera, Lens, Tripod, Flash, & More* at *sdp.io/buybg*.

Figure 6-4: A glamour portrait.

To watch a video on **portrait equipment,** scan the QR code or visit:

sdp.io/PortraitEquipment

Tip: Not only does a shallow depth-of-field provide a nice background blur, but it blurs the skin on the nose, helping to reduce the appearance of pores. This isn't as important if you remove blemishes in post-processing.

Why use a telephoto for portraits? Wide-angle lenses exaggerate features, making noses, eyes, and foreheads look bigger—and while wide-angle portraits can be interesting to look at, they're not flattering. Moderate telephotos help to reduce a person's features just enough to be attractive. Women, especially, tend to look better when shot with a telephoto lens. Figure 6-5 shows three shots from the same session: the first shot at 35mm, the second at 75mm, and the third at 170mm. Notice how the forehead and nose seem to become smaller as you zoom in.

Because a large aperture on a telephoto lens can have a depth-of-field of only a few millimeters, portrait lenses can create gorgeous, smooth background blur, which is important when working outside of the studio. Because the depth-of-field is so narrow, it's critical that you focus crisply on the nearest eye—that's the first place everyone will look, and if the nearest eye isn't sharp, the rest of the photo won't seem sharp. The depth-of-field can be so shallow that the rest of the subject's face can be very slightly out of focus, blurring pores and skin imperfections.

If you include more than one person in your portrait or if you plan to take portraits in front of a background that doesn't need to be blurred, just about any moderate telephoto lens will work. For more information, refer to "Group and Family Photos" later in this chapter. For more information about how to use aperture and depth-of-field to control background blur, read Chapter 4, "Controlling your Camera."

OUTDOOR PORTRAITS

Outdoor portraits, whether planned or spontaneous, have their own set of challenges. Outdoor lighting is notoriously unflattering: the sun creates hard top lighting that accentuates lines and hides the eyes. Even if you find some nice lighting, it will change constantly as the

Figure 6-5: Portraits taken at 35mm, 75mm, and 170mm to show how telephoto lenses show more flattering proportions.

sun moves across the sky and clouds come and go. To take great outdoor portraits, you need to know how to find the best locations and how to handle different lighting conditions.

Tip: As discussed in the Flash section, fill flash almost always improves outdoor portraits—just don't use too much flash.

When planning an outdoor portrait, follow this process:

1. Find a location and background.
2. Within that location, find the best natural light (which might involve moving into shade, choosing a specific time of day, or waiting for the right weather).
3. Add light, as desired, using flash or reflectors.
4. Pick your subject's clothing and pose.
5. Shoot!

OUTDOOR LOCATIONS

The best outdoor backgrounds are those that would make a boring picture without a subject in the frame. Simple lines, such as a pier, a road, or the horizon, can draw the eye through the photo. A grungy background, such as a brick wall, a faded building, or graffiti, adds character to the photo.

If the background is too cluttered, use shallow depth-of-field to create a background blur that

To watch a video on **outdoor portrait locations,** scan the QR code or visit:

sdp.io/OutdoorLocation

focuses the attention on your subject. Depth-of-field is covered in Chapter 4, "Controlling your Camera."

The background in Figure 6-7 was cluttered by a neighborhood. However, I shot the model with a a full-frame camera and a 300mm lens at f/5.6—enough to blur the background nicely, leaving only an impression of trees and sky. Also notice how having the sun behind the model nicely illuminated her hair.

On clear days or days with interesting clouds, get below your model and use the sky as a backdrop, as shown in Figure 6-8. Crouch or have your model stand on a hill. The more you point away from the sun, the deeper blue it will be. Therefore, on all but the clearest and coldest days, you'll need to position the sun in front of the model to get the darker sky in the background. You can use a polarizing filter to help darken the sky.

Because you usually stand above them, you can use the ground as a simple background for children, as shown in Figure 6-9. Zoom in to a telephoto focal length and hold your camera higher than the model's head to fill the background with grass. Unless you're on

Figure 6-6: Choose portrait locations with uncluttered backgrounds and simple lines (60mm, f/5.6, 1/30th, ISO 800).

Figure 6-7: Use short depth-of-field to blur cluttered background (300mm, f/5.6, 1/400th, ISO 100).

To watch a video on **business portraits,** scan the QR code or visit:

sdp.io/Dealership

a golf course, the ground will probably be less than perfect—be prepared to edit out weeds and brown spots in post-processing. Chapter 9 includes a useful video at *sdp.io/EditingLandscapes*.

HAVE THE SUN BEHIND THE MODEL

Having the sun behind the model creates a flattering backlight that creates a rim of light around the model. For profile shots, this accentuates the shape of the face. It also prevents squinting, allowing the model to open

their eyes more naturally. Unfortunately, it casts your model's face in shadow. Unless the background is also in shadow, the background will appear much brighter than the model. Turn on fill flash, or have someone hold a reflector angled toward the model's face.

Tip: The tighter the shot, the more important the lighting. For a full-length shot, perfect lighting on the face hardly matters, because people who look at the picture will see more of the model's body than face. To make a decent headshot, you're need to take control of the lighting. If you're working with natural light, choose an ideal time of day and location.

In Figure 6-10, the sun is behind the model, just off to the left of the frame. You can see the backlighting filtering through the model's hair and providing rim lighting for her coat, separating her body from the background. I used on-camera fill flash for this picture to balance the foreground and background lighting.

If you need to get a specific background behind your subject and you need backlighting, you'll need to know when the sun will be behind your subject as it moves across the sky. Use The Photographer's Ephemeris at *sdp.io/tpe* to identify the time of day (and perhaps time of year) when the sun will be in the right place for your shot.

Figure 6-8: Put the sun at your back and get below your subject to use the sky as a backdrop (220mm, f/11, 1/200th, ISO 200).

Figure 6-9: For children, it's easy to use the ground as a simple backdrop (75mm, f/4, 1/200th, ISO 100).

Figure 6-10: Position the sun behind the model and add fill flash for even front lighting with a pleasant rim light (200mm, f/5.6, 1/125th, ISO 100).

Figure 6-11 shows the effect you can get by placing the sun directly behind the model. The bright light of the setting sun completely overexposes the background, creating a high-key effect that draws your attention to the subject while still providing a sense of location. The bright light shines through translucent subjects, such as the red sweater. It also wraps around subjects, creating rim lighting that separates the far leg from the background and almost completely hides the near leg. I used fill flash for this picture, as described in Chapter 3.

Figure 6-11: Create extreme backlighting by placing the sun directly behind your subject (75mm, f/8, 1/90th, ISO 100).

Figure 6-12: Overcast skies provided a diffuse main light for this seven-eighths portrait (70mm, f/2.8, 1/180th, ISO 100).

WAIT FOR THE CLOUDS

Clouds are nature's diffuser, and the more clouds, the softer the lighting. If you have the luxury of scheduling a shoot around the weather, shoot outdoor portraits on overcast days. If you want to include a blue sky in the portrait, choose a partly cloudy day and wait until the sun goes behind a cloud.

Figure 6-12 shows a cloudy day portrait of the author taken by Chelsea in natural light. The overcast sky provided a diffuse main light, while warm light reflected from the leaves on the ground provided fill. While this portrait doesn't necessarily need it, many cloudy-day portraits benefit from adding fill light from a flash or reflector. Notice that the photo follows the rules of thirds and uses short depth-of-field to reduce the cluttered background to a blur of fall colors.

MOVE TO THE SHADE

The quickest way to provide a pleasant, natural light outdoors to move your model into the shade. Shade provides a soft light outdoors because light is reflected off the surroundings, including trees, buildings, and the ground. Shade also helps prevent squinting.

Figure 6-13 shows two pictures taken just a few feet apart, but the shade (with a bit of fill flash) dramatically improved the lighting.

SHOOTING PORTRAITS AT SUNRISE AND SUNSET

Including the sky in your outdoor portrait makes lighting particularly challenging. However, the sky can be a gorgeous (and free) backdrop, particularly at sunrise or sunset.

To watch a video about **outdoor portraits,** scan the QR code or visit:

sdp.io/OutdoorPortraits

Figure 6-14 illustrates using the rule of thirds, lines, and the golden hour in a single portrait. Because the model was backlit by the setting sun, I added flash to balance the lighting. Because I included the horizon in the picture and I did not use a camera level, I had to straighten the picture in post-processing.

When you include the sunrise or sunset in a portrait, your camera will probably underexpose the model and overexpose the sky. If you use flash, your camera will probably underexpose the sky, hiding the beauty of the background. To properly expose both the model and the sky, follow these steps:

1. In aperture priority (Av or A) mode, turn your flash off and have the subject move out of the frame. Take a picture, and make note of the aperture and shutter speed the camera used. If the exposure is off, adjust the exposure, and re-shoot until the sky is properly exposed.

2. Switch your camera to manual (M) mode, and set the aperture and shutter speed to the previous values. This will properly expose the sky.

3. Turn your flash on and take the picture. The flash should automatically expose the model correctly, and your manual camera settings should expose the sky properly.

4. If the flash overexposed the model, use flash exposure compensation to decrease the light output from the flash.

A quicker (but less precise) way is to point the camera at the sky, press the exposure lock (AE) button, point the camera at the model, and then take the picture.

HAVE THE SUN IN FRONT OF THE MODEL (AND LOW IN THE SKY)

Positioned so that the model is facing the sun directly, the model's face will be illuminated and his or her eyes will have a catch light. It's harder than it sounds, though. The higher the sun is in the sky, the more the hard lighting from direct sun will cast shadows beneath the model's eyes and nose, as shown in Figure 6-15. Once again, using fill flash or a reflector will help.

Another benefit of having the sun in front of the model is bluer skies. The sky is never a single, uniform color—if the sun is to the east, the sky will be bluest to the west. To work around squinting, have the model close her eyes, count to five, and open her eyes wide. Snap as many pictures as possible in the second or two your model has before she begins squinting again.

Figure 6-13: Shade provides much nicer light than direct sun (200mm, f/2.8).

Figure 6-14: Use standard composition techniques when shooting portraits (45mm, f/8, 1/180th, ISO 200).

USE DIFFUSERS AND REFLECTORS

If the shadows are too dark, use a collapsible reflector ($20-$100), as shown in Figure 6-16, to bounce light back onto the model's face, or use fill flash to balance the interior light with the exterior light. Reflectors typically are silver on one side and gold on the other; the gold side warms the lighting a bit.

I carry expandable diffusers and reflectors to soften natural lighting for outdoor portraits. Reflectors are perfect for filling in shadows, while diffusers will help you soften light. When shooting in direct sunlight, position a diffuser between the model and the sun so that the model is in the diffuser's shadow. For softer light, flex the reflector so that the middle of the reflector is curved toward the subject. For more focused light, flex the reflector so that the middle of the reflector is curved away from the subject.

To watch a video about **diffusers and reflectors,** scan the QR code or visit:

sdp.io/Diffuse

INDOOR PORTRAITS

When shooting indoors, start by choosing a location with nice lighting. On cloudy days, a bare window provides a soft, diffused light. On sunny days, pull sheers across a window to turn it into a soft box.

Use the simplest composition possible. Remove all clutter from the shot, and fill the frame with your subject. Try to include only a single element besides the subject in the photo. For example, have your subject lounging on a couch, but don't show pictures on the wall behind the couch.

For best results indoors, shoot during the day with as much sunlight as possible. As discussed earlier, top lighting provided by overhead lights isn't flattering for people, but side

Figure 6-15: When the sun is low in the sky, you can use it as front lighting (160mm, f/11, 1/200th).

Figure 6-16: A reflector on a stand.

lighting streaming through a window and softly reflected off interior walls can be very pleasant. As when working outdoors, avoid direct light. If the sun is visible through a window, use sheers or blinds to diffuse the light.

For traditional portrait lighting indoors, have people stand facing a window several feet away. If the sun is shining directly into the window, draw sheers or thin white curtains to diffuse the light, creating a giant soft box. This type of lighting is called *butterfly lighting*, and it's particularly flattering for women. For Figure 6-17, the model also had a window with white sheers drawn behind him, creating a high-key background often used in stock photography—without spending a dime on backdrops or studio lights. As you can see from the reflection in his eyes, the main light is a bit lower than butterfly lighting should be.

Having the light source directly in front of your subject minimizes texture to hide blemishes, but it also removes depth. Figure 6-18 shows a three-quarters portrait with the window positioned to the left of the frame; if you look closely, you can see the reflection of the window in the model's eyes. Because the main light is illuminating the side of the model's face that's turned away from the camera, this type of lighting is called *short lighting* or *narrow lighting*. Short lighting has a narrowing effect on the face, making it especially flattering for people with round or broad faces. The lighting in this picture could also be called *Rembrandt lighting*, because there is a triangle of light under the model's eye on the darker side of her face. Notice that the background is very dark in this picture because the light was falling on the model's face, but not the background.

For more dramatic lighting, move the model closer to open doors or windows. Even in well-lit rooms, direct sunlight will cause powerful highlights, and everything not directly illuminated will be in dark shadow. If the light is too hard, use sheers or curtains to soften it. If the shadows are too dark, use fill flash or a

reflector to balance the interior light with the exterior light.

When you review your first set of natural light portraits, you'll be shocked by how much darker the shadows are in the pictures than

Figure 6-17: An indoor, natural light high-key frontal portrait with direct front and back lighting (135mm, f/2.8, 1/60th, ISO 400).

Figure 6-18: An indoor, natural light three-quarters portrait with Rembrandt lighting (100mm, f/2.8 @ 1/250th, ISO 1600).

they seemed in person. The human eye has a dynamic range many times greater than that of a camera, which means that what we see in shadows with our eyes is completely black in a picture. Similarly, if something seems bright to your eye, it'll probably be completely overexposed on camera.

While your eye perceives indoors and outdoors as similarly bright, there's a reason you don't wear sunglasses indoors—direct sunlight is about 10-20 times brighter than a well-lit room. Figures 6-17 and 6-18 were taken indoors, using only the sun for light. In both pictures, the extreme difference in brightness between indoors and outdoors causes dramatic lighting and extreme shadows. For Figure 6-19, the model stood in an exterior doorway with the sun providing backlighting. The backlighting creates a rim of light around the model and illuminates her hair.

Figure 6-20 shows the author close enough to the main light to cause a dramatic falloff of light between the nose and the ear, creating deep shadows and a moody effect. Because the light is shining from the side of the frame, it highlights the texture and lines in my face. Because the sheers are diffusing the light, it is

To watch a video on **creating a holiday backdrop,** scan the QR code or visit:

sdp.io/HolidayBackdrop

still soft in this example, as illustrated by the gradual, smooth falloff of light across my face. Hard light would have drawn distinct lines between light and shadow.

CLOTHES

Unless you're shooting fashion, the subject of a portrait is the person, not the clothes. Clothes should never be distracting. Solid colors are better than patterns, and the fewer logos, the better. For waist-up photos, tell the client to wear a long-sleeved shirt so that the upper arms (rarely attractive in a photo) are hidden. Especially in group photos, nobody should wear shorts; the brightness of their legs would distract from the faces.

Black clothes are very slimming in photographs and will look good with just about any background. However, you should avoid shooting black clothes with a black background, or the body can disappear completely.

For casual or glamour shots, be creative; use a hood to frame the face and focus the viewer on the subject's eyes. Fur-trimmed hoods glow nicely when backlit.

People often want to look thinner in their portrait, but they must resist the urge to fit into clothes that are too small for them.

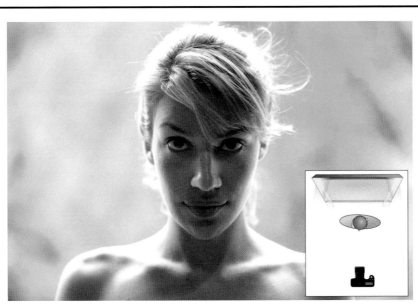

Figure 6-19: Heavy backlighting by the sun creates powerful rim lighting (100mm, f/2.8, 1/250th, ISO 400).

Small clothes pinch the skin and actually make a person look heavier. Even if the clothes look okay while the person is standing, they might be too tight while the person is sitting on a stool.

For traditional portraits, urge the client to choose timeless clothes. If they wear clothes that are too fashionable, the portrait will just look silly sitting on their grandparents' coffee table five years from now.

Urge men wearing a button-down shirt and slacks to get them dry-cleaned before the shoot. Wrinkles become much more noticeable in pictures. If there's any possibility that a strap will show, urge women to hide their bra strap.

For families, it's good if everyone sticks to a theme when picking out their wardrobe to make the group seem unified. For example, everyone

could wear pastel polo shirts and khakis, or jeans and white shirts. Don't have one person wear black and one wear white, or the picture will be too contrasty. For women, tailored clothes that show shape are better than baggy clothes, because it will make them look thinner.

POSING FOR PORTRAITS

You should always go into a shoot with at least two or three poses in mind. Start with traditional poses, such as sitting on a stool with the body turned to the side. Work on making the subject comfortable, and then get more creative with the poses.

The easiest way to have someone pose correctly is to show them a picture. Get a posing book, such as "500 Poses for Photographing Women" and "500 Poses for Photographing Men." A free alternative is to find poses that you like on the web, print them, or save the pictures to your phone or computer. During the shoot, you can flip through them for inspiration. I keep a collection of inspiration photos from other photographers on my iPhone to nudge me in the right direction when I run out of inspiration during a shoot.

The first few times you take someone's portrait, copying a pose from a picture will be challenging enough. Once you get comfortable with the process, however, you can begin to master posing individual parts of the body, as the following sections describe.

POSING MEN AND WOMEN

Women often pose with eye contact and use soft lighting. Special care must be taken for makeup to smooth skin tones as much as possible, darken eyebrows, and bring out the eyelashes. Today, most women expect some level of Photoshopping: removing all blemishes, smoothing skin tones, and bringing out the eyes.

Men can be easier. For portraits, men generally make eye contact. The lighting shouldn't be too hard, but shadows that show character lines on the face are good, even for a fashion shoot. For por-

Figure 6-20: Standing close to the light source creates dramatic lighting (70mm, f/2.8, 1/500th, ISO 400).

traits, the only post-production you need is to remove fly-aways and any blemishes. For fashion, men usually don't make eye contact, but instead act like they just happen to be hanging out next to a gritty brick wall and are far too cool to look toward the camera. Men aren't shot in front of plain backdrops as often as women.

EYES

The eyes are the most important part of most portraits. You should always focus on the eye closest to the camera. Eyes should always be well lit; ensure the eyes are not cast in shadow by the brow (from top lighting) or nose (from side lighting).

Most of the time, portraits look better when the subject's eyes are open a tiny bit wider than normal. Ideally, the eyelids should border the iris (the colored part of the eye). This is especially the case when shooting outdoors or in bright lights; subjects tend to squint. Pupils also look better when dilated, as they would be in a dark room. To provide both of these things, have the subject close his or her eyes for several seconds. Then, count down: "Three, two, one," and have the subject open his or her eyes on one.

Catch lights (reflections of light in the eyes) should typically be high in the eye and off-center, at 10 or 2 o'clock. You can always add catch lights in Photoshop. If you are using multiple lights, you'll end up with multiple catch lights. That's okay; if they're annoying, you can remove all but one catch light in Photoshop.

For traditional portraits, the subject should look directly at the camera. To the viewer, this feels like eye contact. For casual, candid, and boudoir portraits, your subject can look off-camera to provide a feel more like fashion photography. To control the subject's eyes, use a remote shutter trigger, and simply carry on a conversation with them while you walk around the room.

To watch a video about **group photos,** scan the QR code or visit:

sdp.io/Groups

Tip: Don't make too big of a deal about widening the eyes. If your subject overdoes it, he or she will look insane.

SHOULDERS

For most shots, especially those of women, you should have the subject's shoulders turned at an angle to the camera while holding a comfortable, but straight, posture. For women, this also adds shape and definition to the bust. The squarer they are with the camera, the wider the shoulders will appear, and the larger and more powerful the subject will seem. Figure 6-21 compares a traditional portrait with the shoulders square to a portrait with the shoulder turned at an angle.

HEAD TURN

Portrait photographers commonly use four different head angles, as shown in Figure 6-22. Regardless of the angle chosen, you'll usually have the subject's shoulders turned at an angle to the camera.

- **Direct**. The subject faces directly toward the camera. This angle gives the viewer the feeling of being directly connected to the subject. Direct view is common for business headshots.

- **Seven-eighths**. The subject turns their nose very slightly to the side. Both ears should still be visible if they are not covered by hair. By turning the face slightly, the face has more depth and the nose appears less wide.

- **Three-quarters**. For the three-quarter-view, which became popular in 1470s paintings, the subject turns their face slightly to the left or right—but not so

To watch a video about **posing for headshots,** scan the QR code or visit:

sdp.io/HeadshotPoses

far that the nose crosses the line of the cheek. If the nose crosses the cheek, it will look much larger. This pose gives more depth to the face than a direct portrait while diminishing the size of the nose and accentuating the cheekbones.

- **Profile**. The subject faces directly to the side. Profiles are rarely flattering for subjects because they accentuate the shape of the nose, chin, and forehead and diminish the eyes and cheekbones. Profiles can show a great deal of character.

For individual shots, most women look best at three-quarters, while most men look best at seven-eighths. For group shots, everyone should be facing the camera directly or at seven-eighths. If you turn a subject's head in a group shot, have them turn it toward the center of the picture so they are not facing off-camera.

It takes practice to be able to direct posing. It helps to tell subjects to turn their heads towards something in the room. For example, you might say, "Turn your head toward the clock, but keep your eyes looking directly at the camera." You might even need to add objects to the room to make it easier to provide direction. Small children are not good at taking direction, so you'll need to have an assistant holding a stuffed animal and moving wherever children should be looking. Alternatively, you can focus your camera and put your camera on a tripod so that you can walk around and direct the subject's attention yourself. Use a remote shutter release to take pictures.

Figure 6-21: Turn the shoulders to make the body appear narrower.

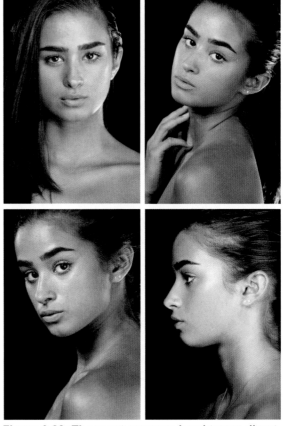

Figure 6-22: The most common head turns: direct, seven-eighths, three-quarters, and profile.

HEAD TILT

Besides turning the head, you should have your subject tilt his or her head slightly to the side. This creates a more dynamic, lively composition.

For the classic *feminine pose*, the subject has her shoulders turned at an angle to the camera, and the head is tilted toward the higher shoulder—the close shoulder in Figure 6-23. The classic *masculine pose* is just the opposite—the subject tilts his head toward the lower shoulder or simply holds it straight up. As shown in Figure 6-24, having a man tilt his head toward the high shoulder definitely gives an oddly feminine look to the picture. It's good to be familiar with the terms and tradition of portrait photography, but don't feel like you need to follow a rule; just have the subject tilt his or her head in a way that looks natural.

If the subject shows a double chin (something that can happen no matter how thin the subject is), have them extend his or her head toward the camera a bit. This stretches out the neck and reduces the double chin. You can also raise the main light so that the face casts the neck in shadow, and raise the camera above the subject's head by standing on a stepladder or having him or her sit on a stool.

Figure 6-23: Feminine, direct, and masculine head tilts on a woman.

Figure 6-24: Feminine, direct, and masculine head tilts on a man.

MOUTH

Smiles are contagious, so get into a good mood before the photo shoot. Chat with the subject so he or she relaxes. Flatter him or her. Have a few cheesy jokes lined up. Kids love knock-knock jokes, and guys love a dirty joke. You can also just chat about the weather, what he or she did last weekend, or what you have planned. The subject will pick up on your mood, so show him or her the expression that you want to mirror.

Full smiles are good for class pictures and family portraits, but little else. Throughout a session, it's a good idea to get shots of the subject with a serious expression, a closed-lip smile, a smile showing teeth, and a full laugh. Some people look best with a full smile. For others, a full smile causes his or her face to bunch up like a Shar-Pei. Keep your camera set to continuous shooting and take dozens of pictures. Take a few seconds early in the shoot to review the pictures and determine which expressions look best for your subject.

> **Tip:** Some people have a slight gap between their lips. That gap won't look good in pictures, so you might need to remind them to pull their lips together.

Most photos you see in the media show people with straight, white teeth. However, most people don't have perfect teeth. In Photoshop, you can select the teeth and then add brightness and reduce the saturation to whiten and remove color. You can also use the clone or Liquify tools to straighten teeth.

HAIR

Use a hair light to show detail in dark hair. In the studio, a hair light is a focused beam of light on the top of the subject's head. Outside of the studio, you can bounce the flash off the ceiling, or just find natural light that reflects off the subject's hair. The harder the hair light the better. Studio lighting is discussed more in "Studio Portraits," later in this chapter.

Dark hair can lose all definition in a portrait and appear to be a single black mass, as shown by the model's hair in Figure 6-25. In the first picture in Figure 6-25, the model had a hair light only on the left side of the frame, causing the hair on the right side of the frame to completely disappear into the black background. Adding some fill light to the right side of the frame better showed that side of the model's hair.

Even with a light background, adding direct light to dark hair brings out the color and shine. Figure 6-26 shows the effect of adding a hair light on either side of a model. In this example, the light adds interest and shows the red color in the hair.

Pointing a gently blowing fan at the face adds a bit of life and movement to hair. Fans that rest on the floor and can tilt upward, such as those designed for construction sites, work best.

Be careful when lighting gray or white hair, because they reflect light extremely well. If you add a hair light to someone with salt-and-pepper hair, it will make it seem far more salt than pepper. Similarly, you can make the person's hair seem darker by leaving it in shadow.

Fly-aways, stray hairs that stand out from the head, are also a problem. Do your best to

Figure 6-25: Without a hair light, dark hair can disappear.

smooth these out during the shoot, because they can be difficult to remove in post-processing. Most importantly, make sure no stray hairs cover the face. Removing a stray hair that crosses the subject's eye could take several minutes during post processing.

If your subject is bald, you don't want his head to be the focus of the pictures. Turn off the hair light, avoid rim lighting, and shoot them from a slightly lower angle.

ARMS

In Chapter 2, "Composition," we discussed the use of lines to draw the viewer's eyes through the photo. In portrait photography, the subject's arms are the most distinct lines. Position the arms at gentle, comfortable angles so that they draw the viewer's eyes toward the face. Avoid having arms completely straight.

Always tell the subject what to do with her hands and arms so that she doesn't let them just hang by her sides. In a seated position, she can rest her hands on her lap. In a standing position, she can put her hands on their hips, in her pockets, or behind her back.

Particularly with women, leave a visible space between the arms and the body. If the arms cover the edge of the body, they make the subject appear wider.

HANDS

Often, it's easier to simply let the hands hang outside the picture or hide them by folding the arms, placing them in pockets, or resting them in the lap. If you do include hands in your portrait, follow these guidelines:

■ Use the hands to draw the subject's attention to part of the picture. In group photos, have subjects put their hands over the shoulders or around the waist of others to move the viewer's eye through the picture.

■ Space the fingers evenly without the fingers touching. People don't do this naturally, so you'll have to help position the hand.

■ Show all or none of the hand. Don't allow just two or three fingers to show.

■ Gently bend the wrist so that it forms a gentle, curving line with the forearm.

■ Avoid having the subject's hands projected toward the camera, because it will make the hands appear larger than normal. If they must be closer to the camera, stand back farther and zoom in more to reduce the distortion.

■ Give the subject a prop to hold. For kids, this might be a stuffed animal. For adults, it might be a flower or a hat.

■ Don't clasp or stack hands. Instead, separate the hands.

■ For a more feminine look, turn the hands so that the sides are facing the camera and you cannot see the backs of the hands. For a more masculine look, show the backs of the hands, and curl the fingers around a small object like a bottle cap. Figure 6-27 shows two portraits showing the backs and sides of a woman's hands—the sides are much more flattering. These pictures also illustrate how moving the arm away from the body makes the waist appear thinner.

Figure 6-26: Hair lights bring out shine and color, especially in dark hair.

For engagement and wedding portraits, it's important to show the rings. In a seated pose, the bride can rest her hands on her lap, with the left hand facing the camera. Make sure the fingers are evenly spaced and that the ring is reflecting enough light to make it catch the viewer's eye.

Hands look terrifying when shot close-up; they're all knuckle wrinkles and veins. If the hands are the main subject of a photo, integrate them into the composition of the picture by using the lines created by the arms, shoulders, and body to draw attention to them.

HIPS AND LEGS

Like the shoulders, the hips should be turned at an angle to the camera to thin the subject. To further slim the subject, turn the hips even farther from the camera than the shoulders to twist the torso. For best results, turn the hips away from the main light.

Like the arms, you can use the legs to show lines in the portrait. Show a space between the legs to thin the subject, and don't allow the legs to be parallel.

When standing, have the subject put most of his or her weight on the back foot so that the body is shifted slightly away from the camera. The subject can bend the other leg slightly.

Figure 6-27: Showing the backs of a woman's hands makes them look large.

GROUP AND FAMILY PHOTOS

Group photos require very different techniques from individual photos. You need far more depth-of-field, lighting must be greatly simplified, and you'll need to take far more shots to get one picture where everyone has a good expression.

The sections that follow provide an overview of taking group photos.

CLOTHING FOR GROUP PHOTOS

If it's just two or three people, have everyone wear muted colors, just like you would for an individual portrait. Avoid bright colors and logos, because those will distract from the faces.

If it's four or more people, it's important to coordinate outfits. The easiest way to do this is to have everyone wear a white button-down shirt and jeans. If you all try to wear a different color, such as blue shirts, the blues never quite look right.

BACKGROUND FOR GROUP PHOTOS

There are a couple of reasons that planning the background for group photos is even more important than it is for individual photos:

- You'll need to use a wider angle lens to fit multiple people in the photo, and that will show far more of the background than a typical portrait lens would.

- You'll need a much wider depth-of-field to get everyone's faces in focus, which will reduce the amount the background is blurred, making it more distracting.

Outdoors, choose a background with minimal distractions, such as trees or a beach. Leave as much room as possible between your subjects and the background. With larger groups, you might need 30 feet or more to get everyone's face in focus and still noticeably blur the background.

Indoors, choose a large room with minimal distractions. Tidy the room up if you need to, and feel free to move potentially distracting objects into different rooms. For example, you might move plants or pictures out of the frame temporarily. Opening or closing curtains can help, too. As with outdoor backgrounds, leave as much space between your subjects and the wall behind them as possible.

LIGHTING FOR GROUP PHOTOS

Whereas you might carefully set up the lighting for an individual portrait to create perfect highlights and shadows, for a group photo, you should simply fill the room with soft light. This can be as simple as bouncing a flash off the ceiling or positioning everyone so that they face a large window.

In a studio environment, position soft boxes in front of your subjects, slightly above your subjects' eye level, and on either side of the camera. A single soft box can work well, too, especially when used as fill for natural light. Make sure that the subjects farthest from the light are well lit, and use reflectors or additional lights as needed.

COMPOSITION FOR GROUP PHOTOS

In group photos, as well as most types of photography, you should strive to fill the frame with your subject and create a background that doesn't distract. Fill the frame with the faces of your subjects, and avoid including their full bodies whenever possible. Framing the shot tight around their faces provides several benefits:

To watch a video about **group photos,** scan the QR code or visit:

sdp.io/Groups

- Because the faces are the most important part of the subject, it simplifies the composition.

- It reduces your need to pose every arm and leg.

- It makes everyone seem thinner by showing less of their bodies.

Be sure to leave room to crop from the left and right sides, especially if you plan to make an 8x10" print.

POSING FOR GROUP PHOTOS

Follow these tips when posing your subjects in a group photo:

- For more than two people, don't put everyone shoulder-to-shoulder. Have two rows, shorter people up-front. If everyone is the same height, you might want everyone to turn sideways (facing the center) and stand back-to-chest so their faces are closer.

- People need to be way closer than they're comfortable being. Everyone should be touching. It's okay to put your arms around other people's shoulders, and sometimes you need to turn people sideways to get them close enough. Remember, the faces are the subject, and you want the faces as close together as possible. It might feel weird to your subjects, but it will look great in the photo.

- Because you can only focus on one person and depth-of-field will cast other people's faces more out of focus the farther they are from your focus point, have back rows stand VERY close to front rows. The closer everyone's face is, the more in focus they will be.

- Arrange your subjects' faces so that everyone is visible. For smaller groups, just look at everyone's face and make sure it's not blocked by someone's hair in front of them. For large groups, tell them that if they can't see the camera, the camera can't see them.

- It really helps to have an assistant— someone who can check outfits, make sure nobody's face is hiding, the kids aren't ruining shots with goofy faces, etc. An assistant allows you to focus your attention on the lighting and camera settings.

- If some people are much taller than others, take off the taller person's shoes to lower them slightly. To raise shorter people, have them stand on apple boxes, chairs, or books. Apple boxes are stackable boxes designed for people to stand on to change their height. Don't ask people to stand on their tiptoes or slouch.

- For babies, the easiest way to equalize the height is to have a parent hold the baby in his or her arms. For small children, have the family sit on the ground, and position the children in front of the parents. To help keep the children's faces in focus, have them lean back against their parent's chest.

CAMERA SETTINGS FOR GROUP PHOTOS

Your biggest technical challenge for group photos will be getting enough depth-of-field so that everyone's face is in focus. Focus on the front row, if there are two rows, or the middle row if there are three or more rows.

For an individual portrait, I typically use a telephoto lens with the smallest f/stop number possible. Using a telephoto focal length helps to show flattering facial features, while the small f/stop number blurs the background to reduce

distractions. For example, I might shoot an individual at 200mm and f/2.8.

Unfortunately, it's usually not possible to use a long telephoto lens with group shots. For example, with a 200mm lens, you'd need to stand very far from your subjects to fit multiple people in the frame. Additionally, because longer focal lengths create a shorter depth-of-field, telephoto lenses are more likely to cast one of the subjects out of focus.

Therefore, as you add more people, you will need to zoom out to fit them in the frame and increase your f/stop number to get the depth-of-field you need:

- For people standing side-by-side, 100mm and f/5.6 is usually good.

- For multiple rows, use the widest angle lens you can (down to about 50mm) while still having a good background. If you want to show less background, step back and zoom in farther. Use an f/stop number of f/11 or higher.

Keep your shutter speed at 1/60th or 1/125th. Then, adjust your ISO or flash output to expose the picture properly, as described in Chapter 4. These suggestions are just guidelines; you will need to take a sample shot and zoom in on your display to make sure that everyone's face is sharp. If some people are out of focus, use a higher f/stop number and take another test shot.

SHOOTING GROUP PHOTOS

Traditional group shots don't leave much opportunity for creative expressions or head positions. Most people expect everyone to simply be smiling and looking at the camera, which makes your job much easier than a traditional portrait.

Getting everyone to smile at the same time can be a challenge, however. The classic, "1, 2, 3, cheese!" still works well. However, you will need to take dozens of shots to get one shot where everyone has a good expression.

If there are children in the picture, you might need to take more than a hundred shots. Kids will make funny faces, hold up rabbit ears behind other people's heads, stick their tongue out, and poke their siblings. Often, there's little you or the parents can do to prevent it, and being too stern can upset the kids or even make them cry, which will definitely ruin the photos.

If the children's behavior is an issue, tell everyone that you're going to take a few silly pictures and then a few nice pictures, and get the kids to agree to the arrangement. For the silly shots, tell the kids to make their silliest face. Let them get it out of their system, and show them the silly pictures. Then, remind them that they agreed to take some nice pictures, and get them to smile for you.

With smaller children, have a squeaky toy that you can use to attract their attention to the camera. Hold it directly above the camera. If the parents or someone else tries to make them smile, that's great, but the kid is going to look directly at them. Therefore, they need to be as close to the camera as possible, or the eyes are going to be pointed off-camera, which looks odd in photos. Never give the kid the toy, or else he or she won't want to put it down.

Parents are going to be trying to get their kids posed and smiling, which means they won't be looking at the camera and smiling themselves. Instruct the parents to look at the camera and let an assistant wrangle the kids and make them smile. You might only have five or ten minutes before small children get tired. Let them take frequent breaks; you won't get good pictures out of them while they're grouchy, anyway.

WORKING WITH KIDS

The biggest challenge with adults is getting them to relax. Kids, on the other hand, require

some planning. This section describes how to work with different age groups. Kids develop at different paces, though, so any given five-year-old might behave more like an eight yearold (and vice-versa). Details about working in a studio environment are provided later in this chapter.

BABIES

There's no talking a baby out of being grouchy, so build it into your schedule. At some point, the baby is going to become uncomfortable, hungry, or even worse—and the parents will need to take a few minutes to address the issue. If you can, provide a bathroom with a changing table and plenty of wet wipes.

Have shots for both a sleeping and waking baby. If the baby is awake, eye contact will make for amazing shots, but you need to be done in five or ten minutes. My favorite shots are:

- **Lying on a white fur rug or a stack of blankets.** This is a great shot to have ready when the baby is sleeping. Give the baby a soft, diffused lighting that matches her innocent character, and deliberately overexpose the picture to give it a high-key look.

- **With a favorite item.** Figure 6-28 shows a baby sleeping in his grandfather's hat.

- **Lying in a nest.** Create a nest from a wreath made of twigs, some moss, and feathers, all of which are available at craft stores. Place a brown blanket in the center of the wreath for the baby to rest in.

- **Close-ups of hands, eyes, and ears.** Have a macro lens ready to get close enough to the baby's features. If you don't have a macro lens, get as close as you can and plan to crop the picture later.

- **Being held.** A close-up of the baby in the parent's hand or cradled in his or her arm.

To watch a video on **photographing a baby,** scan the QR code or visit:

sdp.io/Babies

Today, the most popular shot is on a black backdrop, either with the parent shirtless or with the backdrop draped over the parent's body so that you can only see the hands. Black backgrounds never photograph perfectly, so plan to clean up the black background in Photoshop.

- **With both parents.** The father can stand with his arms behind the mother while the mother cradles the baby, or both parents can face each other while they hold the baby in their hands.

Babies are usually photographed naked. Have the parent pose the baby's legs to minimize the embarrassment the baby will experience in fifteen years when the mother shows the photos to the baby's future boyfriend or girlfriend. To prevent the baby from being cold, make the room very warm.

Avoid using flash, which can upset a baby. Use natural light, the modeling lights on your studio strobes, or video lights (known as hot lights). To get enough light, I position a large soft box with a modeling light just a foot away from the baby, and then use white foam core board as a reflector to fill in shadows.

Dramatic shots of babies are popular, so plan to convert some shots to black-and-white after you copy them to your computer. Don't ever set your camera to shoot in black-and-white, however—it's easy to remove color later, but impossible to add back in.

2-6 YEAR OLDS

Modern children's portraits are very simple:

- **A high-key white background (Figure 6-29).** White backgrounds match even the brightest children's clothes. Have the background cover the floor beneath the child so you can shoot down toward the model. This chapter provides more detail about high-key lighting in the "Studio Portraits" section.

- **Soft front lighting**. A softbox on either side of the camera, or one soft box and a reflector positioned on the other side of the model, will give soft lighting that accentuates the smooth texture and round form of a child's face.

You can tell adults to smile, turn their head slightly to the left, and look at the camera. For a kid, you'll need an assistant (known as a *wrangler*) to wave a stuffed animal while you tell knock-knock jokes and the parent urges the kid to stay on the stool. Each child you add to the picture makes it exponentially more challenging.

A wrangler, as shown in Figure 6-30, is absolutely essential for children under 6. As the photographer, you need to be able to focus on the camera, lighting, and pose. Feel free to give instructions directly to the child, but it's the job of the wrangler to help the child pose and to inspire the right expressions. The best wranglers are women, because both the children and the parents tend to be more comfortable with a female. If you can't find someone to help, set your camera up on a tripod and focus it. Then, take your remote shutter release in your hand and go engage the child—just stay out of the frame.

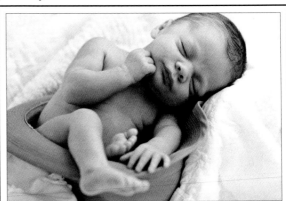

Figure 6-28: Photograph babies by creating a small set around them.

With preparation, practice, and a heavy shutter finger, you can take amazing pictures of young children. Here are some tips:

- **Before the shoot, ask the parents to dress the child in simple clothes**. Avoid heavily branded clothes, t-shirts with writing, and anything with cartoon characters. Kids love them, but bright colors will steal the focus of the picture.

- **Go barefoot**. Kids' shoes are often dirty, and children have perfect feet. Lose the shoes and wait a few minutes for the sock impression to fade.

- **Get to know outgoing children**. Most children will be uncomfortable taking instruction from a strange adult. Spend a few minutes chatting and playing with the child until they seem comfortable with you. The more fun you have with them, the more comfortable they'll be and the better they'll listen.

- **Ignore the shy kids**. It sounds mean, but children who are anxious around strangers will be more comfortable when they receive less attention. Often, shy kids simply need time around you (but not interacting with you) to be comfortable with you. Take your time chatting with the parents before the shoot to let the child get comfortable in their surroundings. When you're ready for the pictures, have the parent show the child where to stand and sit. Hopefully, the child will have relaxed

To watch a video on **photographing children,** scan the QR code or visit:

sdp.io/Children

some by the end of the shoot, allowing you to get friendlier.

- **Have some wet wipes available**. Have the parent clean the child's nose, mouth, and eyes thoroughly. You might not notice the crustics at first glance, but you sure will when you examine the pictures on your computer.

- **Keep the lighting simple**. Kids move around much more than adults, so anything other than soft front lighting will change too much as the kid wiggles about, creating odd shadows.

- **Put a toy on top of your camera**. A stuffed animal in your flash shoe gives you an easy point-of-focus, especially if it makes noise. The toy allows you to say, "Look at the birdie!" and have the child know exactly where to look.

- **Use a non-rotating stool**. Having a child sit on a stool or chair keeps him or her in one place. If the stool rotates, the child will twist it constantly.

- **Play copycat**. Kids this age naturally mimic movements, and the easiest way to get them to move their hands or face is to do it yourself. You can even turn it into a

Figure 6-29: Children on a high-key background with soft front lighting.

Figure 6-30: You need a second person to act as the child wrangler.

game by playing a round of Simon Says.

- **Be a cartoon**. If you want to keep a young child's attention for more than a few seconds, you'd better impersonate television characters. Master an Elmo or SpongeBob impersonation. Memorize some awful knock-knock jokes. Ask absurd questions, like, "So, are you married?" Have five minutes of material ready, and keep it coming until it's time for a commercial break.

- **Play into their egos**. Many kids, even the shy ones, just love to see pictures of themselves. While you definitely don't want to have a display facing the children at all times, you can encourage the child to come out of their shell by showing the pictures you just took on your camera back. This also shows them what you're doing and how it benefits them.

- **Bribe the kids**. The promise of a toy or food (only for after the shoot) might be

just what the kid needs to behave. Sure, it's not great parenting, but you aren't doing a photo shoot every day. Don't give them any food during the shoot or you'll end up Photoshopping it out of every shot. If you must give them a treat, make it a clear drink like juice.

- **Go traditional**. Always get the traditional shots with the child looking at the camera and gently smiling, as shown in Figure 6-31. Even parents who ask for fun and candid shots end up ordering the biggest prints of the traditional shots, and those are the shots that will bring other customers to you. If the model gets tired or grouchy, at least you'll have the basic shots done. Usually, the more relaxed and fun shots will come naturally as the child gets more comfortable.

- **Crouch down**. Like adults, most children look best when the camera is only slightly higher than their eyes.

- **Get above**. Shooting close with a wide-angle lens exaggerates childlike features by making the head and eyes seem larger (as shown in Figure 6-32), creating a fun picture.

- **Have props**. Start with the traditional shots while the child is calm and focused. As he become antsy, toss in sunglasses, teddy bears, bubbles, colorful suckers, sporting equipment, puppies and anything cute. The pictures with props are often the most fun, and they help keep the child's attention. Let him know ahead of time if he doesn't get to keep the toy—the younger your child is, the lower the chance of you getting your prop back without a screaming fit.

- **Parent in the room, everyone else out**. You should have a parent in the room to make the child comfortable, but have the rest of the family wait outside. Too many people are a distraction to the child, and you'll have a hard time getting the child to look at you. Sometimes, you might even need to have the parent wait outside briefly.

Figure 6-31: A traditional portrait.

■ **Reschedule troublesome children.** Everybody has a bad day. For some kids, it's every day. Fortunately, they're only your problem today. Sometimes, a child will be so difficult that you won't get a single picture. If a short break (and possibly a snack) doesn't fix the problem, just give up. Comfort the parents (who are no doubt embarrassed) and reschedule for another day.

Candid, out-of-the-studio portraits are popular now, as shown in Figure 6-33. Usually, parents or siblings will play with the child, either indoors or outdoors. You, as the photographer, will arrange the lighting (which might be natural, on-camera, or a portable studio) and try to grab pictures of the action. My favorite places for candid shots are the child's home (where you can set up proper lighting) and a playground (where you'll be limited to on-camera flash).

You can't ask young children to stand still or turn their heads into the light, so your best bet for lighting children outdoors is to use natural light and photograph them either during the golden hours or on an overcast day. If you must shoot them in the middle of a sunny day, use on-camera fill flash to reduce the amount of shadows. Also, ask the parents to avoid white or black outfits, which will be too contrasty in the harsh lighting.

Take children to an interesting place with attractive backgrounds. Parks, gardens, beaches, and wooded backyards are perfect. It's even better if the child hasn't been there before, because he or she will spend their time exploring.

If you try to chase the kids and take pictures of them, you'll get a great collection of the backs of their heads. Instead, anticipate where the child will be going, and get there first. You might even ask the parent to keep the kids steady, move to an interesting location, and call the kids towards you. Set your camera to continuous shooting and AI Servo (for Canon) or AF-C (for Nikon) autofocus to keep up with the action.

6-8 YEAR OLDS

Many of the same tips apply to 6-8 year olds as younger children, but 6-8 year olds are a unique challenge because they're usually missing some teeth. Some kids are terribly proud of their missing teeth and will smile big for you—usually with great results.

Other kids feel self-conscious about their missing teeth and won't smile for you. That's okay, too. In fact, you should always get some shots with closed-mouth smiles. For the truly tight-lipped, engage them in conversation about their favorite sport, band, or pet, and casually take pictures while they talk. Tell them cheesy jokes, and snap while they're laughing.

Figure 6-32: Shoot from above with a wide-angle lens to create cartoonish proportions.

PRETEENS AND TEENS

The exact age varies, but every kid hits a point when the cute tricks just won't work. Kids in this age range can take direction, but they'll likely act annoyed by the entire process.

Treat them like adults, and they'll usually return the favor. Conversation is important, but don't try too hard. Try to find common ground, like last night's sports event, or a movie you've seen that you think the subject might have seen or be interested in.

If the subject seems tense at all while you're shooting, pretend to adjust the lights while you continue the casual conversation. That'll give them a chance to get used to the surroundings.

STUDIO PORTRAITS

Traditional and some glamour portraits require a studio environment—even if the studio is

Figure 6-33: Candid pictures are perfect for young kids who won't sit still.

nothing more than a backdrop taped to a wall and a couple of carefully positioned flashes. This section describes the basics of a home studio environment that will allow you to create professional portraits on an amateur's budget. Because you're controlling the lighting and the backdrop separate from the camera, you can use very inexpensive camera equipment for traditional portraits—you can easily spend less than $300. The remaining equipment will cost as little as $240: two lights, light stands, softboxes, and backdrops.

For a detailed overview of studio lighting equipment and specific recommendations for every budget, read the "Studio Lighting Buying Guide" chapter of my book *Tony Northrup's Photography Buying Guide: How to Choose a Camera, Lens, Tripod, Flash, & More,* available at *sdp.io/buybg.* For an overview of backdrops, reflectors, stools, light stands, and other studio equipment, read the "Portrait Studio Equipment Buying Guide" chapter of the same book.

CHOOSING A BACKDROP COLOR

Decades ago, photographers used painted muslin backgrounds with lots of texture. Nowadays, most portraits are shot with a solid color backdrop. My most commonly used backdrops are all solid colors: white, black, and green. The white backdrop becomes light gray if I don't light it, and the black backdrop becomes dark gray if I do add a light. I use the green chroma key backdrop any time I want a backdrop of any color, because it's easier to change the color of the backdrop in post-processing than it is to physically switch backdrops.

For shots that show the subject's body, use a backdrop that contrasts her outfit if you want to emphasize the shape of the body. If you want to emphasize her face, use a backdrop of a similar color to their outfit. Figure 6-34 illustrates the difference. Note that in the picture with the white vinyl backdrop, the backdrop is lit so that it appears white rather than gray. In the picture with the black paper backdrop, the backdrop is lit so that it becomes dark gray instead of black.

You can selectively light the backdrop to emphasize or de-emphasize parts of the picture. To avoid shadows and to blur any texture, position the backdrop at least six feet behind the subject.

Once you've chosen the colors you want, you can choose from a variety of different materials: paper, vinyl, and cloth.

STUDIO LIGHTING CONCEPTS

Any given studio light, whether a flash, monolight, or strobe, might play several different roles in a portrait:

- **Main light (also known as the key light)**. The biggest, brightest light, which illuminates the subject's face and body. This is the only absolutely mandatory light.

- **Fill light**. A secondary light that reduces shadows cast by the main light. You can use reflectors for fill instead of a strobe.

- **Kicker light (also known as an accent light)**. A light that adds a touch of illumination to any part of the picture. For example, you might place the kicker light behind the subject to add rim lighting, or you might use it to accentuate a man's jaw line.

- **Hair light**. A narrow, focused light that reflects off the hair to add shine and stop it from blending into the background.

- **Background light**. A light that illuminates the background, especially when you need a bright white background.

Traditional portraits use soft, diffuse main light from a point slightly off to the left or right of the subject, and a bit higher than the subject's face. Having the light slightly above the subject's face gives even lighting across the face, creates a catch light in the eyes, and casts a shadow below the subjects chin. A fill

To watch a video on **camera settings,** scan the QR code or visit:

sdp.io/CameraSettings

light or reflector adds light to the shadows that would otherwise exaggerate features and imperfections.

Figure 6-35 shows a traditional three-light portrait with a reflector for fill light. In the bottom right, the main light provides the primary illumination and is positioned just higher than the subject's head. To the left of the subject, a reflector closer to the ground provides fill light by bouncing some of the main light back to the shadow side of the subject's face. In the upper right, a hair light with a snoot positioned higher than the subject separates the hair from the background. In the upper left, a background light illuminates the backdrop.

Figure 6-36 shows a traditional three-light portrait using the light setup in Figure 6-35, adding lights one at a time. The first picture uses only a soft box for the main light, which results in soft light with deep shadows. The second picture adds a reflector, which helps fill in the shadows. The third picture adds a background light, to bring the white

Figure 6-34: A backdrop with a similar color to the subject's outfit emphasizes his face, while contrasting colors emphasize their clothes and the shape of his body.

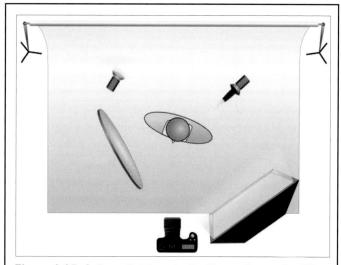

Figure 6-35: A three-light portrait with a reflector for fill.

Figure 6-36: Main light only, with reflector, with background light, and with a hair light.

backdrop from dark gray to light gray. A brighter background light could have created a completely white background. The final picture adds a hair light pointed at the part in the model's hair. This portrait could also benefit from a kicker light to add shine to the model's hair.

There are an infinite number of ways to modify this setup for different effects:

- Make the background darker by turning off the background light.
- Soften the light by moving the reflector closer.
- Create more dramatic shadows by moving the reflector farther away or removing it entirely.
- Add a kicker light behind the subject for rim lighting.

To create soft lighting, use a larger light, and move the light closer. That seems counterintuitive, because light feels harsher as we get closer. If you're getting shadows under the subject's eyes or nose, put a reflector below them—you can even have them hold the reflector, if it's not too distracting.

Light loses power quickly the farther you get from it. Therefore, moving the light closer also increases the falloff of light, creating deeper shadows and increasing your need for fill light. If you position a beauty dish a few feet away from a subject, it will create a soft light. However, because the subject's forehead is so much closer (relatively) to the light than his or her cheeks and chin, the forehead will appear much brighter in the picture.

Move the light farther from the subject, and the light will appear harder because the relative size of the light source is smaller. However, the shadows will be much less noticeable because the difference in lighting between her forehead and chin will be relatively less. Moving the light down, closer to eye-level, reduces the shadows on the face and better lights the eyes. However, it also reduces the shadows under the cheekbones that show the facial structure.

Moving the main light up, down, nearer, and farther can subtly change the lighting on the subject. However, there's no easy way to show it with an example because the size of your studio, the type of light you use, the shape of the model's face, and the subject's pose are the most important factors. The only way to understand how moving the light affects the lighting on your subject is to practice:

1. Start with the main light three feet in front of the subject, two feet off to one side, and about a foot higher than the subject's head.

2. Take a photo, move the light, and take another photo.

3. Continue shooting and moving the light.

Over time, and many different portrait sittings, you will get a feel for where to position the lights to get the effect you want.

As discussed in Chapter 3, "Lighting and Flash," you should also be familiar with broad and short lighting, as shown in Figure 6-37:

■ **Broad lighting**. When the main light casts a shadow on the side of the face farthest from the camera. Broad lighting makes a face appear wider.

■ **Short lighting**. When the main light casts a shadow on the side of the face closest to the camera. Short lighting makes a face appear more slender, and is preferred for most portraits.

You can do decent portrait work with a single soft box (a large diffuser in front of a flash). No matter how diffuse the light, however, you can benefit by filling in the shadows with reflectors. If the softbox is to the left of the subject, a reflector to the right can help to fill in any shadows.

Automatic exposure on your camera will not work when using studio lighting, so switch your camera to manual mode. Choose ISO 100, an aperture of f/11, and a shutter speed of 1/60th. Take a test shot, and examine picture's

To watch a video on **portrait lighting,** scan the QR code or visit:

sdp.io/PortraitLighting

histogram. If it is overexposed, use a higher f/stop number, such as f/16. If it is underexposed, use a lower f/stop number, such as f/8, or a higher ISO. Unless you have a great deal of natural light in the room, adjusting the shutter speed won't change the exposure; you are relying entirely on the studio lighting. Each time you adjust the lighting or move the subject, take another test shot and verify that the exposure is still correct.

USING A WHITE BACKGROUND

Solid white backgrounds convey a happy, fun, and positive mood. They've become common in portraiture, fashion, stock, commercial, and product photography. For that reason, every photographer must master creating a white background. In the industry, many photographers refer to a bright white background as "high key," though that term can also refer to an artistic style where both the subject and the background are very bright.

To create a solid white background, you need to completely overexpose your background

Figure 6-37: Broad lighting is created by turning the nose away from the main light, and short lighting created by turning the nose toward the main light.

without overexposing your subject. That means you'll need much more light on your background than on your foreground subject—about 16 times more light (or four stops of light).

This doesn't necessarily require expensive studio equipment, however. We all share a very powerful and free light source: the sun. For this photo of a radio talk show host and his dog (who was too old to climb the stairs to our studio), I had him kneel in my kitchen mid-day when the sun was streaming through the glass doors behind him. I added three stops of exposure compensation, as I describe in Chapter 4, to properly expose their faces. Because the sunlit background was much brighter than the shade in my kitchen, the camera captured it as almost solid white, as shown in the first unretouched picture in Figure 6-38. It took me just a few minutes in Photoshop to remove the shadows and create a perfect white background.

A makeshift backdrop is convenient for occasional high key photography. If you're a professional, you need to be able to take pictures even when the sun isn't cooperating, and you don't want to spend more time than necessary editing photos. Fortunately, it's easy and relatively inexpensive to setup a white background and lights. In the video at the top right of the page, I demonstrate how Chelsea and I create high-key photos in both a studio environment and in our own kitchen.

USING A BLACK BACKGROUND

Solid black backgrounds convey a serious, dramatic, and sexy mood. They're commonly used for glamour, fashion, and portraits of serious actors, musicians, and politicians.

While creating a solid white background requires having more light on your background than on your subject, creating a black background requires having 4-8 stops more light on your subject than on your background. This is very difficult to do well with natural light; you'll almost always need to light your subject with a flash or monolight, and prevent that light from spilling onto your background.

You can use two techniques to create a black background without using a proper backdrop:

- **Use the night as the background.** Take your models outside at night, or place them in front of an open door, and light them with a flash.

- **Overpower the ambient light.** Set your camera to manual mode, ISO 100, and choose a high f/stop number, such as f/22. Now, select the slowest shutter speed that creates a completely black photo. Next, position a flash or monolight as close as possible to your subject, and adjust the output until your subject is properly exposed. In sunlight, you will probably need to use high-speed sync, as described in Chapter 3.

Figure 6-38: You can use sunlight and white curtains to create a bright background.

In a studio environment, use a black backdrop to reflect as little of the ambient light as possible. Even though the backdrop is black, it will still reflect some light and appear grey in pictures. To prevent the main light from spilling onto the background, attach a grid to any lights that are pointing towards the backdrop, including your main light.

CORRECTIVE POSING AND LIGHTING

Though they won't always tell you outright, most people want to appear thinner than they actually are. There are several things you can do to provide this (other than using the Photoshop Liquify tool):

- Have the models stand instead of sitting. If they must sit, have them shift their weight so that their bodies don't mushroom over the stool.

- Shoot with your camera slightly above the model so that she looks up toward the camera. Have her stretch her neck toward the camera. If you need to, use a foot stool or step ladder to get high enough.

- Shoot facial close-ups and avoid full body shots.

- If you must shoot the waistline, have the subject turn her body to the side (away from the main light) and twist her head and shoulders toward the camera.

- Use short lighting, where the main light illuminates the side of the face farthest from the camera. Use less fill so that shadows are deeper.

- If a subject has a wide face, you can move the main light off to the side to visibly narrow the face. If the subject has a narrow face, turn his face directly toward the main light to broaden it.

- No matter how thin the person is, if there's light from underneath her face, it'll look like she has a double chin. Move the main and fill lights high enough to cast the neck in shadow.

To watch a video on using a **solid white background,** scan the QR code or visit:

sdp.io/WhiteBackground

To watch a video on **low key photos,** scan the QR code or visit:

sdp.io/BlackBackground

USING STUDIO LIGHTING OUTDOORS

Once you start using off-camera lighting, it's hard to go back to natural light. You can use off-camera lighting outdoors; however, there are some special challenges:

- **Fighting sunlight.** In an indoor studio, controlling the light requires overpowering the ambient light. You generally can't do this during the day; the sun will always be your main light. You can use off-camera lights for fill and kicker lights, though.

- **Changing conditions.** Outdoors, your main light, the sun, is constantly moving across the sky. You won't appreciate exactly how fast it's moving until you try to do a two-hour shoot; every twenty minutes or so, you'll need to change poses and fill to adapt to the sun's new position. If clouds are moving across the sky, it might be even more frequent. If you're relying on the sun being low in the sky, you might have less than an hour to finish your shoot. Be sure to choose a flash and trigger that support TTL, which automatically provides just the right amount of light and can help you automatically adapt to changing conditions. For detailed information about hardware, read the "Flash Buying Guide" and "Wireless Flash Trigger Buying Guide" chapters of my Photography Buying Guide, available at *sdp.io/buybg*.

- **Wind.** Indoors, your umbrellas and softbox stay where you put them. Outdoors, a gust of wind will knock them over, possibly breaking something expensive (like your model). A heavy sandbag can help, but then you also need to carry the sandbag. In windy situations, a beauty dish will work better than a soft box, and a small reflector will work better than a beauty dish.

- **No electricity.** Outdoors, you're usually relying entirely on battery power. If you're using a flash and shooting rapidly like you would in a studio, you can run out of batteries in five or ten minutes. Especially if you're using multiple flashes, you can spend half your time swapping batteries. If you're using monolights or a power pack, you'll need a battery pack designed for monolights, such as the Vagabond Minis that I use.

- **Carrying stuff.** You've got to haul in your light stands, light modifiers, lighting, and camera. You'd better bring everything you might possibly need, too.

Don't let these challenges overwhelm you, just start small:

- On your first outing, bring a single light stand with a flash or monolight. Don't even bother with a light modifier. Concentrate on balancing your flash with the natural light. Experiment with having your model in the sun and in shadow.

- Once you feel you've mastered working with a single off-camera light outdoors, add a light modifier (such as an umbrella, beauty dish, or soft box) and a sandbag on your light stand to help stop it from tipping over.

- Now that you understand how your light modifier impacts the output of your flash, gradually add more lights, until you can create any light in any location.

PUTTING LIGHTS IN THE FRAME

Because you're fighting sunlight, your flashes might not be powerful enough to light your

subject from far enough away to keep the light out of the picture. You can work around this by combining multiple pictures into a single shot:

1. Put your camera on a tripod. Pose your subject, and take a picture with natural lighting. You will use this picture as the background.

2. Move the lights into the picture. Shoot for five minutes or so. You will use these pictures of the foreground, and blend them with the background.

3. Repeat steps one and two until you have enough pictures. You'll have to take new background pictures on a regular basis, because the sky and lighting will be changing.

4. After copying the pictures to your computer, combine them to remove the lights from the shot. You can do this in Photoshop by adding the pictures as layers in a single image, and then using layer masks (and a brush with a soft edge) to reveal your subject on the clean background.

TAKING SELF-PORTRAITS

Like any form of photography, portraiture requires practice. If you don't have access to someone who's eager to be in front of the camera, you can take self-portraits to practice lighting, posing, and composition. Self-portrait techniques are also important when taking group and family photos that you want to include yourself in.

It's impossible to compose, focus, and light your self-portrait without a stand-in model. If nobody is available to sit in your while you set up the portrait, you should create a mannequin. Use a Styrofoam head ($4-$10), such as those used for cosmetics and wigs, and impale it on an inexpensive light stand ($15-$30). If you want to check the lighting on your hair, add a cheap wig with a similar hair color and length ($10-$30). This combination of light stand,

Styrofoam head, and cheap wig creates an effective (if somewhat terrifying) stand-in that's also useful for preparing portrait lighting before the model arrives.

With the mannequin version of you in place, you will need to adjust several aspects of your photography to get a great self-portrait:

- **Composition**. Place your camera on a tripod, and compose the shot. Shoot much wider than you would normally, because you can always crop the shot later, but if you accidentally crop your own head out of the photo, you will need to re-shoot. An articulating display that can be rotated forward is useful for framing the shot. However, everyone always looks at themselves in the display rather than looking at the lens, which ruins the eye contact they should have with the camera. Therefore, I only recommend having the camera display visible if you're the only one in the shot. If there are other people in the shot, just be sure to leave plenty of room around yourself, and check the framing after a few shots.

- **Focus**. It's impossible to precisely focus on your own eye while in front of the camera. Therefore, you will need to pre-focus your lens on your mannequin, and then switch your lens to manual focus so that your camera does not automatically re-focus when you take a picture. Otherwise, a tripod or light stand extended to your height works well.

- **Aperture**. For most individual portraiture, I recommend choosing a low f/stop number (such as f/2.8) to blur the background, selecting a single autofocus point, and focusing on the nearest eye. However, self-portrait pre-focusing will never be precise enough to use shallow depth-of-field. Even if you use a mannequin, you will be front- or back-focused by several inches. Therefore, you should select a high f/stop number (such

To watch a video **touring our studio,** scan the QR code or visit:

sdp.io/TourStudio

as f/16) to create a deep depth-of-field and provide a margin of error. This will cause your background to be relatively sharp, rather than blurred, so choose a distraction-free location.

- **Shutter**. I don't recommend using a remote shutter; you spend too much time thinking about pressing the shutter and it often appears in the final shot. Instead, use a remote shutter timer, such as the inexpensive models made by Neewer (which are also available under other generic brand names), which typically cost about $15 USD. Configure the timer to take a photo every one or two seconds. The remote timer will take far more shots than necessary; however, it's very easy to delete all but the best photo.

- **Flash**. If you're using a flash, set the remote shutter timer to take a picture every eight seconds. That's enough time to allow you to pose, and after a few frames, you'll know the rhythm.

POST-PROCESSING

One of the factors that distinguish a snapshot from a portrait is retouching. Every portrait must have some level of retouching. At a minimum, this requires removing blemishes—something that takes only a few seconds with an image editing application. You shouldn't even ask the models if they want blemishes removed; they do, but they'll feel vain asking you to do it. Just do it for them.

Never show models a picture both before and after you retouch it; this can make them feel like you noticed every flaw they have. If you need to retouch a large amount of pictures, you can use software tools to speed the process. I use Imagenomic's Portraiture, available at *www.imagenomic.com/pt.aspx*.

To watch a video on **self-portraits,** scan the QR code or visit:

sdp.io/Self

Even if you're just taking snapshots of your family, every photographer should learn how to remove blemishes. If you lack the patience, computer equipment, or software, you can find photo retouching services online.

CHECKLISTS

I've made a portrait checklist that you can print and keep with you. Better yet, copy it to your smartphone so you never leave it at home. You can download and print the checklist from *sdp.io/checklist.*

PRACTICE

This chapter's practices help you understand lighting and posing when photographing people.

- **Working outdoors**: Bring your favorite model outdoors on a sunny day. Take the following shots both with and without fill flash: sun behind the model, sun in front of the model, sun to the model's side, and model in the shade. Which position worked best? Did fill flash help or hurt? Repeat this practice on an overcast day and at sunset.

- **Head angle**: Find several patient models, both male and female, and have them stand with their shoulders at a 45-degree angle to you. Then, take several different pictures of their faces at different angles. Make note of which poses are most flattering for which people: direct, seven-eighths, three-quarters, or full profile.

- **Head tilt**: Shoot both a man and a woman with masculine and feminine head tilts. Have an objective observer choose which pictures they prefer.

- **Posing**: Search the web for full body portraits and print a dozen or so different poses. You can also collect poses from advertisements in magazines. Have your favorite model duplicate some of these poses. Talk to the model about which poses are comfortable and awkward. Later, look at the pictures. Which poses worked best?

- **Shooting angle**: Shoot full body pictures of a model from ground-level, waist-level, eye-level, and from above. How did each angle change the appearance of the model's body? Which angles lengthened the legs or made the model look thinner?

- **Slimming**: Most people would rather look thinner in pictures. Experiment with poses that make the model look thinner. For example, have the model turn their waist away from you, but twist their shoulders towards you. Vary the lighting and the shooting angle to find the most slimming combination.

- **Watching the details**: So many portraits are ruined by tiny details that are easily overlooked in person, but jump out at you in photos: the bride who didn't put her drink down, the boy with food in his teeth, or the businessman with a crooked tie. As a portrait photographer, it's hard enough to monitor the lighting, focus, and depth-of-field. Once you get comfortable with the technical details, keep your eye out for the details. Take a few shots, and then examine the picture closely. Correct these tiny details, and shoot again.

- **Talking while shooting**: The hardest part of taking portraits is getting non-models to look comfortable on camera. You need to distract them with constant conversation so they feel like they're just hanging out with you. Practice chatting while shooting. It helps if you have some easy conversational topics in mind, like the weather and sports. It also helps to memorize a few jokes that you can recite without much thought.

- **Hair lights:** Create a hair light by using a snoot on a light source. If you don't have a snoot, you can tape a piece of paper around the head of a flash. Find a model with dark hair and use this narrow light source to highlight the top of their hair. Shoot them with and without the hair light. Which works better?

■ **Rim lights:** Create rim lighting by positioning a bright light source behind a model, pointed toward them (but not visible in the frame). Shoot the same poses with and without the rim lights. Notice the effect.

To watch a video on **editing a portrait,** scan the QR code or visit:

sdp.io/EditingPortraits

 Take a quiz!

sdp.io/Quiz6

7
CHAPTER

WEDDINGS

It's only a matter of time before you impress a couple enough that they ask you to photograph their wedding. This is both a compliment to you and evidence of how significantly people underestimate both the importance and challenge of wedding photography.

Before you attempt a wedding, you must be comfortable with lighting and posing portraits as described in Chapter 6, "Portraits." Wedding photography isn't technically any more difficult than portrait photography; all the same fundamentals apply. The challenges of shooting a wedding are largely non-technical:

- Between the bridal party and their family, someone is going to be upset.
- You usually have no control over the location and timing.
- Most of the people involved will hate having their pictures taken.
- During the posed shots, everyone will want to get away as fast as possible so they can enjoy the reception.
- During the rest of the wedding, people will be busy and you'll need to get pictures of them without getting in the way.
- Alcohol.

And here's the biggest challenge a wedding photographer faces: you absolutely have to get it right the first time. If you get back home and discover you left your camera in the wrong mode, you can't reshoot, and the bride and her mother are going to be *very upset*.

The good news is that a pair of competent portrait photographers, with good equipment and careful planning, can do a good job as wedding photographers (and save their friends thousands of dollars). In fact, as friends, the couple can be more comfortable around you than they would be with an unknown photographer, and your pictures can be more intimate.

To watch a video overview of photograhing a wedding, scan the QR code or visit:

sdp.io/Wedding

PLANNING

The wedding photography process starts by meeting with the bride and groom. Sometimes, their parents will want to meet with you, too. You'll discuss the types of pictures they want and the style they like. It's good if they bring samples from bridal magazines or the Internet, so you can get a feel for whether they prefer traditional, artistic, or casual. Bring the pictures to the wedding, or copy them to your phone so that you can reference them.

In addition to their stated style preference, you should plan on taking traditional pictures. Many couples specifically do not want posed pictures, asking instead for candid photos. Agree to take mostly candid shots, but insist on a few posed pictures for the parents and grandparents.

Ask the names of the most important people in the wedding, including the bridesmaid, best man, the wedding party, parents, and grandparents. Get the phone numbers of the parents, the bridesmaid, and the best man, in case you are unable to reach the bride or groom. Make a list of the group shots that they want and who should be in each one. Keep this list with you at the wedding—I like to put the list both on paper and in my phone so that I have it no matter what.

Visit the wedding location a week or two beforehand, at about the same time of day as the wedding. Make note of where the bride and groom will enter and exit, the path they will walk, and where the ceremony will be held. Find out exactly which direction the bride and groom will be facing during the ceremony so that you will be able to see both faces.

Choose where you will stand for each set of pictures, the lens that you will use, and how you will bounce the flash. Identify spots that have nice lighting for individual portraits. Choose backdrops that show off the unique characteristics of the location without distracting from the subject. While you're there, take some pictures of the location. If the sunlight is unflattering at that time of day, consider coming back at sunrise or sunset for better shots of the location.

If you discover that the bride and groom will be facing into the bright sun during the ceremony, you should warn them. Not only will this create unflattering lighting for the picture, but they'll be uncomfortable and squinting.

During the planning phase, you should create a checklist of equipment to bring for the wedding. Be sure to include:

- Snacks and a bottle of water for yourself
- A towel to wipe the sweat from your brow
- Extra batteries for your camera and flash
- Extra memory cards
- Wireless flashes and light stands, if extra lighting is required for the posed shots
- Your shot list (get one at *sdp.io/checklist*)

PROCESS

Though weddings vary, the following sections provide a good overview of what you'll need to do during each major phase.

GETTING READY

Typically, the getting ready process starts with the bride and bridesmaids meeting up and getting their hair and makeup done. Shoot the bride leaving the house, travelling, and preparing the dress. Find a decorative way to shoot the dress and shoes (as shown in Figures 7-1 and 7-2) before, or while, the bride puts

Figure 7-1: Isolate moments to reduce clutter in a picture.

them on. Shoot wide-angle shots that show the overall scene, but also shoot close-up shots that isolate a moment, as shown in Figure 7-1.

Photograph the bride putting on makeup and doing her hair. Even if she has a professional helping her, you might ask the makeup artist to step away and have the bride pretend to put on lipstick so that you can get a clean shot without the makeup artist in the frame. While the bride is more important, one of the photographers should spend some time with the groom and the groomsmen. Catch him tying his tie, having a cigar, and drinking.

There's always about an hour of waiting around before the ceremony begins. Use this time to photograph the flowers and the wedding hall's details and decorations.

PROCESSION

While the groom waits for the bride, photograph the groom and each of his groomsmen individually and as a group. Walk up and down the aisles and photograph people as they wait. Engage children by waving or saying hi, and crouch down to photograph them from eye level. Photograph the ushers seating people, especially the mother of the bride.

When the wedding party begins walking up the aisle, position the lead photographer directly

in their path with a normal zoom lens, such as a 24-105mm or 24-70mm. Don't be shy; to get this shot, you'll have to be in front of the entire audience. To get the procession shots, the photographer should set her camera to continuously autofocus with a shutter speed of 1/250th to 1/500th to keep the moving subjects sharp. Continuous autofocus never works perfectly, so use the continuous shutter mode and take more shots than you think you need.

The assistant photographer should be positioned either to the front or the sides of the aisles with a telephoto zoom lens, such as a 70-200mm, and should get profile shots of the wedding party as they walk down the aisle and reaction shots of the guests as they see the bride. When the bride walks down the aisle, focus on her closest eye, and allow depth-of-field to cast everyone else gently out of focus, as shown in Figure 7-3.

> **Tip:** Leave room to crop! The most popular wedding print size is 8x10", and that requires cropping one inch off both ends of your photo. The framing will cover about half an inch all around the picture.

If the wedding is outdoors, hard sunlight can create very harsh lighting on people's faces. Your only option is to use a touch of fill flash on your subjects to reduce the shadows on their face, as discussed in Chapter 3. Check your shots regularly to verify that you're not using too much flash.

Figure 7-2: Photograph the shoes and dress before the wedding.

Figure 7-3: Use depth-of-field to show that the bride is the center of attention.

CEREMONY

If you feel like you're in the way during the ceremony, you're probably doing it right. The lead photographer should be directly in the aisle, shooting the bride, groom, and officiate, as shown in Figure 7-4. Your shutter will sound like a bass drum in the quiet hall, so don't shoot more than necessary, and use the quiet or silent shutter feature if your camera has it. Watch the eyes of the bride and groom, and shoot when you can see them both in profile. Try to capture the moments when they look at each other or wipe a tear away. Be sure to capture anything that makes the ceremony unique, such as interesting gifts or rituals. You might not be able to make every shot a work of art, but it's critical that you document it.

The assistant photographer should be positioned in front of the pews and to either side so that he can shoot the bride and groom head-on as they look at each other, as shown in

Figure 7-5. It's okay to capture an out-of-focus bride in part of the frame when shooting the groom (and vice-versa); it provides context to the shot and gives the viewers the feeling that they are experiencing it from the perspective of the bride or groom. Move to both sides of the wedding party so that you can shoot both the bride and the groom. Additionally, the assistant photographer is responsible for capturing reactions from the guests during the ceremony.

When the bride and groom exchange the rings, the lead photographer should shoot wide-angle to capture both the bride and the groom in the shot. The assistant photographer should zoom in to get close-ups of the rings. It won't always be possible to see the rings in the shots; just do your best.

As the bride and groom prepare to walk down the aisle together, position the lead

Figure 7-4: Stand in the aisle to shoot the bride, groom, and officiate during the ceremony.

Figure 7-5: Stand in front of the pews and shoot the bride and groom from the sides.

photographer in front of them, at the end of the aisle. If it won't block the bridal party, the assistant photographer should find a spot behind them to take pictures of them walking away, as shown in Figure 7-6. If there's not a spot available, the assistant photographer should stand off to one side and shoot the couples walking down the aisle from an angle. Both photographers should switch to continuous autofocus (to keep the moving couples in focus) and a low f/stop number (to reduce the visible clutter in the background).

Now, breathe a sigh of relief; the hardest part is over.

POSED SHOTS

After the ceremony, bring the wedding party and anyone in the group shots to your location. Start with shots of the flower girl and ring-

bearer with the bride and groom, because if you wait too long, the kids will mess up their outfits. Then, work from biggest to smallest, starting with the largest group of people and working your way down to the shots of just the happy (and no doubt relieved) couple. You'll find a complete list of shots at the end of this chapter.

For the large groups, find a stairwell, as shown in Figure 7-7. The bride and groom should always be in front, followed by the wedding party. Ideally, everyone would be in shade, but locations don't always allow that. As an alternative, you could stand on a ladder and shoot down on people.

If you must arrange a group on a flat surface, position the couple in the center, and have the other participants balanced on either side, facing inward, as demonstrated by Figure 7-8.

Be sure you have enough depth-of-field to get everyone's faces in focus. Take a test shot, and then review the shot and zoom in to everyone's faces, especially people on the front and back row. For more information, refer to the Group Photos section of Chapter 6.

Lighting so many faces can be very difficult, especially outdoors. Make sure everyone has

Figure 7-6: Look for candid, sincere moments throughout the wedding.

Figure 7-7: Position large groups on steps so that you can see everyone's faces.

the same lighting; you don't want half the group in shade, and half in direct sunlight.

The shade of a tree acts like a huge diffuser, creating flattering light across a large group. However, having your subjects in shade can make them 4-6 stops darker than the background. To better balance the foreground and background lighting, use two off-camera flashes located on either side of you, raised slightly above eye level, and pointed at your subjects. Use manual mode on your camera to properly expose the background, and then increase the flash output until your subjects are properly exposed. Figure 7-8 shows the results of this technique: bright, even lighting in the shadows and a balanced exposure for the background scene.

The hardest part of a group shot is getting everyone's expression right. To get everyone's eyes open, have the group close their eyes, and on the count of three, open their eyes and smile. Take many different pictures—it will be difficult to find one shot with everyone smiling. If you can't find one shot, you can use an image editing application to mix-and-match expressions from different photos.

The assistant photographer won't need the camera during the posed shots. He or she will be undertaking these responsibilities:

- Rounding up the right people for each shot.
- Checking everyone's outfits for odd creases and dirt.
- Telling children how important it is to their family that they stop screaming.
- Keeping kids' fingers out of their noses, mouths, pants, etc.
- Taking people's drinks and food out of their hands.
- Helping to organize people during the group shots and keeping everyone's eyes towards the camera.
- Creatively guiding the photographer on how to compose the shots.
- Monitoring the background to ensure nobody accidentally walks through a shot.

Figure 7-8: Position the couple front-and-center with family facing in, and watch the lighting!

■   Watching the lighting to ensure people's faces are shaded.

The lead photographer will take the actual photos. During group shots, you'll have the job of making everyone smile, so tell a few cheesy jokes, or just tell everyone to say cheese. Unlike during the ceremony itself, you do have the opportunity to re-shoot if something goes wrong, but you'll need to notice the problem right away. Therefore, it's important to continually review the shots. In particular, look for the following:

■   **Sufficient depth-of-field to ensure everyone's face is in focus.** When reviewing the pictures, zoom all the way in to ensure everyone's face is sharp. You should always focus on the groom's or bride's eyes, and then adjust the f/stop higher until you have the depth-of-field you need.

■   **Sufficient front lighting.** Regardless of where the light is coming from, you should add a bit of fill flash, as shown in Figure 7-9. If you're shooting outdoors in sunlight, use fill flash set to -1.5 stops. This should be enough to add a catch light and fill in any shadows in the face, without washing people out or making them blink.

■   **Flattering angles.** Keep people's heads and bodies turned in ways that make them look as beautiful as they feel, as discussed in Chapter 6, "Portraits."

As you narrow the shots down from big groups to just the bride and the groom, you can get more and more creative. Use interesting elements of the wedding and location to create pictures as unique as the couple. For example, Figure 7-10 creatively shows the three most important members of the wedding party: the groom, the bride, and their dog (not necessarily in that order). Don't forget to get a close-up of the rings on their fingers.

If you have to shoot a group of people one at a time, start with the most energetic, outgoing person. A ham in front of the camera will be a good example for everyone else, helping to reduce their natural self-consciousness. Make a point of engaging the entire group in your conversation to loosen everyone up.

RECEPTION

Once you dismiss the wedding party from the group shots, it's time for them to relax. You're

Figure 7-9: Quick-and-easy outdoor posed pictures: find shade, add fill flash, and use short depth-of-field.

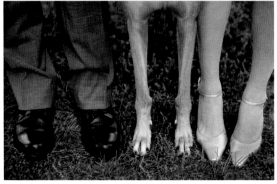

Figure 7-10: Find creative angles of your subjects.

Take a quiz!

sdp.io/Quiz7

still on the clock, though. When the best man and bridesmaid give their speeches, get a close-up of them with the microphone and a group shot of them with the bride and groom. Grab some shots of the crowd laughing and applauding. Be sure to photograph the food, as shown in Figure 7-11.

During the dancing, have one photographer shooting close-ups from ground level. If possible, have the other photographer above the dance floor on a balcony or ladder, shooting a wide-angle shot that shows the dance floor. When the guests begin dancing, take a few shots from this high perspective with a slow shutter speed to blur the motion. Look for emotion, and zoom in tight on the faces, as shown in Figure 7-12.

You can rest during the meal; people would prefer not to be bothered, anyway. Typically, the wedding party will feed you. Take a few moments to photograph the reception hall's details and decorations.

THE RING SHOT

During the meal, borrow the bride's and groom's rings and find a creative way to shoot them using the wedding's decorations, as shown in Figure 7-13. You can stack them nicely on an invitation, Bible, flower, or decoration. If you have one available, shoot them with a macro lens (as described in Chapter 12, "Macro"). Lighting can make these shots amazing; use off-camera flash to provide directional lighting, or bounce the light off a reflector.

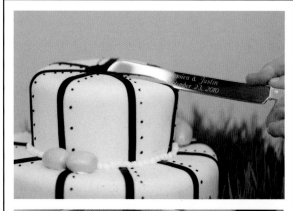

Figure 7-11: Photograph the food if it's especially unique or attractive.

Figure 7-12: Find emotions, and zoom in tight.

SHOT CHECKLIST

You can download and print a checklist for photographing a wedding from *sdp.io/checklist*. Not all shots will apply to all weddings.

PRACTICE

This chapter's practices help you prepare for photographing a wedding.

- **People walking (simulating the aisle).** Set your camera to continuously autofocus. In a room roughly as well lit as the ceremony venue, have someone stand beside you, and then walk fifty feet away from you. The model should then turn and walk back towards you. After every six frames, switch between wide-angle showing his or her entire body and zoomed in to his or her face. Afterwards, see how many photos are in-focus.

- **Using bounce.** In a room of roughly the same size (especially ceiling height) as the reception venue, practice using bounce flash to take people's portraits. If you have a flash diffuser, use it. Bounce in different directions and note the effects. Shoot enough to use all the batteries in your flash. Note how many total shots you got from the batteries and how long it took the flash to recycle throughout the shoot.

- **Using off-camera flash.** Practice using manual exposure on your camera and controlling the output from one or two flashes to balance the exposure of the foreground and background.

- **Shooting outside.** If part of the ceremony or reception will be outside, go to the venue with subjects and photograph them in different locations. Place them in the sun and in the shade. Shoot them with and without fill flash. Use a low f/stop number and a high f/stop number. Which combinations gave you the best results?

- **Posing individuals.** Work through the practices in Chapter 6, "Portraits," to better understand how to pose people.

- **Posing groups.** Assemble a group of people to photograph. It's okay if they're unwilling, because that's what you'll experience during a wedding. Try to direct them into attractive group poses, get everyone's expression right, and light everyone nicely. Repeat this practice both indoors and outdoors.

- **Shooting rings.** Practice shooting two rings in a decorative way. For information about how to get close up, read Chapter 12, "Macro."

Figure 7-13: Bring a macro lens for the ring shot.

The most important lesson in photography is learning to photograph what you love. It's only what you're passionate about that you know well enough to capture the essence of. If you love animals, whether domestic or wild, you'll quickly discover that photographing them is one of the most challenging and rewarding types of photography.

This chapter begins with a general discussion of wildlife photography technique that is applicable to most scenarios and animals, including getting eye contact, approaching animals, and using flash. After that, this chapter discusses specific types of animals, including pets, birds, and insects. Finally, I'll cover how to get great pictures at zoos and provide basic information about post-processing pictures of animals.

> **Quick—take the picture!** With still life, I encourage you to take your time and find the perfect angle and composition. With animals (and children), moments are fleeting. Take the picture first, and then try and find a better angle. Chances are good that your subject will move and ruin the shot you imagined. If you find something better, you can always delete your first picture. It's a shame to miss a decent shot because you thought you could do better.

EYE CONTACT

The eyes are the most important element of an animal picture; focus on the eyes, and don't shoot unless you can see at least one eye clearly. The first photo in Figure 8-1 doesn't work because the fox kit has his head turned away and you can't see the eyes. Patience pays off, though, and a moment later the fox made eye contact. Keep your finger off the shutter until you have a clear shot of the eyes.

APPROACHING ANIMALS

The first few times you take pictures of wildlife, you'll be shocked when you look at the picture and realize how far you seem from the subject.

Here's the problem, and it's one of the biggest challenges in photography: your brain makes a lot of adjustments to what your eyes see. When you're looking at a wild animal, your brain zooms in on the subject, and it blocks out everything else around it. Your brain doesn't do this when you look at the photo you took, though; suddenly you'll see that the animal is a tiny spot in the middle of a cluttered background.

Even with a telephoto lens, you'll want to get as close as you can to the animal without endangering yourself or scaring the animal. When you spot the animal, take a quick snapshot from where you are. If your next steps

Figure 8-1: The two shots are nearly identical, but eye contact makes all the difference (400mm, 1.4x teleconverter, f/8, 1/125th, ISO 800).

scare it, that might be your best picture. Then, use these tips to approach it:

- Appear non-threatening by meandering like a grazing deer. Humans are natural predators, and our instinct is to approach animals directly. Animals have learned to be threatened by this approach, so they respond with either fear or aggressiveness, neither of which you want.

- Don't move too slowly; this resembles stalking behavior.

- Don't look directly at the animal while you're moving; instead, keep an eye on it from your peripheral vision. Predators make eye contact. (My 7-year-old daughter taught me this one while hand-feeding a chickadee. The conversation went like this: Madelyn: "Don't look at the birds or they'll leave." Me: "Who taught you that?" Madelyn: "The birds.")

- Move as quietly as possible. Roll your feet gently as you walk and look for solid surfaces to step on. You can walk silently on a large rock, but no matter how ninja-like you are, dried leaves crinkle when you walk across them.

- Appear as small as possible. Crouch down, or better yet, lie prone on your belly and crawl forward. The more of your body you can hide behind bushes, grass, and rocks, the less of a threat you will seem to the animal.

- Work alone. It's a good idea to work with another photographer while you stay still and wait for animals to approach you, because they can help alert you to approaching animals. However, if you're approaching an animal, it's better for one person to go ahead while everyone else waits.

- In the woods, wear camouflage. The more of your body you cover in camouflage, the closer you'll be able to approach. You'll still disturb the animal at some point, but I've found that camouflage allows me to approach 30%-50% closer. Wearing green or brown clothing isn't the same as wearing camouflage; the complex patterns in camouflage are more difficult to spot than solid colors. LensCoat makes neoprene camouflage covers for your camera, lens, teleconverter, and tripod, too. Be sure to choose camouflage that matches your environment, and avoid areas with hunters, because some of them will shoot at anything that moves.

For the health of wildlife, you should always do your best to avoid disturbing animals. They'll let you know when you've gotten as close as you can. If they stop eating and watch you, you've gotten as close as you're going to get until they relax again. If their ears perk up, the hair stands up on the back of their necks, or growl or hiss, or they flee, you've gotten too close and have disturbed them. You might have interrupted their feeding or nesting, or caused them to abandon their offspring. Learn from your mistake and avoid repeating it during your next encounter.

Never approach an animal unless you're sure that you can do so without endangering the animal or yourself. If you see a nocturnal animal, such as a raccoon, in the daylight, stay away from it. Stay away from all baby animals,

Figure 8-2: Getting this close to the snapping turtle required staying hidden and crawling (400mm, 2x teleconverter, f/16, 1/250th, ISO 640).

because there might be a threatened parent nearby.

I had been trying to get a close-up photo of this snapping turtle in Figure 8-2 for months, but every time I approached he would disappear into the water. To get close enough, I had to crawl on the ground, staying hidden behind a rock wall. Then, I slowly lifted my camera and took the shot. I only had time for a couple of pictures before he disappeared into the water.

While you move, keep your camera in a ready position. Every few steps closer to the animal, take another picture. You don't know when the animal will decide you're a threat and take off, so taking the occasional picture will ensure your time hasn't been completely wasted.

Planning Your Pictures for Great Shots

Good wildlife photography requires a really big telephoto lens and a bit of luck. Great wildlife photography requires planning, patience, and persistence so that you're ready for that lucky moment when an animal finally does exactly what you dreamed they would do. Most people won't have the patience to take a great wildlife photo, which will make yours all that much more remarkable.

Note: This section describes the labor of love that goes into making great wildlife photographs. If the labor part seems too laborious, don't be discouraged just yet. Often, it all amounts to simply getting up an hour earlier and stopping by a pond on your way to work a couple of times per week.

Taking a great wildlife photograph is a 5-step process:

1. Find a location.
2. Learn the animal's behavior.
3. Choose a background.
4. Find (or make) a hiding spot.
5. Pick the best time for lighting, weather, and tide.

The first step is to find a great location. You might already know the spot—perhaps it's a path near your house that deer frequent, a bridge on your way to work where you often see shore birds, or even your own bird feeder. If you don't know a spot, here are some ways to find it:

- Ask wildlife enthusiasts in your area where they've seen interesting animals.
- Join a bird and nature club and go on its outings.
- Use an app, such as the Audubon iPhone and Android apps, to identify a wildlife hotspot.
- Use the web to find spots near you. For example, search for "birding <town> <state>."

You can even make your own great location, as I describe later in this chapter in the section titled, "Creating a Song Bird Studio."

Once you find a location, visit the spot and watch the wildlife for an hour or two. Bring your camera, but make understanding the animals' behavior your primary goal. Make note of what they do, which direction they face, and how often they repeat it. Decide on the shot you want to get, and then decide where you need to be to get the shot.

For example, your goal might be to photograph an osprey as it hits the surface of the water to catch a fish. To get that shot, you will need to find a spot where osprey regularly fish. Then, you will need to find a place to sit or stand where you can photograph the surface of the water.

Choose an angle that gives you the desired background. Simpler backgrounds are better, so avoid angles with trees or houses in the shot. It's often better to be above or below an animal, so that the background is the ground, water, or sky, rather than trees or buildings. The simpler background makes it easier for your camera to focus on your subject, too, which is particularly important when photographing moving subjects.

With your spot selected, find a place for yourself to hide and wait. Your comfort is important here, because if you're not comfortable, you're not going to be patient enough. Bring a stool to sit on. Bring a monopod to support the weight of your camera while it is in the ready position. Bring insect repellent to keep the mosquitos off you.

Finally, plan the time of day. The golden hours are usually ideal, because the sun will provide nice front, back, or side lighting. Front lighting is usually the best, so choose a time of day when the sun will be behind you when you are in your sport. Clear skies are ideal, because the direct light from the sun will be enough to let you use a fast shutter speeds to freeze motion

Figure 8-3: I spent hours in the woods allowing the robins to become accustomed to me (400mm, f/5.6, 1/180th, ISO 1600).

Figure 8-4: Pick a spot where you think wildlife will appear, and wait (235mm, f/5.6, 1/3000th, ISO 800).

with a higher f/stop number to get the entire animal in focus.

These were the techniques Greg de Toit used to get close-up photos of different animals in a watering hole. He needed to be at eye-level with the drinking animals, and wanted to use a wider-angle lens than most photographers use when shooting dangerous animals. So, he submerged himself completely in the water and waited patiently, taking pictures for a total of 270 hours.

While my own patience pales in comparison to Greg's, I've spent many hours waiting in the woods for animals to appear. To photograph the nest of robins (Figure 8-3), I first chose an angle that would give me a view of the nest clear of leaves and branches. Then, I approached the nest slowly over the course of hours, allowing the birds to become accustomed to me.

You don't have to be quite as committed. You can simply put your camera on a tripod and crouch, hidden in bushes, until the ducks appear at your favorite pond. I photographed the mallard duck in Figure 8-4 by waiting near a bridge for a couple of hours in the early morning with the sun to my back.

Study hunting techniques to photograph the most elusive animals. Learn to identify places where animals rest, eat, and pass through. Learn to camouflage yourself, and your scent, to give yourself more time to photograph the animals.

USING A HUNTING BLIND

Hunting blinds are the ultimate camouflage for the stationary photographer. Blinds allow you to get very close to animals, eliminating the need for an expensive telephoto lens. With proper planning, you can use a hunting blind to fill the frame with a 75-300mm lens—even with the smallest birds.

Pop-up hunting blinds cost $30-$120, and can fit individuals or up to three photographers with their tripods. They fold up small enough to let you carry them on a short hike, and set up in about 3 minutes. You can buy them online, or at any store that sells hunting supplies.

Additionally, you'll need some camouflage netting that you can hang over the windows in the blind (and over your protruding lens) and a folding stool that you can carry with you.

Hunting blinds hide your movement from animals, making them much more effective than simply wearing camouflage. This allows you to relax more than you would be able to while crouched in a bush, enabling you to spend more time in the field. The inside of a hunting blind is black. Therefore, black clothes and a dark hat are more effective than camouflage while inside the blind.

Choose a location for your hunting blind with an attractive background, such as a flowering bush. Front lighting is ideal, so find a location in direct sunlight, with the sun in front of the birds (and thus behind you). The lower the sun is in the sky, the more attractive the light.

Birds will need a place to perch. If there's not an ideal perch with a nice background, find a large branch and bury the largest end of it about 6 inches into ground in front of your background. Setting up a perch gives the birds a place to land, and allows you to control the bird's placement in the light and against the background.

Animals in the area will initially be disturbed when you set up a hunting blind. However, birds generally reappear in about ten minutes, and will remain unaware of your presence as long as you're quiet and you don't move your camera lens too suddenly. Animals that later come across the hunting blind, such as deer or fox, might not notice the blind at all.

To watch a video on **using a blind,** scan the QR code or visit:

sdp.io/UsingBlind

When photographing songbirds, I typically set up the blind 6-10 feet away from where I want the birds to perch. For larger animals, set up the blind at a distance that will allow you to almost fill the frame with your subject.

When working at close range with small animals such as songbirds, you might need an extension tube to focus closely enough. Extension tubes are hollow tubes that fit between your lens and your camera body, moving the lens farther from your camera's sensor, thus reducing the minimum focusing distance (and eliminating your ability to focus on far away subjects). A 24mm extension tube with support for autofocus is perfect for most telephoto lenses. For more information about extension tubes, refer to Chapter 12.

While the hunting blind is designed to hide your movements, it's still important to minimize how much you move around. Use a tripod to hold your camera upright with the lens slightly protruding from the blind so that you don't have to lift your camera when a subject comes into view.

Some animals will be scared by the sound of your shutter. Many new cameras support a quiet shutter mode that can help. If your shutter continues to scare animals, you'll still be able to get one shot—take your time and make sure you have eye contact before you press the shutter.

The longer you spend in a hunting blind, the better your results will be. It's tempting to occupy yourself with a book or smartphone. However, the minute you look away, your subject will appear, and you'll miss your shot. A better option is to listen to music or an audiobook with a single ear bud, keeping one ear open to listen for animal sounds.

USING SOUND TO ATTRACT BIRDS

Hunters have used bird calls to attract birds for hundreds of years. Today, there's a much easier alternative: using a smartphone or other audio player to play back pre-recorded calls.

Using bird calls is remarkably effective. Some species of birds will immediately begin to sing back to you, and often begin moving from perch to perch looking for the potential partner or threat to their territory. This is perfect for the photographer, because every spot they perch on is another opportunity to photograph them.

I occasionally use bird calls with a hunting blind. I'll save a bird call as an MP3 file on my smartphone and configure the song to repeat. Then, I'll turn up the volume and place my smartphone in the area where I want the bird to pose. If I plan to try different songs, I'll simply poke the smartphone's speaker from the bottom of my blind.

If the volume on your smartphone isn't loud enough, you can connect inexpensive battery-powered speakers. With a long enough cord, this can even allow you to control the song from the safety of your tent while broadcasting from a nearby location.

The Macaulay Library (*macaulaylibrary. org*, run by the Cornell Lab of Ornithology) is the most comprehensive source of animal sounds on the Internet. However, they start with a human voice, making them less than ideal. The Cornell Lab of Ornithology's website (*allaboutbirds.org/*) has calls without the human introductions, but they don't automatically loop, meaning you'd have to manually replay them. YouTube has videos featuring many different birds, and many of those videos are quite long; however, their quality varies. You can also try searching the Internet for "*<species>* mp3" to see if anyone has shared their own sounds.

If you use the Google Chrome web browser, install the FVD Video Downloader extension. Then, you can easily download almost any bird call that you can play on a website. Once downloaded, copy the audio file to your smartphone and play it using the audio player's repeat capability.

Most birds have multiple calls with different meanings. The ideal calls are meant to attract mates. These calls are often effective at attracting both genders—for example, a female might be drawn in by the call of a male bird, but another male bird might also appear to defend its territory. Other calls might be territorial or act as a warning, which can actually scare birds away from your area. For best results, research the species you wish to photograph, and experiment with different calls. Calls from aggressive birds, such as crows or blue jays, can cause other species to hide or leave the area.

Avoid using compilations of different bird sounds. These are intended to be relaxing to humans, and they often feature calls that will deter birds from your area.

Avoid using bird songs for more than a few minutes at a time. While there's no scientific evidence showing they harm birds, if the song is effective, it will briefly distract the bird from its regular tasks of feeding, mating, and nesting. In my experience, the birds get bored of the song too quickly to cause them any harm, but switching songs to a different species on a regular basis should greatly reduce any risks.

FLASH

You wouldn't want to photograph a person in direct sunlight, but we're not as worried about casting unflattering shadows on animals. Indeed, with animals, you want as much light as possible. Try to position yourself between the animal and the sun, so that the sun is behind your back. The lower the sun is in the sky, the better. This will provide nice front lighting for the animal. Use the Photographer's Ephemeris at *sdp.io/tpe* to find the exact direction of sunlight at any day and time on any spot on the earth. For example, if you're going to shoot wildlife at a watering hole, you can use the tool to determine which side of the watering hole to be on so that you shoot the side of the animals that's illuminated.

Flash does for animals many of the same things it does for people: fills in the shadows, adds a catch light, and helps the subject stand out from the background. Use a flash when:

- The sun is not creating a catch light in the animal's eyes.

- The light is too dim to keep your shutter speed above 1/125th or 1/250th (with an ISO of 400 or less).

- You need to freeze rapid movement, such as flapping wings.

- The light and sound from the flash will not disturb the animal.

Like using flash on people, I suggest using aperture priority (Av or A) or shutter priority (Tv or S) and using the same exposure you would use without flash. This will cause your camera to use the flash only to fill in the shadows, and it will keep the background well exposed.

The challenge with animals is the need to keep your distance. Light from a flash falls off rapidly—by the square of the distance from the subject, for those mathematically inclined. Most external flash heads feature zooming flashes that spread the light into a narrow cone when using telephoto lenses, but they typically only zoom to around 100mm. If you're photographing a bird at 400mm, the vast majority of the light from your flash is falling outside the frame, wasting battery power and increasing the flash recharge time.

To get more out of your flash when using a telephoto lens, attach a flash extender. I personally use the Better Beamer (as shown in Figure 8-5), which gives you two to three extra stops of light when shooting telephoto. It's

Figure 8-6: Two consecutive frames, with and without fill flash, and the superiority of a natural catch light.

Figure 8-5: Using a monopod and flash extender with a 500mm telephoto lens.

lightweight, though it does make your camera even clumsier—I find that I often brush it against branches when hiking. By reducing the battery power required for each shot, it allows your flash to recycle faster and lets you get more shots out of your batteries.

Figure 8-6 shows three shots of a white-breasted nuthatch. The first is in shadow without flash, the second is in shadow with flash, and the third with a natural catch light. The flash adds a small catch light when the bird is in shadow and brightens the foreground, but it's much less attractive than a natural catch light. Of course, you can control the flash, which you can't do with sunlight.

If you need to get even more power out of your flash, increase your ISO speed. Increasing the ISO one stop halves flash's light output. Of course, it increases the noise in your picture, too. Noise is particularly problematic with wildlife pictures, which usually need to be cropped.

USING MOTION SENSORS AND TIMERS

If you don't have the patience of a *National Geographic* photographer, but you're brave enough to leave your camera outside for long periods of time, you can outsource your photography to a motion sensor. Motion sensors detect movement and trigger your camera's sensors, allowing you to leave your camera for hours or days at a time. As shown in Figure 8-7, I set up my camera to take a picture if anything left this fox den.

I use The Time Machine from *bmumford.com* with an infrared sensor, but many people use the less expensive Triggertrap from *triggertrap. com*. When an animal breaks the infrared beam, the camera snaps a photo. Figure 8-8 shows the infrared beam placed over some strawberries, waiting for a woodchuck or squirrel to trigger The Time Machine.

This technique allowed me to finally photograph a beaver that had been gnawing on a tree in my yard in the middle of the night. The white box in the foreground of Figure 8-9 is the infrared receiver. The black cord runs to the transmitter, positioned on the other side of the beaver. I could easily remove the cords in post-processing to create a more natural picture.

As an alternative to using an expensive motion sensor, you can simply use a remote shutter release with a timer. Set the timer to take a picture every ten seconds. You will have to sort through thousands of pictures, but you'll get the shot. Even though I own a motion sensor, I use a timer when it is impossible to position the IR beam (for example, when a bird's nest is inaccessible).

With automatic photography, you can't focus, zoom, or frame based on the subject's movements. So, follow these guidelines to get as many pictures as possible to turn out:

- **Shoot wide-angle**. You can always crop later. Animals will approach from odd angles, and you don't want to cut part of them out of the picture. When photographing a bird's nest, leave extra room above the nest—the parent will be standing upright when it feeds the chicks.

- **Pre-focus your lens**. While your camera might be able to autofocus before taking the picture, you'll have no way to control what it autofocuses on. Focus your lens where you expect the animal's face to be, and set the lens to manual focus so the focus does not change.

- **Shoot rapidly if the animal is moving**. If the animal is passing through the area with the motion sensor, set your Time Machine (or other remote trigger) to take at least one picture per second when the animal is present. That way, you'll increase your chances of getting a flattering angle.

- **Shoot slowly if the animal is stationary**. If the animal will be staying put (for example, if it's eating bait you've placed in the frame), take one picture every five or ten seconds. This will keep your camera from filling up your memory card with redundant pictures.

- **Get the most depth-of-field possible during the day**. Getting close and using a wider-angle lens is a good way to get deep depth-of-field. During the day, set your camera to shutter priority (Tv or S) and use a shutter speed fast enough to freeze motion, such as 1/125th for larger animals or 1/250th for smaller animals. Your camera will use the smallest aperture possible to achieve that shutter speed. Increase your ISO as necessary to get more depth-of-field. Because you can't anticipate exactly where the animal will be, pre-focusing is less than perfect, and deeper depth-of-field will increase your chances of getting a usable shot.

- **Get the most out of your flash at night**. You'll have to use a flash to photograph animals after dark. Your flash will certainly scare the animal off, so you'll only get one or two pictures before the animal leaves. To allow the flash to recharge between shots, do not take a picture more than once every two or three seconds. To reduce the power output and get the most out of your batteries, set your camera's ISO to the highest acceptable setting. This will also increase the reach of your flash, helping to light the background more evenly.

- **Save your batteries.** Turn off image preview and image stabilization to reduce power consumption.

- **Charge your batteries**. Automatic photography has a great deal of false positives—shots where something other than your subject, such as a leaf, triggered your camera. Make sure your lens and camera have enough power to get through the session.

- **Change your batteries.** Have a second battery charged, and swap it out in the middle of a particularly long session.

- **Clear your memory card**. You'll probably take hundreds of unsuccessful pictures

Figure 8-7: Attach your camera to motion sensors to automatically photograph activity at a location.

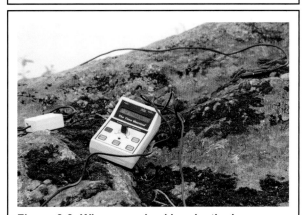

Figure 8-8: When an animal breaks the beam, The Time Machine triggers the camera.

Figure 8-9: A beaver caught by The Time Machine.

before you get one usable picture. You might consider using JPEG instead of raw to fit more pictures onto your memory card.

Tip: Use your motion sensor to set up a photo booth at your next party. Just point your camera at a blank wall and set it to fire any time someone steps in the frame. Then, wait for the alcohol to kick in.

PETS

Unlike every other member of the animal kingdom, pets actually want to be close to you. That alone makes them great models. If your pet will hold a pose long enough for you to take a decent picture, he just might become a star.

DOG PORTRAITS

Every pet deserves a proper portrait, such as Figure 8-10. You will always need at least two people: one to work the camera, and one to position the dog. The person positioning the dog should have treats available, but should only use them if she has a difficult time getting the dog's attention. Many dogs are obedient enough to sit and stay without regular rewards, and some dogs find the treats too distracting. Because the dog will spend most of its time looking at the person with the treats, that person needs to stay as close to the photographer as possible. If it's a well-behaved dog, you can have her sit and stay, have the person with the treats walk away, and then have the photographer call the dog's name to have her look at the camera.

To get a proper headshot of the dog, have the photographer sit and get the camera at its eye level or below. The photographer will need to sit or crouch. Choose an f/stop number of f/11 or higher; you need more depth-of-field for dogs than for people, because their noses are much farther from their eyes.

You can't position a dog as precisely as you can a human model. In fact, with some dogs, you'll be lucky if you can get them to stay in front of the backdrop. If you have studio lighting, accommodate this by setting up your lights close to the floor and positioning them to cover a broad area. Move your light stands farther back so that you can move around and reframe the picture without getting them in the shot. For dogs with dark hair, use a hair light, just like you would with a person. The first few frames with flash might startle the dog, so plan to waste a few frames while the dog gets accustomed to the lighting.

For more information about shooting portraits and working with studio lighting, read Chapter 6, "Portraits."

Figure 8-10: A traditional pet portrait.

PETS IN ACTION

My labradoodle, Sandi, loves catching snowballs in her mouth. I never managed to capture this with a single picture, but I can show it with a sequence of three photos, as shown in Figure 8-11.

To create this effect, set your camera's shutter to continuous shooting and hold the shutter down throughout the action. Then, display the pictures together. If you are displaying the pictures online, you should use your image

processing software to combine them into a single image. If you are displaying prints, you could buy three frames and display them next to each other.

My cat, Sam, is strikingly ugly (and not just on the outside, either). To try to make him cute, I took the photo in Figure 8-12 of his favorite activity—hiding behind blankets and clawing at any exposed body part. I lit the picture with a medium soft box attached to an external flash and took dozens of photos to capture the moment just before attack.

BIRDS

Birds are amazing subjects because of their amazing diversity. Birds have adapted to almost every environment on Earth, and their striking colors (or lack thereof), varying shapes, and complex behaviors are all designed to help them survive.

Photographing birds is challenging for many different reasons:

- Birds are small and would rather you not get close to them.

Figure 8-12: Capture animals at play to show their personality (shot on film).

Figure 8-11: Use a sequence to show action (24mm, f/6.3, 1/640th, ISO 800).

- Birds like to hide in trees, where branches and leaves can ruin your pictures.
- Birds are often photographed against the sky or water, which can confuse your camera's autoexposure.
- Birds don't like to pose, but head position and catch lights are vital to taking a good picture.
- Birds can fly, but you cannot.

The sections that follow will show you how to address each of these challenges.

USING TELEPHOTO LENSES

We love birds, but the feeling is not always mutual. With the exception of human-friendly species such as pigeons, birds would like to stay far enough away from you that you can't get a clear picture. The smaller the bird is, the closer you need to be.

Naturally, you should follow the advice at the beginning of the chapter for approaching and waiting for animals. While you can get a lovely picture of a goose or a swan with a 200mm lens, you'll need to buy a big telephoto lens with a focal length of 400mm to 1000mm for smaller birds. The bigger and more expensive the lens, the better; however, even 1000mm won't allow you to get close enough to many birds.

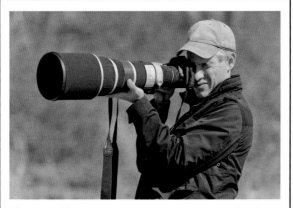

Figure 8-13: Brace your arm against your body to allow yourself to support a heavy lens for a longer period of time.

For detailed information about wildlife equipment and specific camera and lens recommendations, read *Tony Northrup's Photography Buying Guide: How to Choose a Camera, Lens, Flash, Tripod, & More.*

SUPPORTING TELEPHOTO LENSES

Telephoto lenses are awkward to hand-hold. For birding, I recommend attaching a monopod to your lens' tripod mount, as shown in Figure 8-5. Monopods don't completely support your camera like a tripod, but they're easier to carry and they make it easier to move from place-to-place.

While I prefer to use a monopod, I often hand-hold my big telephoto lenses. No matter how strong you are, your left arm will get tired after several minutes of supporting the lens, resulting in shaky pictures. Whenever possible, I find a window frame, rock, fence, or wall to rest it on. In zoos, I'll press the edge of the lens hood directly against the glass to steady the lens.

When improvised support is not possible, I press my left elbow against my chest, support the lens with my left hand, and lean back so that the weight of the lens is supported by my body, as shown in Figure 8-13. To further reduce camera shake, I lean my left side against a tree or wall. The bigger you are, the longer you'll be able to hand-hold the lens. Notice that the lens in Figure 8-13 has a black covering on it to make it (slightly) more discreet.

If you plan to stay in one place for an extended time, use a tripod with a Gimbal head. Gimbal heads are expensive, but they're worth it if you have an extremely heavy lens.

AIMING TELEPHOTO LENSES

Big telephoto lenses give you severe tunnel vision, showing you a view of the world only a few feet across. The first time you pick up a big lens to take a picture of something, the view through the lens will be shaking so much that you probably won't be able to find your subject.

Like everything else in photography, using telephotos takes practice. If your lens supports image stabilization, hold the shutter button halfway down to activate it and remove some of the shakiness. If possible, support your lens with a tripod or monopod.

Use landmarks to help find your subjects. For example, if you saw a sparrow in a tree that you wanted to photograph, you might make note that it is just to the left of the tree trunk, and directly above a broken branch. When you put the camera to your eye, don't look for the bird. Instead, look for the tree trunk or the broken branch, and navigate from there. Also keep in mind that your lens is several inches lower than your eyes. If you're shooting between branches and leaves, you'll have to stand on your tip-toes when you hold the viewfinder to your eye to get an eye-level perspective.

The tunnel vision caused by looking through a lens can hide what's happening around you. While you have your eye to the camera waiting for a chickadee to hop to a branch with a clear view, you might be missing other activity around you. Every ten seconds or so, lift your head up and look around.

BALANCING DEPTH-OF-FIELD, SHUTTER SPEED, AND ISO

Depth-of-field is one of the greatest challenges of using a telephoto lens. The longer the lens and the closer you are to the subject, the shorter the depth-of-field becomes. At the focal lengths you use for birds (400mm to 1000mm), if you're close enough to fill the frame, lower f/stop numbers (such as f/4 or f/5.6) can cause parts of your subject to be out of focus.

To watch a video on **wildlife equipment,** scan the QR code or visit:

sdp.io/WildlifeEquipment

If your subject has a cluttered background, use the lowest f/stop number possible to blur the background. If your subject has a clear background, or if there is room behind your subject, use f/11 or f/16 to get the sharpest pictures possible. Strive to stay at ISO 100 or 200. If your shutter speed falls below 1/250th, however, you might need to increase the shutter speed. If a subject is staying in one place, you can use a lower shutter speed, such as 1/90th, along with a higher f/stop number or lower ISO. The slower shutter speed means more of your pictures will be blurry, however, so take dozens or hundreds of pictures to get just one sharp picture.

To ensure at least some shots are sharp, take a few shots at a fast shutter speed (such as 1/1000th) using a high ISO. Then, use slower and slower shutter speeds and lower and lower ISOs. The slower you go, the more shots you should take to improve your chances of getting a sharp photo. Often, I'll take more than 100 shots at 1/45th to get one sharp.

> **Tip:** Confused by the technical stuff? Refer to Chapter 4, "Controlling Your Camera," for a refresher on aperture and depth-of-field.

Figure 8-14 shows slightly cropped pictures of a Black-capped Chickadee taken at f/8 and f/27 (but both at 700mm). The branches and tree trunk in the background of the first picture are much blurrier than in the second picture. The second picture is much grainier; to keep the same shutter speed while increasing the f/stop number, I had to increase the ISO from 100 to 3200. Viewing the two photos close-up, the first is clearly superior because of the reduced noise and nicer background blur.

> **Tip:** It's easier to photograph birds in trees in the winter when there are fewer leaves to block your view.

GETTING CLOSE ENOUGH

When people see big telephoto lenses, they often assume that you're taking close-up or even microscopic pictures. Unfortunately, that couldn't be farther from the truth. Even if you go all-out and spend $8,000 on a big telephoto and hide in camouflage near a bird feeder, you won't be able to get full-frame pictures of common songbirds like sparrows, finches, and chickadees. They're too small and telephoto lenses don't focus close enough.

For example, a typical minimum focusing distance for a 600mm lens is 18 feet/5.5 meters. At that distance, most songbirds will only fill about half the frame. That's okay—you can crop the picture later and still get good results. If you use a camera body with a crop factor, you'll be that much closer.

To overcome a lens' minimum focus distance, use extension tubes. Extension tubes attach between the lens and your camera body, just like a teleconverter. However, they're completely empty, with no optical elements at all. Moving the lens away from the camera body allows the lens to focus closer than its minimum focus distance but prevents you from focusing far away.

I regularly use a 20mm extension tube with my 500mm lens allowing me to get a few feet closer to birds. That's enough for me to fill about half the frame with a small songbird. The birds aren't especially comfortable with that distance, so I have to be quiet and camouflaged. For more information about extension tubes, read Chapter 12, "Macro."

Figure 8-14: Telephoto lenses have very short depth-of-field (400mm, 1.4x teleconverter, 1/250th, f/8, ISO 100 and f/27, ISO 3200).

EXPOSING STATIONARY BIRDS

Birds are a challenge to expose properly for two reasons:

- Birds often have either a bright sky or water as their background, which will cause the camera to underexpose the bird.

- Because you can't always get close enough to birds, there can be more background than foreground in the frame.

- Many birds have a light-colored belly and a dark-colored back to camouflage them while flying and on the ground.

While spot metering can help, spot metering tends to be quite unpredictable. Instead, use evaluative metering (sometimes known as matrix metering) and adjust the exposure compensation as necessary.

When the subject is as small in the frame as birds will be, viewing the histogram can be misleading because it will show the exposure of the background. Therefore, after taking a few pictures, you should zoom in to view your subject and verify that both dark parts and light parts of the bird are equally well exposed. With dark birds, you might need to overexpose by one stop, depending on how accurate your camera's metering is. With light birds, you might need to underexpose.

Finally, shoot raw. Raw captures extra detail in both shadows and highlights, and you can recover one or two stops of overexposure and underexposure on your computer. For more information about shooting raw, read Chapter 4, "Controlling Your Camera."

POSING BIRDS

Birds, especially smaller birds, move constantly. Even when they're not running or flying, they're continuously looking around for danger. As a photographer, this is just

> To watch a video on **Tracking Osprey, Owls, and Eagles,** scan the QR code or visit:
>
> **sdp.io/TrackingOsprey**

like working with a professional model who changes her pose slightly between every shot. Just like with a model, you'll need to shoot constantly and delete all the pictures that didn't work.

Figure 8-15 shows a series of photos of a red-tailed hawk dining in the snow (with a few frames omitted). Even at 4 frames per second, every single frame had the bird's head in a different position. In the first frame, the bird's head is blurred. In the second, its nictitating membrane (that's a bird's third, translucent, eyelid) is closed. In the third, its head is turned too far to get a catch light from the setting sun. The fourth is the keeper, because the bird's head is perfectly positioned for a catch light.

You're forced to pose birds with patience and luck. These traits make a great bird portrait:

- Everything is sharp, which requires snapping a picture between a bird's jerky movements.

- There is a natural catch light in the eyes.

- The head is turned at a perfect profile or towards the camera at an angle; birds look silly when directly facing the camera.

- The bird is not blocked by leaves or branches.

A picture of a bird hunting, eating, or caring for its young is far more interesting than a picture of a bird perching.

PERCHED BIRDS

As you might have learned in the portrait photography section, shooting from below is rarely flattering. Plus, having the sky as the background will cause the subject to be in a dark shadow. The picture of a Harris hawk on the job (Figure 8-16) isn't bad, but it would be much stronger if I had shot it from the same level as the bird.

For best results, find a location where you can photograph birds from eye level. If you have trees near your house, an open window on the second floor might work. As the picture of the Gouldian Finch in Figure 8-17 shows, the ideal position is with the bird's body in front of the branch. When framing the picture, use the branch as a compositional element, as described in Chapter 3, "Composition."

Wildlife photographers often use bait to attract animals to a location that's easy to photograph. For birds, this is as easy as setting up a birdfeeder in your backyard. Choose your food based on the type of bird you'd like to see, or get multiple bird feeders for different types of birds. For the best pictures, hang the bird feeder a few inches below your eye level.

Even if you don't want the bird feeder in the shot, it'll attract birds to your house, and you can shoot them as they sit in nearby trees. I set up a bird feeder in a location with a nice background (Figure 8-18), put my camera on a tripod, attached a flash for fill, and used a remote shutter release to trigger the camera from a distance. The food I chose was specifically marketed for finches, and these goldfinches seemed to have approved.

However, you'll never get *great* shots by leaving your camera on a tripod and triggering the shutter with a remote release or timer. While this allows you to get close to the birds without spooking them, you can't frame the

Figure 8-15: You can't pose a bird, so keep shooting and hope it strikes the perfect pose (200mm, f/8, 1/180th, ISO 100).

picture or focus the camera. To get great shots, stay with your camera, focus for each set of shots, and keep the tripod flexible enough to move with the birds.

Most feeders are circular, which means birds might land at any part of the feeder—including behind it. To increase the number of good poses you get with a feeder, use tape to block all openings except the one that's perfect for your shots.

HUMMINGBIRDS

Photographing hummingbirds is different than photographing song birds:

- They require different feeders.
- Most are very small, requiring you to get closer to them.
- Most species are comfortable around

humans, and if you stay still for five or ten minutes near a flower or feeder, they'll fly close enough to you to get a good shot.

- They usually stay still (either hovering or perched) for only a few seconds while they feed.
- When hovering or flying, their wings move extremely fast.
- Many hummingbirds defend their feeder, meaning you might only get a single visitor.

Besides putting out a hummingbird feeder, you'll need a faster shutter speed to keep hovering hummingbirds sharp. Hummingbirds flap their wings a full stroke in one direction around 1/25th to 1/200th, depending on the

Figure 8-17: Shoot perched birds from their same height when possible and position the branch so that it does not block their body (150mm, f/5.6, 1/160th, ISO 3200).

Figure 8-16: Shooting birds from below provides an unflattering angle (135mm, f/5.6, 1/125th, ISO 800).

Figure 8-18: Use a birdfeeder to lure birds to your level (105mm, f/18, 1/250th, ISO 640).

species and their behavior. Therefore, any shutter speed in that range will allow you to capture most of a full stroke and nicely blurred wings. Set your camera for shutter priority, 1/125th, and auto ISO. The shot in Figure 8-19 was taken at 1/250th, and it captured most of a full stroke of the wings.

If you want to freeze the wing motion, you'll need a shutter speed of at least 1/1000th, but usually more like 1/4000th. With most telephoto lenses, this will require an ISO of 800-3200 on a sunny afternoon and even higher on a cloudy day. Even a shutter speed of 1/1000th might capture half an inch of movement in the wings, however. Figure 8-20 shows a picture of a female ruby-throated hummingbird shot at 1/1500th and ISO 1600, and the wings are still noticeably blurred.

If you do manage to get a fast enough shutter to freeze the wings, they will be in a random place in each frame, so you'll need to take even more pictures than normal to get one with the wings in a pleasing location—completely forward or back. If you use a flash with hummingbirds and a slower shutter speed, you're likely to get an interesting (if somewhat odd-looking) effect: ghosting. With ghosting, the wing will be both frozen in one place (when the flash fired) and blurred (while the shutter was open). Naturally, you will need to use your flash's high-speed sync option.

Tip: If you want a picture of a hummingbird at a flower and don't feel like chasing the birds around your garden, add a few drops of hummingbird food to one flower, set up your tripod, and wait.

If you plan to use a remote flash to freeze the wings of a hummingbird, choose a remote flash solution that supports high-speed sync like the PocketWizard, and position the flash as close to the feeder as possible. Because you will need a great deal of light to freeze the hummingbird at a moderate ISO speed, you might need multiple flashes to provide enough light and give you a recycle time fast enough to get multiple shots while the bird is in the right spot. Getting the proper exposure will require some trial and error. This technique will likely result in a black background because the light falloff behind the subject will be severe. If you don't like the black background, use another flash to illuminate the background.

Another challenge to using a flash to photograph hummingbirds is their iridescence. The smaller the point of light, the more oddly colored their feathers will appear. For best results, use a diffuser or soft box over your flash, or bounce the flash into an umbrella.

Hummingbirds will perch while sipping nectar, if a perch is available. When they're perched, your chances of getting a clear picture improve drastically. However, I prefer to capture them hovering, as that's how most people

Figure 8-19: A red-billed streamertail, known locally in Jamaica as a doctor Bird (500mm, f/5.6, 1/250th, ISO 400).

Figure 8-20: A shutter speed of 1/1500th is too slow to freeze a hummingbird's wings.

think of a hummingbird. Therefore, I cut the perches off my feeders. Unless you happen to find a hummingbird perched, you should set your camera for continuous autofocus and continuous shutter, and take dozens of shots.

To watch a video on **bird studios,** scan the QR code or visit:

sdp.io/BirdStudio

CREATING A SONG BIRD STUDIO

As with all types of photography, taking great pictures requires planning the subject, background, and lighting. A bird feeder gives you some control over the subject and lighting, but the best bird photos feature the birds in their natural environment—perched in a tree. To get the benefits of a bird feeder with the appearance of a natural environment, create a song bird studio by adding branches near a bird feeder, and then optimizing the background and lighting. Before and after they eat, the birds will perch on the branches, posing perfectly for you.

First, get a bird feeder (preferably one that is squirrel-proof). Place it away from other trees and bushes where birds might prefer to land, fill it with seed, and wait a week for the birds to discover it. You don't even need a direct view of the bird feeder. Then, find a tree branch that is four or five feet long. Remove any leaves and branches too small for birds to perch on; these branches just block the foreground or clutter the background. Dig a hole 6-12 inches deep and stick the branch securely in the ground a few feet from your bird feeder. Figure 8-21 shows my bird studio, set up outside my office door so that I can take pictures from my desk. Figure 8-22 shows a diagram of a typical bird studio.

Set up your camera and telephoto lens on a tripod so you don't have to lift your camera up; any movement will startle the birds. Position yourself in a lawn chair as close to the perch as your camera can focus. If you take some pictures and still want to get closer, add an extension tube to your lens, as described in "Approaching Animals" earlier in this chapter. Get comfortable, and then focus your lens on the perch so that when a bird does land, you will be able to focus quickly. If your lens has a focus limiter that prevents it from trying to focus at longer distances, use it; this will improve autofocus speed.

Now, wait for twenty minutes or so until the braver birds begin returning to the bird feeder and perch. When a new bird arrives, wait until it takes a turn at the feeder; it will be less easily scared once it has sampled the food. Move as gently as possible so as not to startle them. The longer you stay, the better your pictures will be.

Choose a location with good front lighting and a nice background, if possible. Ideally, the sun would be behind you and low in the

Figure 8-21: A bird studio: at left is a birdfeeder (with a tufted titmouse), at right, a tree branch embedded in the ground acts as a perch for pictures. In the background, a remote flash attached to an umbrella.

sky. The background should be green leaves, at least five feet in the distance. You don't want the background too close, or you won't get a nice blur. If you don't have a nice background, take an out-of-focus picture of trees, make a large poster of it, and put it behind your perch. Alternatively, you could just paint a large board with varying shades of green, or buy a camouflaged tarp. It will be out of focus anyway.

If you can't find good lighting, use a remote flash, as described in Chapter 6, "Portraits," to fill in the shadows and add a catch light to the eyes. Place the flash as close to the perching area as possible, and raise it slightly higher than the branches. Point the flash into an umbrella to soften and spread the light, and aim the umbrella so that it illuminates the entire perching area. Remember to put a sandbag on the light stand to keep the wind from blowing it over. Figure 8-23 shows a close-up of a picture taken with and without the off-camera fill flash (at -1.5 stops) and umbrella, with the sun behind and to the left of the bird.

Bird studios increase your chances of getting those perfect bird pictures: great lighting, nice pose, and a pretty, blurred background. As the chapter cover and Figure 8-24 illustrate, they allow you to get close, detailed pictures with clean backgrounds.

If you don't have a convenient place to set up a bird studio near a door or window, use a blind, available anywhere that sells hunting supplies. Portable blinds resemble small camouflaged tents, and can be bought for $50 to $100. Be sure the blind has enough room for a stool and your tripod.

> **Tip:** For perched birds, focus using one-shot (for Canon) or AF-S (for Nikon), and refocus on the bird's eye every few frames. Continuous autofocus tends to move around too much, causing you to miss more shots. If you don't regularly refocus, small movements (including your own), combined with the short depth-of-field of telephoto lenses, will cause your subject to fall out of focus.

After a few days, you'll notice that you get the same birds over and over. To keep it interesting, try to outdo yourself:

- Use a decorative perch with leaves, berries, and flowers.
- Add extension tubes to your telephoto lens and get closer than its minimum focusing distance.
- Get the perfect catch light in their eyes.
- Fill the frame with the smallest birds.
- See how slow your shutter speed can be by decreasing your ISO, increasing your f/stop number, and taking hundreds of pictures with the hope that the bird holds still for just one of them.

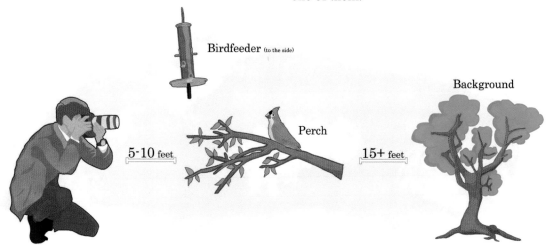

Figure 8-22: The smaller the bird, the closer you should be.

- Document interesting behaviors.
- Take close-up video, if your camera supports it. Search for other photographer's pictures of the same bird, and get a more beautiful or more detailed picture.

Also, be patient. While some birds will be there year-round, many birds are migratory. Especially during the spring and fall, you will get random visitors that you might only see once.

FLYING BIRDS

Photographing birds in flight is challenging. Set your camera to shutter priority (Tv or S) with a shutter speed of at least 1/500th. Often, you will need a shutter speed of 1/1000th or 1/2000th to stop motion blur, but it depends on the bird. Start with a slower shutter speed so that you can use a lower ISO and a higher f/stop number, and increase the shutter speed and ISO until you get the head and body of the bird sharp. I prefer to use a shutter speed just fast enough to freeze the head and body but slow enough to blur the wingtips so the bird does not appear frozen in air.

Set the autofocus to servo mode so that it continually focuses on the moving subject. If the background is the sky or the water, try enabling all focus points. If the background is land, trees, or buildings, your camera might try to focus on them rather than the bird, and you will get more pictures if you enable only the center focus point. Different cameras and lenses have different capabilities, so finding the ideal combination for different backgrounds and

lighting requires experimentation.

Any time you focus on a living thing, you should focus on the nearest eye. That level of precision is impossible with flying birds, however. Often, the camera will focus on the nearest wingtip, and the depth-of-field will be shallow enough that the wing is in focus but the bird's eye is out of focus, ruining the shot. To overcome this, use a higher f/stop number, such as f/8 or f/11. To do this in shutter priority mode, simply increase your ISO. Depending on how bright the sky is, you might end up using ISO 800 or ISO 1600. The higher ISO setting will increase the noise in your picture, but it is more important that you get the eye in focus and keep a shutter speed fast enough to freeze the motion.

Use continuous shutter mode to rapidly take as many pictures as possible. I typically take 500 pictures of a single bird in a session just to get one shot that I want to share. Because the exposure can be difficult, and you might need to recover the shadows or highlights to balance the exposure of the bird and the sky, I recommend shooting raw.

The large size of raw images can fill your camera's buffer too quickly, however, preventing you from taking more shots for several seconds while the camera writes the pictures you've already taken from the buffer to the memory card. It might also fill up your memory card. Buying a high-speed, large

Figure 8-24: A tufted titmouse happily tricked into posing in a bird studio (500mm, f/4, 1/250th, ISO 1000).

Figure 8-23: A tufted titmouse with and without off-camera fill flash (cropped).

capacity memory card can solve this problem, but they can cost as much as a low-end camera body. If your memory card is causing problems and you don't want to upgrade, simply switch to JPEG. While it's not ideal, taking large numbers of pictures is more important than capturing each image's raw data when shooting moving subjects.

Chelsea photographed the soaring bald eagle in Figure 8-25 at 1/1500th, which was fast enough to freeze the motion of a large soaring bird. However, it would not have been fast enough to freeze the motion of smaller birds. As you shoot, check your results and adjust your shutter speed to the slowest shutter speed that gives sharp results.

If you're using a super-telephoto lens, you'll find that it's very difficult to even find a flying bird in the viewfinder. Telephoto lenses have a tiny field of view. If you're using a zoom lens, start by zooming out all the way. Keep the flying bird in the center of your viewfinder, and then zoom in—holding the shutter button down halfway so that the camera maintains focus on your bird.

If you're not using a zoom lens, keep your left eye open to help spot the bird. Keeping both eyes open takes some practice, but it's the best way to avoid tunnel vision when using a telephoto lens. It's also a good way to spot other animals out of frame.

Smoothly pan your camera with the bird as it moves, attempting to keep it in the center of the frame. Leave plenty of room around the bird, or else you'll lose shots because you accidentally clipped part of the bird's wing. You'll need to crop the photo later, but that's almost always required when panning.

When shooting birds flying overhead, exposure is almost always a challenge. While your instinct might tell you to use spot metering, I prefer evaluative or center-weighted metering. Spot metering determines the exposure from a very small part of the picture, which will work well when the bird is centered in the frame. However, flying birds tend to move around in the frame, so spot metering will result in some frames being metered off the sky, wildly changing the exposure.

The sky in the afternoon will be much brighter than the subject, casting the underside of the bird into a shadow. With darker birds, you might get nothing but the silhouette of the bird. If this happens, use exposure compensation to increase the exposure by one or two stops until the bird itself is well exposed. This might cause the sky to be overexposed. If the sky is overcast, that's okay, because an overcast sky will usually appear completely white, anyway.

If the sky is clear, use exposure compensation to increase the exposure until the sky is almost overexposed. Check the histogram and use your blinkies, as discussed in Chapter 4, "Controlling Your Camera." The sky might not look great on your camera's preview, but as long as it is not overexposed you will be able to correct it in post-processing. For example, in Adobe Lightroom, you can decrease the luminosity of the blues to correct the color of the sky to match what your eye saw, while still maintaining proper exposure for the bird. In Photoshop, you can even replace a white background with a gentle blue gradient to completely paint a new sky.

If you don't want to perform post-processing, add a polarizing filter to darken the sky if it is overexposed. However, polarizing filters block about two stops of light, which will require

Figure 8-25: Use the lowest shutter speed that still freezes the motion of the bird to minimize noise and maximize depth-of-field (500mm, f/5.6, 1/1500th, ISO 400).

you to increase your ISO two stops to maintain proper exposure of the bird. The reduced light can also slow down your camera's autofocus system. Therefore, using a polarizing filter is not ideal for flying birds, but it's the best option if you don't want to darken the sky in post-processing as described in the previous paragraph.

Your best option is to shoot when the weather and time of day provide ideal lighting. The shot of a Great Egret flying overhead in the first shot in Figure 8-26 has a nice blue sky and great rim lighting because I took it early in the morning on a cold, clear day. Had the sun been higher in the sky, or if the sky were overcast, the sky would have been too bright and the lighting would have been flatter, as the second shot of the osprey shows in Figure 8-26. The golden hours are ideal, but even three hours after sunrise and before sunset provide much better lighting than mid-day.

When a bird is flying overhead, you'll probably need to shoot hand-held. This can be extremely tiring, so you'll need to let your camera hang when you're not shooting, and lift only when you see a bird flying. When a bird is flying closer to the ground or water (as shown in Figure 8-27), use a monopod or a tripod with the head loose enough to allow you to pan the camera with the moving bird.

> **Tip:** Avoid using a teleconverter when shooting flying birds. Teleconverters slow down your camera's autofocus, and autofocus speed is critical with moving subjects.

You'll notice most of the flying pictures in this section show water birds. Their behavior makes them easier to photograph while flying; they tend to soar slowly at low levels looking in the water for food. While difficult, it is possible to photograph flying songbirds. Here is the method I use:

1. Set up a feeder to attract the songbirds.

To watch a video on **insects,** scan the QR code or visit:

sdp.io/Insects

2. On a day with bright sun, watch the behavior of a particular bird over twenty minutes. You should see a repeated pattern, such as perching on a branch, flying to the feeder, and then perching on a different branch.

3. Choose one of the repeated flights to photograph where the bird is near eye level and flying to the side, rather than towards or away from you.

4. Autofocus your lens on one of the bird's perches, and then switch your lens to manual focus to prevent it from autofocusing again.

5. Set your camera to ISO 3200, shutter priority, $1/1000^{th}$, and continuous shutter.

Figure 8-26: Shoot birds overhead early in the morning when the sky is clearest (500mm, f/5.6, 1/2000th, ISO 125 and 500mm, f/8, 1/1000th, ISO 250).

6. Wait until the bird repeats the flight you planned to photograph, hold the shutter button down, and try to keep the bird in the frame.

INSECTS

We're all accustomed to seeing, and being annoyed by, insects. When you capture them in a macro photograph, though, you get more insight into their life, activities, and bright colors. In fact, insects might be the most rewarding animals to photograph, because they're brightly colored, plentiful, and accessible.

I encourage you to experiment with insect photography using your existing camera equipment.

Once you attempt to take some insect pictures, you'll find that it's difficult to get close enough and the pictures are often blurry. Solving these problems requires a combination of technique and equipment. For detailed information about macro photography equipment and techniques, read Chapter 12, "Macro."

Focusing on insects is a massive challenge. I use two different approaches:

- Set the lens to autofocus and set the camera to AI servo with the center focusing point. This will cause the camera to attempt

to continually keep the subject in focus. Depending on your equipment and the lighting, this might work well or the camera might spend all its time hunting for focus, never finding the subject.

- Set the lens to manual focus, adjust the focus to the minimum focusing distance, and then move the camera towards the subject until it's in focus. Rather than adjusting the focus ring on your lens, you'll focus by leaning towards or away from the subject. When the subject is in focus, hold down the shutter and take several pictures.

Whichever technique you choose, you'll find that most of your pictures are out of focus—hence the need to take many pictures. Even if the subject is still, you're not. Because macro photography has an incredibly small depth-of-field and you'll be hand-holding your camera, you'll find that your body moves forward and backwards enough to throw your entire subject out of focus.

With some patience, you can take amazing insect photos using your existing lens and several inexpensive extension tubes (as described in Chapter 12, "Macro"). The ideal insect photography gear requires a DSLR and the following equipment:

- A telephoto macro lens with a focal length of 100-200mm. I use a Sigma 150mm macro lens, which costs about $1,100.

- A ring flash. Ring flashes mount to the front of your lens so they can light your subject more evenly. If you try to light an insect with a flash mounted over the body of your camera, the light will be very uneven and partially blocked by the lens. Ring flashes cost anywhere from $50 to $500.

You don't always need a ring flash; if it's a bright day and you're shooting a subject that holds still for a few seconds at a time (like a butterfly), set your camera to ISO 800 and shutter priority (Tv or S) with a shutter speed of

Figure 8-27: Use a monopod when birds fly close to the ground (500mm, f/11, 1/2000th, ISO 800).

1/250th. Using shutter priority will cause your camera to use the aperture with the most depth-of-field possible. Natural light *always* looks better than a ring flash, but you almost always need a flash to avoid camera or motion blur.

If you are using a ring flash, start with your camera set to manual mode (M), ISO 200, a shutter speed of 1/250th, and an aperture of f/11. If the background appears too dark, increase the ISO to 400 or 800. If parts of your subject are not in focus, set the aperture to f/16 or f/22.

Notice that the equipment list didn't include a tripod. As a rule, tripods are a requirement for macro photography—but photographing living insects requires you to constantly refocus and chase them with the camera, and only hand-holding gives you the flexibility you need.

CATERPILLARS AND BEETLES

For your first insect photography assignment, start with a larger, slow-moving insect. caterpillars or beetles are perfect model; the japanese beetle in Figure 8-28 waited as long as I needed to set up the shot. Remember, focus on the eyes.

Experiment with different apertures and shutter speeds, manual and automatic focus, and using a flash or natural light. Examine your pictures on your computer and determine which settings made the pictures turn out, and which failed.

This american dagger moth caterpillar in Figure 8-29 is much less dangerous than it sounds. I found him crawling across my patio, aligned as much of his body as possible with the plane of focus, and focused on his eyes. I needed to use an aperture of f/9 to get a fast enough shutter speed to hand-hold the photo, causing too short a depth-of-field at macro range.

Caterpillars, in particular, aren't good at getting away. If you find a good (albeit unwilling) model, carefully move it to a location with

good lighting and a nice background. I found the gorgeous *Lophocampa caryae* larva (Figure 8-30) near a stream in a forest. The forest was too dark for decent macro photography, and his black and white coloring was too contrasty for flash photography. So, I moved him onto a red flower that was illuminated by a spot of light streaming through the forest canopy.

BUTTERFLIES

Once you're comfortable with slow-moving insects, it's time to move up to butterflies. Butterflies flutter from spot to spot, and they're basically impossible to photograph when they're moving. Instead, wait for a butterfly to stop for a moment.

To get the butterfly in focus, you'll need to align the plane of focus with the butterfly's wings. The lens must be perpendicular to the

Figure 8-28: Use slow-moving insects to practice technique (150mm, f/16, 1/160th, ISO 200).

Figure 8-29: Align the insect's body with the plane of focus (150mm, f/9, 1/80th, ISO 3200).

butterfly's wings; if the wings are tilted towards or away from you, the tips of the wings will be out of focus, as they are with this sara longwing (*Heliconius sara*, Figure 8-31).

Butterflies usually stand upright, which means your camera will be level with the ground when the butterfly's wings are closed, but you'll need to stand over the butterfly and point your camera towards the ground when the wings are open. Notice that every part of this eastern tiger swallowtail (*Papilo glaucus*, Figure 8-32) is in focus.

Different species of butterflies hold their wings in different positions at rest—either spread or closed. Most of the color is hidden when a butterfly's wings are closed, so your best pictures will be of those species that keep their wings open.

If you can't get sharp pictures, try using a ring flash. A ring flash surrounds your camera lens,

providing even light for close-up subjects. If you were to use a traditional flash with a close-up picture of a butterfly, the lens would probably block part of the light, and the shadows would be extreme. I photographed the butterfly in Figure 8-33 with a ring flash and without. With the ring flash, the butterfly's coloring is brighter, but the background is dark (because it was not illuminated by the flash), and the picture feels less natural. While I prefer to work without a flash, it's often impossible to get a fast enough shutter speed without it. I always bring my ring flash when doing macro photography, but I only turn it on when I need it.

Tip: Butterflies move slower in the cold, so you have more time to shoot them while they hold still if you get up early in the morning.

Figure 8-31: If a butterfly's wings are not aligned with the plane of focus, the wing tips will be blurry (150mm, f/6.3, 1/160th, ISO 500).

Figure 8-32: Align the plane of focus with the wings (150mm, f/16, 1/125th, ISO 400).

Figure 8-30: If you can do it safely, move insects to a nicer location (150mm, f/8, 1/125th, ISO 800).

Butterfly gardens, which are like zoos for butterflies, are scattered throughout the country. Look for a butterfly garden near you to quickly get practice photographing dozens of different species.

DRAGONFLIES AND DAMSELFLIES

Dragonflies and damselflies (which look like small dragonflies) behave similarly to butterflies—they fly from spot to spot and stop to rest for a few seconds at a time. Butterflies are much better models, however, because they thoughtfully choose to land on colorful flowers. Dragonflies typically choose ugly branches.

Thoughtless as they are, dragonflies' bright colors make them excellent subjects. You can try chasing a dragonfly from spot-to-spot, but your movements will probably scare him off before you have a chance to focus. You might have better luck by setting your camera up at one of his favorite stopping points, holding very still, and waiting for him to return.

With butterflies, it's critical that you align the sensor with the wings so that the wings are also in focus. This isn't as important with dragonflies and damselflies, because their wings are translucent. Instead, strive to keep the body aligned with the sensor, as shown in Figure 8-34.

I've found that dragonflies and damselflies are quite stubborn when they're eating. If you happen to find one with a fresh kill, he'll likely

hold still for you (Figure 8-35), and you'll be rewarded with a very interesting picture—like this crop of a picture of a damselfly eating an even smaller bug.

Dragonflies shed their skin, and when they do this, they'll hold still for a couple of days at a time while their fresh skin dries out. This makes them very vulnerable to both birds and photographers. If you happen to find a molting dragonfly (Figure 8-36), take your time, set up your tripod, and hold the branch still.

BEES AND FLIES

Like butterflies, bees and many species of flies are brightly colored and move from flower to flower. Bees and flies are quite a bit smaller than butterflies, though, and their round shape means they often need even more depth-of-field to stay in focus.

Figure 8-34: Align the dragonfly's body with your camera sensor (150mm, f/10, 1/160th, ISO 400).

Figure 8-33: A butterfly with a ring flash and with natural light (150mm, f/22 and f/4.5, 1/160th, ISO 800).

Bees and pollen-collecting flies are even more predictable than butterflies or dragonflies; they'll return to the same flower over and over. If the same bee or fly doesn't return, one of his siblings certainly will. Take advantage of this and stake out the prettiest flower (Figure 8-37). Keep your camera roughly focused on the flower and wait until the bee returns. If your arms get tired, use a monopod to support the weight of the camera. A tripod will probably not give you the flexibility you need. If it's windy, consider tying the branch the flower is on to a stake to help hold it still.

Once you get some experience photographing still bees, try photographing them as they approach a flower (Figure 8-38). You'll need to watch their movements so you can anticipate where they'll be as they approach the flower and pre-focus on this area. Your shutter speed should be fast enough to freeze the motion of the body of the insect, but leave the wings at least a little blurred.

Houseflies aren't the most beautiful subjects, but they're interesting in close-ups. Unfortunately, they don't tend to land in the most attractive locations. To attract a fly to a particular spot, spray it with water, as I did for Figure 8-39.

SPIDERS

Spiders are one of the most overlooked animal subjects; that also means they provide the most opportunity to create striking pictures.

For spiders that make webs, you want hard top lighting that highlights the individual fibers. To highlight them further, use a spray bottle to gently mist the web with water, as shown in Figure 8-40.

Spiders spend most of their time waiting, which gives you some time to set up a tripod. Generally, I set my macro lens to the minimum focusing distance, and then move the camera closer to the spider until it's in focus. When I'm hand-holding my macro lens, I simply shift my body forward until the spider's eyes are in focus, and gently press the shutter button.

Figure 8-36: A molting dragonfly (400mm, f/11, 1/160th, ISO 500).

Figure 8-35: A tiny damselfly eating his kill (150mm cropped, f/10, 1/160th, ISO 400).

Figure 8-37: Pick a flower and wait for the bee to land (150mm, f/18, 1/160th, ISO 1000).

Though spiders stand still, their webs bounce in the wind enough to move the spider out of focus. If you can't wait for the wind to stop (mornings and evenings are the best times), then set your camera to continuous shooting and take dozens of pictures. Keep your shutter speed above 1/250th, and use the highest f/stop number possible to maximize your depth-of-field. At macro range, it's a challenge just to have the entire spider sharp, so don't worry about background blur.

Zoos

It feels a bit like cheating. After all, no *National Geographic* photographer is known for taking pictures of animals in captivity. Nonetheless, I love photographing animals in zoos, because that's where the animals are, and some

thoughtful folks have put up barriers so they can't run away from me.

Tip: Take pictures of the signs so you can identify the animals later.

If you find yourself shooting in low light in the zoo, follow the techniques for shooting in low light.

FENCING

The biggest problem with zoos is fencing. It's never good, but you can completely hide it. If you use the right technique, you won't see the fencing in the picture—instead, you'll get a somewhat low contrast, unsharp picture, just as if you had used a very dirty lens.

If possible, place your lens directly against the fence and shoot through a hole. Dark, shaded fencing is better than shiny, illuminated fencing. If the holes in the fence are too small to fit your lens through, or if there is fencing in the background, use the biggest aperture possible to create the shortest possible depth-of-field. If you can blur the fence enough, it'll disappear completely, though blurring the fence will leave your picture very low contrast—a problem that you can mostly fix in your photo editing software.

Figure 8-38: Pre-focus on a flower and shoot rapidly as the bee approaches it (150mm, f/16, 1/160th, ISO 200).

Figure 8-39: Spray a leaf to attract flies (150mm, f/9.5, 1/125th, ISO 400).

Figure 8-40: Use water droplets and light to illuminate a spider web (150mm, f/4, 1/350th, ISO 400).

Figure 8-41 shows me photographing an injured great horned owl through small black fencing. I held the lens as close to the fencing as possible, resting the lens hood against the fence. I used a telephoto lens (500mm) and a small f/stop number (f/4.0), and got as close to the subject as possible to completely blur the fence. Back at home, I used Photoshop to adjust the black and white points of the picture to increase the contrast and make it a usable photo. Notice that the picture shows the owl facing the camera; owls are one of the few birds that look more attractive head-on.

If you can't completely hide the fencing with depth-of-field, review the "Controlling Depth-of-Field" section of Chapter 4, "Controlling Your Camera." In a nutshell, zoom in as far as possible, get as close as you can, and use the lowest f/stop number. You can't hide the fence if the animal is too close to the fence; find an angle with as much distance as possible between the fence and the animal. Figure 8-42 shows two pictures of a japanese squirrel in a zoo, taken through the same type of fencing. For the second one, the squirrel moved about a foot farther away from the fence, giving enough distance to allow the short depth-of-field to blur it out completely.

Figure 8-41: Blur fencing by putting your lens as close to the fencing as possible (500mm, f/4, 1/160th, ISO 3200).

Figure 8-42: Wait until the animal moves away from the fence and use short depth-of-field (200mm, f/2.8).

GLASS

If you must shoot through glass, there are several things you can do to improve your pictures:

- **Find a clean section of glass.** Kids dirty the glass they can reach, so you might get better results by holding your camera above your head.

- **Hold your lens against the glass.** Not only will this steady your shot, but it will make sure any reflections in the glass are as out of focus as possible.

- **Block reflections on the glass.** You have a lens hood to keep reflections off your lens. To keep reflections off the glass, hold your hands or hat above the portion of the glass you're shooting through.

- **Use a polarizing filter.** Polarizing filters help reduce reflections. They also reduce the light, so you might need to increase your ISO to keep your shutter speed up.

For more information, refer to the "Washed-out Pictures" section of Chapter 5, "Problem Solving."

CAMERA EQUIPMENT

Different zoos require different equipment. If I could only have one lens, it would be a 75-300mm f/4-5.6 zoom, which costs about $150. If you're willing to spend over $1,000, choose an 80-400mm or 100-400mm telephoto zoom. They are often not long enough to get close to the animals, so you will need to crop many photos, which is standard—most wildlife photos are cropped. If money isn't a concern, a 500mm lens, especially with a 1.4x teleconverter, is long enough for most zoos without being too heavy to carry—but it's still cumbersome and attracts a great deal of attention. On the upside, people always clear a path when they see a lens that big.

In smaller zoos, the animals tend to be much closer, but they're protected by chain link fencing. In that case, choose a medium-telephoto lens with a huge maximum aperture. My lens of choice for this type of zoo is my 85mm f/1.8. Being a prime lens, it doesn't give me the flexibility of zooming. However, the huge aperture does wonders for blurring out fencing.

Aviaries (bird enclosures) are typically open-air, allowing you to get close to the mostly-tame birds. However, they also tend to be very dark. Unless the zoo is very empty and the birds are sleeping, you probably won't have any luck with a tripod. Instead, choose a telephoto lens with image stabilization, concentrate on good hand-holding technique, shoot wide open, and use a higher ISO speed if necessary.

TIMING

Some animals are wonderful models; they're constantly active, changing position, angle, and expression, just like a real model. Other animals (I'm talking to you, lions) sleep constantly. For better results, find out the animal's feeding times, or get there early on cool days—the crowds will be smaller and many of the animals will be more active.

The Golden Hours still count when you're at a zoo. This old film shot (Figure 8-43) of a lioness, taken at Busch Gardens in Florida (one of the best zoos for photographers in the United States), is made interesting only by the warm lighting cast by the setting sun.

AQUARIUMS

Aquariums usually allow you to get within a foot or two of the creatures, so any lens should work. You might be tempted to attach a polarizing filter to cut down on the reflection from the glass, but the 2 stops of light loss isn't worth it when photographing the relatively dark underwater environments.

To watch a video on **aquarium photography,** scan the QR code or visit:

sdp.io/Aquariums

Lighting is the biggest challenge with an aquarium; you might need to shoot at ISO 1600 or higher, which will create noisy pictures. Don't bother with the flash; it'll reflect off the glass and the water. With practice, you can get useable pictures that'll make your friends think you went SCUBA diving (Figure 8-44).

Because you can get relatively close to the animals, you don't need a big telephoto lens for the aquarium.

Focusing is a challenge in aquariums. Most of the fish move constantly, and the low light inside aquariums makes it difficult for cameras to autofocus. Take many pictures, because persistence pays off. Wide apertures pay off, too; a lens with a low maximum f/stop number (such as f/1.8 or f/2.8) will pass on the most light to your camera's autofocus sensors.

Get as close to the glass as possible. For best results, keep a lens hood attached, and gently rest the edge of the lens hood against the glass. This will help reduce glare and stabilize your shots.

POST-PROCESSING

You don't need to remove pimples from a bird, but you can definitely benefit from bringing pictures into Photoshop. Figure 8-45 shows an example: a cedar waxwing in the snow underneath a holly bush. Unfortunately, the snow isn't as clean and pure as it looks to our eyes. Ten minutes in Photoshop cleaned up the snow and background, showing a pure scene more like I saw with my eyes.

Besides removing stray background objects, you should fix flaws in feathers and fur, reduce noise (especially in blurred backgrounds), dodge dark areas such as black feathers and eyes, and add catch lights if the natural lighting didn't provide it.

Figure 8-43: Use the golden hours at outdoor zoos.

To watch a funny video about **people who annoy wildlife photographers,** scan the QR code or visit:

sdp.io/Annoy

Figure 8-44: At the New Orleans aquarium, a seahorse (200mm, f/2.8, 1/60th, ISO 3200) and a clown fish (200mm, f/2.8, 1/750th, ISO 6400—in hindsight I should have lowered the ISO to 1600).

To watch a video on **editing wildlife photos,** scan the QR code or visit:

sdp.io/EditingWildlife

Figure 8-45: Use post-processing to clean the background (500mm, f/5.6, 1/500th, ISO 800, +2 stops exposure compensation).

PRACTICE

This chapter's practices help you understand how to photograph animals, both domestic and wild.

- **Pets**. Make two portraits of a pet: one posed, and one in action. For the posed picture, select a location with nice lighting and a pleasant background. For the action picture, play with your pet and try to capture his or her movement.

- **Working through fencing**. Go to a zoo. Set your camera to aperture priority and choose the lowest f/stop number your lens supports. Find a dark spot of fencing that is not illuminated by sunlight, and press the front element of the lens as close to the fence as possible.

- **Shutter speed**. Go to a zoo. In an indoor exhibit, set your camera to shutter priority. Take dozens of pictures of different animals at 1/30th, 1/125th, and 1/250th. You will need to adjust your ISO to allow the higher shutter speeds. Which shutter speeds provided the most clear pictures?

- **Depth-of-field**. Go to a zoo. Choose an exhibit where you can get fairly close to an animal, set your camera to aperture priority, and zoom in as close to the animal as possible. Choose the lowest f/stop number your lens supports, and take a picture. Was the depth-of-field sufficient to show the entire animal in focus? If not, choose a higher f/stop number and take another picture. Review the picture, and repeat the process until you identify the f/stop necessary. If camera shake or motion blur becomes a problem at higher f/stop numbers, increase your ISO.

- **Lighting and posing**. At a location with birds (such as near a bird feeder, at a beach, or in a park with pigeons), take continuous pictures of birds with the sun high in the sky. Use fill flash for some of the pictures. Which head and body angles look best? Notice how their head and body movements alter the catch light. Repeat the process with the sun low in the sky. Was the lighting better or worse?

 Take a quiz!

sdp.io/Quiz8

- **Approaching animals**. Without putting yourself in danger, try to get as close as possible to a wild animal and take a picture of it. Plan to spend at least five minutes approaching the animal. You'll have more success in parks with people, because the animals are already habituated to humans.

- **Panning**. Find a running dog or a soaring bird, set your camera to shutter priority, and take pictures of it by panning your camera with the movement. Adjust the shutter speed so that you get some background blur without blurring the animal's face too much. Do not use flash.

- **Close-up**. Using your lens with the highest magnification, photograph any still subject as close as possible. Magnification is often listed on the lens, such as 1:4 or 1:1, with 1:4 requiring you to stay farther away and 1:1 being ideal. Experiment with different shutter speeds and apertures to prevent camera shake while providing sufficient depth-of-field. You might need to select a higher ISO to provide both. With your newfound macro photography skills, attempt to photograph insects, capturing as much detail as possible. Only use flash if you happen to have a ring flash.

- **Post-processing**. Using your favorite pictures from the previous practices, use Photoshop or another image editing application to improve the picture. Fix lighting, color, and contrast. Then, remove unnecessary obstructions.

The world around you is a beautiful place, whether you're surrounded by snow-capped mountains, grassy plains, or manmade roads and buildings. To the casual observer it seems to stand still, and all but the most dramatic scenes go unnoticed. Once you learn to appreciate landscape photography, you'll see our Earth for what it is: an ever-changing terrain, painted with dynamic light, and washed in uncontrollable weather. To understand landscape photography is to know the gifts each season brings, to never again take the sun for granted, and to love water in all its forms: humidity, clouds, rain, snow, ice, rivers, lakes, and oceans.

Taking a great landscape photo, however, requires planning, patience, and persistence. You need to find the best vantage point for your subject, choose the right season, pick the time of day with the best lighting, and then return to the same spot day after day (and sometimes year after year) to get the weather and other conditions just right. Sometimes, though, you might just get lucky. When you do, your understanding of landscape photography will allow you to capture and share the magnificence around you as you see it.

By definition, landscape photographs portray a world untouched by humans, free of people, structures, and anything manmade. I expand the definition of a landscape to include all outdoor, open space, still life photography, including cityscapes. I'll also cover other elements of nature, including sunsets and sunrises, flowers, forests, streams, rivers, and waterfalls.

COMPOSITIONAL ELEMENTS

As described in Chapter 2, "Composition," standard composition techniques, especially the rule of thirds and symmetry, work well for landscape photography. In addition to those techniques, the best landscape photos show depth by including three elements:

To watch a video with landscape tips, scan the QR code or visit:

sdp.io/LandscapeTips

- **Foreground.** The most commonly forgotten element, the foreground is typically at the bottom of the picture and it provides the viewer with a sense of distance from the background. In a mountain landscape, you might have flowers in the foreground. If you're shooting a beach sunset, you might have sand or shells.

- **Middleground.** In a mountain landscape, the middleground might be a lake, trees, or a winding road. If you're shooting a beach sunset, the middleground is the ocean. Also, I think I made up the word *middleground*.

- **Background.** The furthest subject from the viewer. In the case of a mountain landscape, this is the mountain range itself. If you're shooting a beach sunset, the background is the setting sun.

If you include a foreground, middleground, and background, your landscape will have the depth that you see in person (Figure 9-1 next page). For best results, follow the rule of thirds, and divide the picture horizontally into three, roughly equal areas. Avoid putting the horizon in the middle of the picture. If the sky is interesting, place the horizon in the bottom third. If the sky is dull, place the horizon in the top third, or even higher. The chapter cover shows a church steeple in the Swiss Alps; the grassy hill and the steeple form the foreground, the distant town in the wooded hills forms the middleground, and the snow-capped Alps and sky are the background.

Still, it might be tough to make a simple landscape interesting. To make your landscape more interesting, use trees, rivers, roads, or bridges to create lines that draw the eye through the landscape. Whenever possible, incorporate an additional subject to provide scale and a focal point, such as a person, a bird, the sun, or the moon.

Tip: Don't let a dull afternoon sky ruin your picture. If you can't come back in the morning or evening or when the weather is nicer, you can always delete the sky in Photoshop and replace it with something nicer. When you do have a nice sky, take pictures of it for later use! When you combine multiple images, it's called a comp. Comp is short for composition or composite.

PLANNING

Great landscape photos are made over the course of weeks, months, and years. Regardless of your skills and equipment, you can't just plan a trip to Yosemite and get an Ansel Adams shot. Great landscape photos require:

- **Location**. Finding the right spot is the first challenge. Often, though, the best viewpoints require hours or days of hiking.

- **Lighting**. You're at the mercy of the sun, moon, and clouds for your lighting. As described in Chapter 3, "Lighting and Flash," pick your time of day (usually within the golden hours) to get the right lighting. Stay after the sun sets and take a night shot, as described in Chapter 11, "HDR."

- **Weather**. Landscapes typically include the sky. While a clear blue sky with puffy white clouds is the traditional ideal, many of the greatest landscapes feature thunderclouds. At night, clear skies and no moon can fill your picture with stars.

- **Season**. Every spot changes throughout the year. Flowers bloom in the spring. Summer heat gives a hazy sky. In the fall, leaves become warm shades of orange and red (for a week or two). In the winter, leaves are sparse, but a pure white snow can highlight every branch, freeze lakes, and cover mountainsides.

Landscape photography doesn't happen in a studio where you can control everything; with landscape photography, nature controls everything, and you simply pick a spot and wait for the right moment. Because of this, your best landscape photos may be near your

Figure 9-1: Multiple layers add depth, especially if they overlap (35mm, f/6.3, 1/200th, ISO 100).

house. Grabbing an award-winning landscape shot while on vacation requires a great deal of luck—but it's still worth a shot. Find locations by looking at other people's pictures and using Google Earth (*earth.google.com*). Get there before sunrise or sunset, and plan to hang out for a couple of hours. Watch the weather during your trip, and plan your visit to the spot when the weather happens to cooperate.

There's no flash big enough to light a landscape photo, but you still have a great deal of control over lighting. Unfortunately, it requires a lot of patience, because you have to wait for Mother Nature to give you the right lighting.

As discussed in Chapter 3, use the golden hours—the hour after sunrise and the hour before sunset. It depends on your location and which compass direction you're shooting the landscape from, but sunrise and sunset can provide completely different lighting effects.

Pack your gear ahead of time, get there early (plan to arrive a full hour before your ideal light), setup your tripod, and wait. Don't just take one photo—take a picture at least every few minutes. Even though the lighting might change too slowly for you to notice, when you look at the pictures later, you'll see how dramatically the light changes during the golden hours.

While direct overhead light and the haziness of the afternoon are rarely flattering, you can still get great shots outside of the golden hours. To determine exactly where the sun will be at any point during the day, and hence know which side of the mountain, lake, or waterfall you want to be on to keep the sun at your back, use the Photographer's Ephemeris (a free download from *sdp.io/tpe*).

As if waiting for sunrise or sunset wasn't enough, you also need to plan around the weather and the season. If you know the spot you want to photograph, you can't just show up before sunrise and snap a few shots and know you got the best picture. You need to plan to show up several days in a row, because the sky, haze, and fog will be a little different every day.

To watch a video on **fall,** scan the QR code or visit:

sdp.io/FallColors

Then, come back in the winter, spring, summer, and fall. To get the most amazing shots, you might even need multiple visits within each season. Figure 9-2 shows the same section of a pond in three different seasons. As you can see, a landscape will look very different just after a snowfall, and fall colors are only at their peak for a couple of days.

Figure 9-2: Landscapes change dramatically between seasons.

Tip: Get out your parka and snowshoes— the colder it is, the clearer your picture will be, and the bluer the sky will be.

ADAPTING

In the introduction, I mentioned that great landscape photography requires both planning and persistence. The reason it requires both is that no matter how carefully you plan a shot, it can still go awry.

For example, I planned a trip to Vermont in October to photograph the brightly-colored foliage. I carefully researched the days of the peak colors, and selected days when the forecast called for clear skies. I selected locations that would be nicely illuminated by the rising or setting sun during the golden hours.

Despite my planning, none of my shots turned out. Days before the trip, a heavy wind storm blew the most brightly colored leaves from the trees. Despite a weather forecast of clear skies, the sun almost never peeked through the clouds.

You can, however, adapt your photos to the conditions:

- Use HDR techniques to maximize contrast, color, and detail.

- If the sky is cloudy, shoot subjects on the ground.

- If the sky is hazy, use it to show depth.

- If you don't get the colors you hoped for, convert your pictures to black and white.

- Find isolated spots of color, and shoot them close-up.

FINDING A LOCATION

Most people get interested in landscape photography only after they find a great location; perhaps they drive through a fog-filled valley on their way to work, or walk their dogs around a still, reflecting pond in the woods.

Make the most of these spontaneous landscape opportunities by traveling slowly and deliberately. Rent a car instead of taking a train. Walk instead of taking a cab. When you see a photo opportunity, stop.

Figure 9-3 shows a picture from the countryside of Peru that was only possible because we chose a car instead of a train, because we alloted extra travel time, and because we weren't afraid to ask the driver to stop.

If you're serious about landscape photography, though, you will seek out great locations. Fortunately, you can use the Internet to find great landscape photography spots:

- Install Google Earth. In the Layers panel, make sure that Photos\Panoramio is

Figure 9-3: Travel slowly and deliberately so you can stop for photo opportunities.

selected (it is turned on by default). Now, simply zoom into a location, and click the photo icons to see people's pictures of that spot. Browse around to find great locations that you'd like to visit.

- Do an image search (for example, using *images.google.com*) for the name of a state or town. Find out where pictures you like were taken.

- Seek local advice; photographers know the area they live in better than anywhere else. Search blogs and forums for recommendations from other photographers for a specific location. For example, you might search for "Boston photo ops," "New York City skyline view," or "Yosemite photography."

- Fall foliage moves south, so for different weeks, different locations will have the best colors. Search for your location and "foliage report" to find the best spots.

Once you get to your location, it can be hard to get the right perspective. There might be buildings, people, or other obstructions in the way. Getting the best landscape shot often requires you to change your location horizontally (by walking or driving to a different spot) or vertically (by finding a nearby rooftop, driving to a nearby hill, or even taking flight in a helicopter or hot-air balloon).

CAMERA SETTINGS

For landscape photos, your priorities are to make everything as sharp as possible and to capture the greatest amount of dynamic range (and hence the greatest details in both the highlights and shadows). Most cameras have a landscape mode—look for an icon showing mountains. Landscape mode chooses settings that maximize depth-of-field and dynamic range, and typically you can simply choose that setting and focus on the non-technical aspects of your photography.

When manually choosing settings for landscape photos, use these settings:

- Focus on the most important part of the picture. Use precise focusing techniques (as described in Chapter 4, "Controlling Your Camera"). If there's no particular focal point (a problem unto itself), focus about $1/3^{rd}$ of the way through the picture.

- Set your camera to capture raw (if possible) for the greatest possible dynamic range.

- Set your camera to aperture priority (Av or A) mode.

- Use a moderate aperture, such as f/11.

- Set your ISO speed to 100, or as low as possible.

- Allow the camera to determine the exposure. If the shutter speed is below $1/30^{th}$, place the camera on a tripod. If you use a tripod, also use your camera's built-in timer to delay the picture by a couple of seconds after you press the shutter. If available, enable mirror lock-up to further minimize the amount of shake you introduce by taking the picture.

- Verify that the camera is level, either by carefully examining the horizon, by using a bubble level attached to your camera's flash shoe, or by using your camera's electronic level.

- Bracket the exposure so that you can combine multiple pictures to balance the shadows with the highlights (usually the sky). For detailed information, refer to Chapter 11, "HDR."

With these settings, take a test picture. Examine the picture on your camera's display by zooming in as far as possible. Specifically, ask yourself:

- **Is the point you focused on clear?** If not, place the camera on a tripod. If that's not possible, verify that image stabilization is turned on. If necessary, choose a higher ISO speed to increase the shutter speed.

To watch a video about **focus stacking,** scan the QR code or visit:

sdp.io/StackLandscapes

- **Are both the foreground and background in focus?** If not, try focusing closer. If that does not solve the problem, use a smaller aperture, such as f/16. If you still need more depth-of-field, try focus stacking, discussed next.

- **Are the tree leaves clear?** If trees appear blurry, the wind may be moving them too much. Use a lower f/stop number or a higher ISO speed to increase the shutter speed.

- **Are you capturing the full dynamic range?** If the histogram shows overexposed or underexposed areas, bracket your exposure. If you are already bracketing, expand your bracketing range. Refer to Chapter 11 for more information.

- **Is the sky overexposed?** If so, attach a polarizing filter, and rotate it to the point that the sky appears darkest when viewed through the viewfinder. If the sky is still overexposed, use exposure compensation to reduce the exposure by ½ stop. Further reduce the exposure until the sky is no longer overexposed.

FOCUS STACKING

When taking a picture with a nearby foreground and a distant background, you might not be able to get both in focus, even when using the highest f/stop number. If you don't mind post-processing, you can use a technique called focus stacking. With focus stacking, you'll separately focus on the foregound, middleground, and background, and then combine the pictures in post-processing,

For detailed instructions, refer to the video on this page.

Figure 9-4: Cityscapes require finding a viewpoint outside or above the city.

CITYSCAPES

Cityscapes, as shown in Figure 9-4, are the single best way to capture an entire city in one shot. Planning and composition are just like in traditional landscape photography. Some of the locations that might work for you include:

■ **Towers, walls, or skyscrapers**. Tall buildings elevate you above obstacles that would otherwise ruin your view. For example, the upper-right photo in Figure 9-4 includes a picture of Salzburg, Austria, as taken from a tower that used to be used to protect the ancient city. Because the buildings in Salzburg are so low, I could not get a good outline of them against the sky. In New York City, you might visit the Empire State Building. In Seattle, you might visit the Space Needle (the view from which is shown in the upper-left photo in Figure 9-4).

■ **Opposite shorelines of lakes or rivers**. Most cities are along a body of water. If the city is built on a lake or river, look for viewpoints along the opposite shore. The picture of Seattle from across the water (the lower-right photo in Figure 9-4) was taken from Harbor Avenue, a street on the opposite side of Seattle's harbor. Similarly, the best places to get a view of the New York City skyline are the opposite shores of the Hudson and East rivers, and in Boston, visit Piers Park, which is across the harbor.

■ **Boats**. For cities on the ocean, such as Boston, the best viewpoint is the ocean. Research ferries and tours to find a cheap way to take to the water, and plan your trip around the ideal light. If the city is on the East Coast, take out the boat at sunrise so the sun illuminates the city. If the city is on the West coast, visit at sunset.

■ **Hills or mountains outside the city.** Don't get too far away from the city, or the hazy sky will ruin the sharpness and contrast of your picture. Use Google Earth to find hills that might have a view. First, center your location on the city. Then, hold down the shift key on your keyboard and drag with your mouse to view the earth from close to ground level. You can then pan around the city with your mouse, looking for elevated locations that provide a clear view of the city. Of course, when you visit the location in person, you might find that it's obstructed by trees or buildings, but it's a start.

■ **Helicopters or airplanes**. Higher viewpoints provide a rarely seen view of the city and make buildings feel more three-dimensional than traditional eye-level photographs. Helicopters can often be chartered for just a couple of hundred dollars. Air tours are not available for all cities—in particular, security concerns prevent flying over Washington, D.C.

Timing is very critical—you'll notice that I don't have any cityscapes of San Francisco, one of my favorite cities. I found the perfect spot on

Figure 9-5: Sunset pictures taken at 200mm and 700mm.

top of a hill just outside the city, but every time I visited, the hill was immersed in a thick cloud that made photography impossible.

Most of the time, you'll be far enough from the city that you'll need a telephoto lens to fill the frame. For best results, bring zoom lenses that cover the 100-400mm range.

SUNSETS AND SUNRISES

The sunrise and the sunset are staples of landscape photography, but they're much harder to do well than you might expect. The first lesson to learn is that you need to zoom way in: while most landscape photos are taken with wide-angle lenses, you'll need to use a telephoto lens if you plan to include the sun in the picture. In this instance, big lenses are preferred. Figure 9-5 compares two telephoto photos, taken at 200mm and 700mm. Even at 700mm (a length typically only used for birding and some sports), the sun takes up only a small portion of the frame. With a wide-angle lens, the setting sun would have been a tiny spot.

Sunsets are excellent for creating silhouettes. To create a silhouette, simply position your subject in front of the setting sun. If your camera's autoexposure settings don't create a silhouette, use exposure compensation to underexpose the picture by two stops.

Most people know that the sun rises in the east and sets in the west. Unfortunately, it's not that simple, and to get an ideal direct shot of a sunrise or sunset, you need to know exactly where the sun is going to be. Depending on the time of year, and where you are on the globe, the sun will rise and set in completely different places on the horizon. For example, Connecticut has southern-facing shores. However, because it's fairly far north, the sun rises and sets over the ocean to the south in the winter. In the summer, the sun rises and sets over the land to the north.

Be aware that official sunrise and sunset times are based on the true horizon, and will only be accurate if the horizon is at sea level. If there are hills, trees, or buildings, the sun might set 20-30 minutes earlier.

Figure 9-6: Often the best sunset/sunrise shots are away from the sun (45mm, f/8, 1/60th, ISO 400).

The closer you are to the equator, the faster the sun sets. For tropical locations, the sun will only be near the horizon for a couple of minutes. If you are near the North or South Pole in the summer, twilight can last for months. Therefore, the closer you are to the equator, the less time you'll have, and the more important it will be to plan where you're going to shoot and to get there early.

Some of the best sunrise and sunset shots don't include the sun. When the sun is low on the sky, it illuminates the clouds and fills the sky with rich blues and oranges. I photographed this chapel in Austria (Figure 9-6) many times over the course of several days, but the only picture that worked was this photo, taken as the sun set, because of the compelling colors in the sky.

FLOWERS

The most successful flower photos show only the flower itself. Most camera lenses can't focus close enough to fill the frame with the

flower, however. For that reason, a macro lens is the best choice for flower photography.

As with all types of macro photography, shooting close-up gives you a very short depth-of-field. This helps to make the flower stand out from the background, which, in gardens, is typically cluttered. To get the most out of your narrow depth-of-field, position the camera's sensor parallel to the most important part of the flower. Shooting an open flower straight-on will allow you to get all petals in focus.

Figure 9-7 was taken with a 150mm macro lens wide open at f/2.8. As you can see from the cropping, the background is extremely blurred. This cropping of the same photo shows just how shallow the depth-of-field is—only a very small portion of the center of the flower is properly in focus. Experiment with different apertures to find the best compromise between a nicely blurred background and sufficient depth-of-field.

Wind is a serious problem when photographing flowers outdoors. If you can clip a flower and bring it indoors, you'll find it much easier to get a clear picture. Otherwise, bring a stake and some small-gauge wire to stabilize the flower. For the ultimate in wind-blocking, use a shooting tent that you can place over the flower, such as the PhotoFlex LiteRoom. If you don't want to kill the flower and you can't stake or cover it, use a shutter speed of at least 1/250th—which can be a challenge if you need a high f/stop number of more depth-of-field.

You can use just a bit of flash to bring out the colors in the flower and to darken the background. For smaller flowers, you will need to use a ring flash, as you would with other types of macro photography. Because the subject is so close to the flash, the light falloff behind the subject will be severe, giving you a dark or completely black background. This isolates the subject, but I prefer flowers to have a more natural background. Figure 9-8 illustrates the light falloff with flash—the leaves to the left of the flower were

Figure 9-7: Use a small f/stop number to blur the background and reduce distractions.

immediately behind it. There were leaves to the right of the flower, too—but they were far enough away (just a couple of inches) that the flash didn't reach them.

If you're not happy with the background, bring your own. Place a white, black, or green background behind a flower—a simple piece of foam core board works well. You might even create your own background by taking an extremely out of focus picture of a garden, which will result in blurred green colors, and getting a print of the picture to use as the artificial background. Leave as much distance as possible between the flower and the background.

As with other types of outdoor photography, weather is a major influence. Overcast days will give you the ideal soft lighting. If you can't wait for clouds, have someone hold a diffuser over the flower so that the flower is in the shadow of the diffuser. Figure 9-9 shows a rather large diffuser, but you can buy smaller diffusers that fold small enough to fit in your pocket.

Raindrops add peace and beauty to flowers, as shown in Figure 9-10. The most gorgeous

Figure 9-8: Use a ring flash to bring out the flower's colors while darkening the background (150mm, f/16, 1/160th, ISO 400).

Figure 9-10: Shoot flowers after a rainfall, or bring a spray bottle (75mm, f/2.8, 1/500th, ISO 400).

Figure 9-9: Use a diffuser to soften the light on a flower (photo by Christine Mercado).

Figure 9-11: Wait for a bee (or a fly in this case), to show the flower's role in the ecosystem (150mm, f/16, 1/160th, ISO 200).

flower pictures are taken moments after a rainstorm ends. If you can't wait for the next rain, bring a spray bottle and add your own drops. To get a prettier background, crouch down so that you're level or even below the flowers. If crouching tires you too quickly, bring knee pads.

> **Tip:** Shooting during the golden hours when the sun is low on the horizon will provide interesting side lighting and shadows, and the warm light can bring out the colors in the flower.

An interesting flower becomes even more engaging when you show its larger role as a reproductive organ and food for insects. If you're patient, wait for a bee, butterfly, fly, or even a hummingbird to visit your flower, as shown in Figure 9-11. Because you'll need to quickly focus on the insect and re-frame the photo, you won't be able to use a tripod. For more information, refer to Chapter 8, "Animals."

FORESTS

The lighting in forests is very challenging, but it can also be extremely rewarding, as shown in Figure 9-12. The bright sun filters through the trees, causing spots of light on the forest floor. As a result, forest pictures are always high contrast—especially if you include the sky in your picture. Therefore, you need to watch your histogram carefully to make sure you capture as much of the dynamic range as possible.

If you're in a dense forest, point your camera straight up and use the sun as the focal point, as shown in the second example in Figure 9-12. The picture will be extremely contrasty; the bright sky will hide the trunks of the trees in shadow. Fill flash won't help you here, because the light would be too uneven. However, you can add fill after the fact in your favorite photo editing application.

If part of what you hope to capture is the grandness of the trees, be sure to include a person in the picture for scale. The largest example in Figure 9-12 shows giant redwoods. However, because there are only other redwoods for scale in the picture, the viewer would assume that they are

Figure 9-12: The scale and dynamic range make forests challenging subjects.

To watch a video about **waterfalls,** scan the QR code or visit:

sdp.io/Waterfalls

To watch a video **editing a landscape photo,** scan the QR code or visit:

sdp.io/EditingLandscapes

standard pine trees. If you look closely at this example, you can see a person in the bottom center of the frame.

STREAMS, RIVERS, AND WATERFALLS

Like any moving subject, capturing the essence of water requires carefully selecting your shutter speed. Using a high shutter speed seems to freeze water, isolating individual droplets. Longer shutter speeds blur the movement of water, creating a soft, silky look. For streams, rivers, and waterfalls, a longer shutter speed usually creates a better picture. For oceans and larger bodies of water, you might want to use a short shutter speed to catch waves in motion.

When you want to blur moving water (as shown in Figure 9-13), use a shutter speed of at least a second or two. Naturally, because you're using a slow shutter speed, you'll absolutely need to use a tripod. Unless you're in a really dark forest, this will probably cause your photo to be overexposed (though a little overexposure can be okay). To compensate for that, use the lowest ISO speed your camera supports, and the highest f/stop number your lens allows.

If your photo is overexposed even with a low ISO speed and small aperture, consider using a neutral density (ND) filter, also known as a stop-down filter. ND filters block incoming light uniformly, reducing the exposure by as much as several stops. A 0.3 ND filter blocks 30% of the incoming light, reducing your exposure by about one-third of a stop. A 0.6 ND filter blocks 60% of the incoming light, reducing your exposure by a little over one stop. A 0.9 ND filter blocks 90% of the incoming light, reducing your exposure by a little more than 3 stops.

Figure 9-13: Use a long shutter speed to give water a soft look (50mm, f/22, 1.5 seconds, ISO 100).

If you're in the habit of putting on a polarizer every time you go outdoors, take it off before you take a picture of water. Polarizers block reflections. In the case of water, they block the sunlight glinting off the surface, removing any ripples and depth from the picture. If you're shooting a waterfall and you absolutely need a slower shutter speed, and you don't have an ND filter, you can try using your polarizing filter. They block about two stops of light, and at a very long exposure, enough reflected light will still get through the filter to show the waterfall as white.

PRACTICES

This chapter's practices help you understand how time of day, weather, and season change scenes, as well as how to photograph waterfalls.

- Pick a nice spot near your home or workplace. The location must be convenient, because you'll be visiting it often for the exercises that follow. It's OK if it's just your backyard or a park between your home and work. At that spot, take as many varied pictures as you can. Crouch low, and climb up higher. Turn your camera sideways. Zoom in, and zoom out. At home, copy the pictures to your computer and pick your favorite angle.

- Using that same location, do these practices:

  ○ Set a reminder: Once a month, at the same time of day, take a picture. This will give you a sense for change between seasons.

  ○ Take pictures during different weather conditions: clear, partly cloudy, overcast, hazy, drizzling, rainy, and snowing. This will give you a sense for changing weather.

  ○ Take four pictures throughout the day: during sunrise, mid-day, at sunset, and at night. This will give you a sense for how a location changes throughout a single day.

 Take a quiz!

sdp.io/Quiz9

- Create a cityscape by capturing the skyline of your nearest city. Use tools such as the Internet and Google Earth to find a location ahead of time. Use Google Earth and The Photographer's Ephemeris to identify the time of day with the best lighting.

- Find a location that is either elevated or on the ocean, where you can see the sun rise or set. Determine when the sun will rise or set, and get to the location 30 minutes early. Capture the sunrise or sunset with both wide-angle and telephoto lenses. Which focal length created the best picture? How long did it take for the sun to rise or set? How did your pictures change over the course of the sunrise or sunset? Take the same shot over the course of five days. How did the sky vary? Is there any way you could predict which days would have the nicest colors?

- Practice photographing flowers. Shoot from above, beside, and below. Take pictures on sunny days and cloudy days. Wait until bugs land on the flowers. Spray flowers to add droplets. Back at home, examine the pictures. Which were your favorites?

- Bring your camera and a tripod to a stream or waterfall. At first, simply hand-hold the camera and use automatic settings. Take pictures at different angles until you find the composition you like. Then, put your camera on a tripod, set it to shutter priority, and choose the lowest ISO setting possible. Take pictures at $1/30^{th}$, 1/4, 1 second, 2 seconds, and 5 seconds. At which shutter speed did your pictures become overexposed? If you have a polarizing or neutral-density filter, attach it to your lens and try the overexposed pictures again. Examine how the longer shutter speed affected the look of the water.

10
CHAPTER

NIGHT PHOTOGRAPHY

At night, photos no longer represent an instant in time; shutter speeds are measured in whole seconds rather than fractions. Leaves gently blowing in the breeze become an impressionist painting. Waves crashing against the shore become a mysterious fog. The sky fills with millions of distant suns, each slowly circling the North Star. Without the overpowering daylight, you are free to paint the world around you with flashlights and fireworks.

Whereas landscape photography is relatively simple technically, night photography will push your brain's left hemisphere to its limit. Your camera's autofocus, exposure, and white balance systems will fail. Your trusted tripod will teeter and shake. Your pictures will have so much noise that you can barely find the stars. You'll be cold, tired, and at some point, scared.

But it's all worth it. With night photography, you capture a world seldom seen. While casual photographers are enjoying the light of their television sets, the night photographer is exploring moonlight, streetlights, and firelight.

GEAR

Here's what you need:

- A camera that allows manual exposure
- A sturdy tripod (though it's okay to start out with a travel tripod)
- A headlamp for lighting your gear
- On cold nights, a lint-free cloth to clean the dew off your lens

In rural areas without street lights, you'll also need:

- A bright flashlight for illuminating your subject so you can focus
- A remote shutter release with a timer for exposures of longer than 30 seconds, if your camera doesn't have a timer built-in
- Something to entertain yourself while you wait for those long exposures

To watch a **night photography introduction** video, scan the QR code or visit:

sdp.io/NightIntro

While you might not need these items, they can be useful:

- A camera level, if your camera doesn't have one built-in
- An extra battery

TAKING YOUR FIRST NIGHT PHOTO

Your first night photo should be an easy one: turn on the lights inside your house, set your camera to automatic, walk out your front door, and take a picture of your home. Don't even bother with a tripod.

Now, copy the picture to your computer and take a look at it. Here's what you'll find:

- The lights are overexposed, and the dark areas are underexposed.
- When you zoom into the picture, the noise fills the dark parts of the picture with red, green, and blue specks.
- Quite possibly, the picture is shaky.
- The lights are tinted orange, blue, or green, or some combination of different colors.

Nonetheless, the picture is cool, and it might just be the most interesting snapshot you've taken of your house.

TAKING YOUR SECOND NIGHT PHOTO

With your first snapshot under your belt, you can begin to solve the problems. Repeat the previous shot of your home, but do this:

- Put your camera on a tripod.
- Set your camera to aperture priority, f/5.6, ISO 200, and raw.
- Select a delayed shutter.

- Autofocus your camera on a bright light, and then switch the lens to manual focus to prevent the focus from changing. (You will need to refocus if you move your tripod.)

Now, take the picture again. This time, listen to the shutter; that will let you know how long the exposure was. Always listen to the shutter, and over time, your ears will tell you when you've properly exposed a shot.

Taking your Third Night Photo

The second night photo required much more work than the first. Even so, it was just a test shot. We're just going to use the second shot to prepare for our third shot:

- **Check the composition**. Often, you're so concerned with the technical details of a photo that you overlook some aspect of the composition. Check the edges of the frame and make sure nothing important is cut off.

- **Check the focus**. Zoom all the way in on your preview and make sure that it's in focus. Because of the low light levels, focusing is notoriously difficult in the dark.

- **Make note of the shutter speed**. Preview your picture and view the shooting information. Make a mental note of the shutter speed and what that shutter sounded like.

- **Examine the histogram**. The histogram—not the preview—tells you whether the photo was properly exposed. The histogram should peak in the right 1/4th.

Not only can you not trust your camera's photo preview, but if the preview looks good, your picture is probably underexposed. If the picture looks as bright as daylight, then the exposure is correct. You'll darken it in post-processing, but your picture will have less noise than if you expose it less. The histogram should peak near the right. If the exposure is not in the right 1/4th of the histogram, you should use exposure

compensation to double the exposure for the next frame. If your shutter speed is already at 30 seconds, double your ISO.

Processing your Photo

This is a photography book, not a software book, so I don't dedicate too many words to post-processing. However, every night photo better than a snapshot requires some editing:

- Decrease the brightness so that it looks like a night photo.

- Adjust the white balance/color temperature so that lights appear as you expect them to.

- Straighten the picture. (It's really hard to level your camera in the dark).

- Convert your photo from raw to JPG so that you can share it.

The Difference 5.9 Seconds Makes

I already know what you're going to say:

- "I get bored waiting 30 seconds for a photo at ISO 100. I'll use ISO 3200 and my picture will be ready in a couple of seconds."

- "What's the point of over-exposing the pictures just to darken them on my computer? I'll just use autoexposure."

- "Why bother with a tripod? I'll just use high ISO and image stabilization and hand-hold the shot."

I know you're going to say these things, because I thought those same things when my night photography teacher, Lance Keimig (*www.thenightskye.com*), lectured me about using low ISO and long shutter speeds. In fact, it took me years to realize the error of my ways.

Figure 10-1 shows two unprocessed pictures of the Boston skyline just after sunset with their histograms (taken at Piers Park in East Boston).

The first was autoexposed at ISO 800 and 1/90th, while the second was manually exposed at ISO 100 and 6 seconds. At a glance, the first picture looks better—after all, the second picture looks too bright to have been taken at night. Also, counting the delayed shutter, the second picture took more than 1000 times longer and required a heavy tripod.

Remember, though, the preview lies: trust the histogram, and increase your exposure until it fills the right quarter. The third photo in Figure 10-1 shows the brighter of the two pictures after decreasing the exposure, removing sensor dust, and straightening the horizon; as you can see from the colorful sky, the raw file contained

To watch a video on **editing night photos,** scan the QR code or visit:

sdp.io/EditingNight

sufficient detail to properly expose the sky even though the histogram seemed to indicate that it was overexposed.

In post-processing, I adjusted the exposure of the two pictures so they were the same. Figure 10-2 shows an extreme close-up of the same two pictures after processing. The shorter exposure has more noise, less detail, and too much contrast. The longer exposure has a smooth sky and the lighting better shows the

Figure 10-1: A night photo that seems to be exposed properly (f/4, 1/90th, ISO 800), one that is actually exposed properly (f/8, 6 seconds, ISO 100), and the final result after processing.

round form of the two buildings. The longer exposure has so much more detail that you can see an extra row of windows on the taller building. While either might look good on your Facebook page, only the second picture would look good printed or even just full screen on your computer. Professionally, every stock agency would reject the first picture, while the second was not only accepted by stock photo agencies, but is selling well commercially.

> **Tip:** As long as you're using a tripod, turn off image stabilization to save battery power during those long exposures. For some lenses, image stabilization actually introduces shakiness while your camera is on a tripod.

For more information about using histograms and understanding noise and ISO, refer to Chapter 4, "Controlling Your Camera."

Figure 10-2: High ISO and underexposure lead to high contrast and noise. Low ISO and a higher exposure reduce noise and contrast.

HAND-HOLDING

When you simply can't use a tripod and make a long exposure, you might be able to hand-hold a decent shot. Just use these tips:

- Use image stabilization.
- Shoot with the smallest possible f/stop number, and choose a lens with a maximum aperture of f/1.8 or f/2.8.
- Use a high ISO.
- Use continuous shooting and take lots of shots.

URBAN NIGHT PHOTOGRAPHY

Because there is so much artificial light in a city, urban night photography is much less technically challenging than rural night photography. Cities still pose several challenges, however:

- **Artificial light**. Because different lights have different color temperatures, you'll always get an odd array of colors that your eyes didn't notice. Usually, the colors of the artificial lights are very warm, so pushing the overall color balance to the cool side will help. However, fluorescent lights are a bit green, and LEDs are quite blue. There won't be one white balance that will work for every light in a picture, so you'll have to pick the one that looks the best overall.

- **Movement**. Cities are filled with movement, including cars, trains, people, and sometimes boats. With a long shutter speed, cars become white and red stripes, for their headlights and taillights. People become ghost-like blurs. Trees and grass become ethereal, as shown in Figure 10-3. This movement can be beautiful, but it needs to be deliberate. The shutter speeds you need vary depending on the speed of the movement, so experiment with different shutter speeds to find the most attractive effect. Pictures of boats in water never work; they just appear blurry.

- **Dynamic range**. Cities are mostly shadows with spots of bright lights. If you expose to capture the bright lights, the shadows will be dark and noisy. If you expose to capture the detail of the shadows, the lights will be overexposed. It's usually best to overexpose the lights. If you shoot in raw, you can often recover the blown-out highlights. Another way to better capture the highlights and shadows is to bracket your shots and combine them in post-processing using HDR techniques, as described in Chapter 11, "HDR."

- **Skies**. At night, clear skies appear dark. While a star or two might be bright enough to appear in your photo, generally, the city lights will wash them out. After the sun sets, cloudy skies are more interesting because they reflect the city lights and add texture to what would otherwise be a black sky. The light reflected back to the ground also helps to reduce the dynamic range of the picture.

- **Water**. Water is prettiest when it's still, because the surface of the water reflects light. Unfortunately, moving water just appears blurry with long exposures. When shooting ponds, lakes, and rivers, try to choose nights with no wind. Oceans never stop moving, but the waves against the shoreline take on a pleasant, feathery appearance.

For best results, shoot at twilight, known as "the blue hour." As the sun touches the horizon, street lights automatically turn on, and people flip on their office and home lights. It's these lights that give the city a night-time feel. For ten or fifteen minutes while the sun sets, you'll have the best lighting: the sky will be bright enough to show some texture, the sunlight will fill in the shadows just a bit, and most of the city lights will be on.

To watch a video on **photographing a city at night,** scan the QR code or visit:

sdp.io/NightCity

RURAL NIGHT PHOTOGRAPHY

Night photography is easiest in urban areas with street lights. As you move away from artificial lights, especially on moonless nights, you'll discover new challenges that come along with working in near-darkness. The sections that follow describe how to cope with these challenges.

TIMERS/REMOTE SHUTTER RELEASE

For reasons I can't explain, most cameras don't allow you to pick a shutter speed longer than 30 seconds. That's generally fine for photographing cities at night, even at ISO 100. Venture into the wilderness, especially on a night with no moon, and you often need shutter speeds of 3-5 minutes to properly expose a picture.

Most cameras include a Bulb mode that keeps the shutter open as long as you keep your finger on the button. So, you could hold your finger on the shutter and watch the clock until five minutes have passed—except that you'll certainly shake the camera and you just might pass out from boredom.

Figure 10-3: Leaves become blurry with long exposures (45mm, f/7.1, 30 sec, ISO 200).

To watch a video on **remote shutter timers,** scan the QR code or visit:

sdp.io/ShutterTimer

A better option is to get a remote shutter release that includes a timer. *Amazon.com* and *ebay.com* sell "timer remote control" devices for specific models of Canon and Nikon cameras for less than $30—don't spend more to buy a name-brand model. They'll allow you to specify any shutter speed while your camera is in Bulb mode, so you can keep your shutter open for several minutes. You can also set up your remote shutter release to take pictures on a regular basis—for example, one picture every five minutes so that you can create a time-lapse video from a series of pictures of a plant growing or the light changing.

Remote timers only control your shutter speed when your camera is in Bulb mode. If your camera is in any other mode, the settings on the camera determine the shutter speed, but you can still use the remote timer to trigger the camera.

> Tip: For many Canon cameras, you can install the Magic Lantern Firmware on your camera to add support for longer shutter speeds. Use it at your own risk, however, because it is not supported by Canon, and frankly, it can be a bit flakey. For more information, visit *magiclantern.wikia.com/.*

Using Bulb mode and a remote timer overrides your camera's autoexposure system. Without autoexposure, experimentation is the easiest way to determine how long to keep the shutter open. Attach your remote timer, set your camera to Bulb mode, set your ISO to 100, and take a shot at 30 seconds, and if the histogram shows all the data in the left half, then adjust your timer to take another shot at two minutes—two stops longer. Use the timer to quadruple the shutter speed again until most of the data is in the right half of the histogram.

FOCUSING IN THE DARK

It's difficult or impossible to focus on dark subjects with very little contrast. Nonetheless, autofocusing is almost always better than manually focusing. Here are three techniques you can try to autofocus your camera in the dark. Unfortunately, they only work when focusing on nearby subjects:

- Attach an external flash to your camera (even if you don't plan to use it). Many external flashes have infrared transmitters built in that the camera can shine on subjects to assist focusing.

- Illuminate your subject with a flashlight. Carry a powerful flashlight that allows focusing the beam. Use the brightest setting and the narrowest beam possible. Shine the flashlight on your subject, and then focus on the illuminated spot.

- Have someone stand near your subject and shine a flashlight at the base of your tripod. Then, focus on the flashlight. This technique requires two people, but you can use a low-powered flashlight.

If none of those techniques work, you can attempt to manually focus your camera. Typically, if it's so dark your camera can't autofocus, your eye won't work any better. Instead, you can use the focus distance markings on most lenses, and estimate the distance to your subject. The closer your subject, the more important it is for your estimate to be accurate. If you resort to estimating the focus distance, use a higher f/stop number to increase the depth-of-field, which allows your estimate to be less accurate.

STARS AND METEORS

Stars make an amazing backdrop. The darker the night and the clearer the sky, the better the stars will look. Here's how to get great pictures of stars:

- **Get away from the city**. Lights reflect off the atmosphere, causing the night sky to glow.

- **Shoot well after the sun has set**. Even after the sun has disappeared below the horizon, it will light the night sky.

- **Shoot before the moon rises**. The moon reflects sunlight. Even bounced off the moon, that light is bright enough to illuminate the Earth and obscure the stars. Check the moon rise and set times for your area, and plan your shoot for when the moon's on the other side of the Earth.

- **Choose a clear, cold night**. Just as a hazy sky obscures the horizon, it will blur bright stars and completely hide dim stars. Day or night, lower humidity creates sharper pictures of faraway subjects.

- **Shoot towards the dark part of the sky**. Even on a night with no moon, parts of the horizon will be brightly illuminated. When you shoot with a long enough exposure to capture the stars, those parts of the sky will appear very bright.

- **Get closer to the stars**. The higher you are, the less the atmosphere will obscure the starlight. The next time you're on top of a mountain, spend the night—and bring a tripod.

While stars are quite good at holding still for long exposures, the earth is spinning quite fast. Just like shooting from a moving car, long exposures cause everything to be blurred. Star trails (as shown on the chapter cover) can be beautiful, and many people do them intentionally to amazing effect.

To minimize star trails, keep your shutter speed at 30 seconds or less. Depending on the direction you're facing, you still might see visible star trails at 30 seconds—or you might be able to get away with a shutter speed up to a minute.

You can also deliberately create star trails using one of two different techniques:

To watch a video on **star trails**, scan the QR code or visit:

sdp.io/StarTrails

- **One long exposure**. Choose a low ISO setting (such as ISO 200), a moderate f-stop number (such as f/5.6 or f/8), set your camera to Bulb mode, and use a remote timer to set a shutter speed of ten minutes or more. The exact settings will take some experimentation, because the brightness of the sky and stars can vary. This approach doesn't require post-processing, but non-moving lights (such as the glow near the horizon) will be brighter than the stars (as shown in Figure 10-4). Additionally, depending on your camera, noise can be amplified with very long exposures.

- **Image stacking (the preferred method)**. Use a timer to take a series of thirty-second photos, and then combine them using an image stacking tool. For example, to create one hour exposure, you would take 120 thirty-second photos. Image stacking provides a darker sky and brighter stars. Image stacking can also automatically align pictures, fixing problems created by a tripod that moves slightly (something that is almost impossible to avoid over long periods of time).

Either approach requires a remote timer and manually focusing your lens. If you can't see the stars well enough to manually focus, focus near the infinity marking on your lens, take test shots with a high ISO (so you don't have to wait as long), and refocus until the stars are sharp.

If you choose to use image stacking, set your camera to Manual mode with a shutter speed of 30 seconds, an ISO of 400, and an aperture of f/5.6. Experiment to determine the correct ISO and aperture settings to properly expose the stars with a 30-second shutter speed; if your first picture is too dark, decrease the f/stop number or double the ISO, and try again. Set your camera to continuous shooting, so that it will continue to take pictures as long as the shutter is held down. Then, use your remote timer to lock the shutter open (which simulates you holding down the shutter button). Your camera will continue to take pictures every 30 seconds until you stop it, it runs out of batteries, or it fills the memory card.

There are many different ways to perform image stacking. You can do it natively in Photoshop, manually using layers, or with the Stack-a-Matic script (*sdp.io/stackamatic*), or by using stand-alone applications such as StarStaX (*www.starstax.net*), Image Stacker (*sdp.io/istacker*), or StarTrails (*startrails.de*). Star Tracer (*sdp.io/tracer*) can even fill in gaps in your star trails created by delays taking the next picture (for example, if you need to change the battery) and can lengthen star trails, allowing you to pretend you spent hours out in the dark, rather than just a few minutes.

Whichever approach you choose, plan to wait for hours while the software processes your pictures. The more pictures and the larger the files, the longer the processing will take. If the script or application outputs a file with each image in a separate layer (as the Stack-a-Matric script can), merge the layers before saving it—otherwise your file might take several gigabytes of space.

When you're done, you'll have several straight, dashed lines through your picture created by the blinking lights on airplanes. Airlines can be very inflexible about rerouting their flights around your pictures, so your best bet is to remove the lines in post-processing. It's more easily done with image stacking, since the airplane would only appear in one or two frames.

Battery life is also a problem, especially on cold nights. If you use image stacking, bring an extra fully charged battery, and swap it out as quickly as possible when the battery begins to run low. The time it takes you to swap the battery still might leave a tiny gap in your star trails. To extend your battery life, you could invest in a battery grip that stores two batteries.

Check your lens for moisture every 20-30 minutes, and use a lens cloth to dry off your lens' front element. It gets dewy and cold at night, and the condensation is unavoidable. This is another good reason to use image stacking; when you clean the lens, you'll no doubt move the camera slightly. Image stacking software can automatically adjust for the alignment change.

You can help reduce moisture by storing your camera in a sealed plastic bag or the trunk of your car and allowing it to gradually acclimate to the temperature before you begin taking your pictures and after you bring your camera back inside. Using a lens hood helps, too. The most reliable technique is to attach one or two disposable hand warmers to your lens with a rubber band.

You should also monitor the sky for clouds. If clouds roll in, no matter how whispy they are, they will ruin your star trails. With image stacking, simply release the remote shutter and stack the images that were not ruined by clouds.

To create really exciting star trail pictures, choose a perspective with something interesting in the foreground, such as a building, a tree, or a rock formation, and shoot wide-angle to show enough stars. If it is not naturally lit, use light painting techniques (described later in this chapter) to illuminate it. You only need to illuminate it for a moment for the light to be added to your final picture.

Star trails move in a circular pattern revolving around the North Star (if you're in the Northern Hemisphere), as shown on the chapter cover, or the Southern Celestial Pole. Actually, you're on the Earth, and the Earth is spinning on its

North/South axis, so if you're looking up at the relatively motionless stars near either axis, you'll see them appear to be rotating around the axis point. If you're not pointed at your hemisphere's pole, stars trails will be slightly curved lines, as shown in Figure 10-4.

In the Northern Hemisphere, you can find the North Star by finding the big dipper. The two stars at the end of the big dipper's scoop (the two stars farthest from the handle) are called the "pointer stars" because they point to the North Star. Unfortunately, there's no star at the right location that you can use in the Southern Hemisphere. You'll just have to find south using a compass and experiment with long exposures to align your picture.

As with all night photography, shooting stars requires some post-processing. You'll probably need to bring the black point up to hide noise and distracting light. You should also pull the color temperature towards the cool end of the spectrum to better show the different colors stars give off.

THE MOON

First, if you've seen some awesome landscape with the moon huge in the sky, let me tell you the bad news: it's fake. Pictures with the moon

To watch a video about **photographing the moon,** scan the QR code or visit:

sdp.io/Moon

prominent in the sky are always compositions (known as comps). Someone takes two shots: a night shot with a wide-angle lens, and a shot of the moon with a super-telephoto lens. Then, they blend them together in photo-editing software.

To get a decent picture of the moon, use the biggest telephoto lens you have. Use manual mode, and start at 1/125th, ISO 100, and f/5.6. Adjust the shutter speed as needed so the moon is bright but not overexposed. You'll have to take dozens of shots to get a good one, because even on a tripod, it's difficult to hold the camera steady when it's pointed at the sky.

For the ultimate in detail, use RegiStax to combine dozens or hundreds of pictures of the moon. For detailed information, watch the video on this page.

FIREWORKS

Fireworks are often people's introduction to night photography. I wouldn't recommend you start with fireworks, though, because

Figure 10-4: A single 30-second exposure.

To watch a video about **fireworks,** scan the QR code or visit:

sdp.io/Fireworks

shooting fireworks is much more technically challenging than just about any other type of night photography: they're difficult to focus on, they're constantly moving, the lighting conditions are extreme and dynamic, you don't have time to review your pictures and re-shoot, there's a crowd of screaming people around you, and you're probably drunk. Or maybe that's just me.

There are two different techniques for photographing fireworks. The first produces the best results by using a remote shutter release to lock the shutter open. After you shoot, however, you'll want to combine multiple shots together using your computer. The second technique is the classic approach photographers used when they shot film, which doesn't require post-processing.

WITH A REMOTE SHUTTER RELEASE

My favorite technique is to set my camera for a 5-second exposure and continuous shooting and then simply lock the shutter open for the entire show. After I unload the pictures into my computer, I can layer the best shots on top of each other to recreate how I remember the show. To take pictures of fireworks using a remote shutter release, follow these steps:

1. Attach a wide-angle lens to your camera. I like to work at 24mm. It's better to be too wide-angle than to cut off part of the explosion; you can always crop later.

2. Attach your camera to a tripod. If people are standing, you might need a tripod that is tall enough to hold the camera over people's heads.

3. Set your camera to Manual mode, ISO 200, f/5.6, with a 5-second shutter speed. Shoot raw image files, so you can adjust the exposure on your computer. Turn your flash off.

4. When the first fireworks go off, quickly attempt to autofocus on the fireworks while they're bright. Then, switch your lens to manual focus. If you can't autofocus on the fireworks, switch your lens to manual focus and adjust the focus to infinity.

5. Use your remote shutter release to lock your shutter open.

6. After a few pictures, release the shutter and check the histogram for the last couple of pictures and make sure it's not overexposed. If it is, lower the ISO to ISO 100, increase the f/stop number to f/8, or both.

7. Restart the timer, sit back, and enjoy the show. When it's done, stop the timer.

Figure 10-5: For best results, photograph individual fireworks and combine them on your computer.

This technique does a nice job of capturing individual fireworks. To illustrate the entire fireworks show, combine the prettiest fireworks into a single picture (as demonstrated by Figure 10-5). In Photoshop, you can do this by adding different fireworks pictures as layers and setting the layer blending options to Screen. Then, move the layers around so the fireworks don't overlap too much.

WITHOUT A REMOTE SHUTTER RELEASE

If you don't have a remote shutter release, or if you're a purist who prefers not to use photo-editing software, you can photograph fireworks by taking long, 30-second exposures that capture multiple explosions. However, because the explosions tend to happen at the same spot, they won't appear like you remember them—they'll be overlapping. To take pictures using this technique, follow the steps in the previous section. However, you will not need a remote shutter release and you will choose a 30 second shutter speed.

When the fireworks start, cover your lens (for example, with a hat) and press the shutter button. It will stay open for 30 seconds, during which time you won't be able to see through the viewfinder. Just as fireworks explode, uncover the lens. Recover the lens as an explosion starts to fade to avoid capturing too much of the smoke. Uncover the lens with each explosion.

Whichever technique you choose, you won't get good

pictures out of the grand finale, because firing fireworks off too quickly in the same spot creates a great deal of smoke. Subsequent fireworks illuminate that smoke, making your picture appear blurry.

INCLUDING PEOPLE

Night photography requires long exposures that blur movement. This gives you three options for including people in your pictures:

- **Light them up**. You can combine flash with a long exposure—simply turn your flash on. After the flash fires, have the

Figure 10-6: Hold still for half of a long exposure, and you will appear translucent (top: 50mm, f/4, 2.5 minutes, ISO 400; bottom: 24mm, f/4, 30 seconds, ISO 800).

subjects continue to hold still to allow the camera to properly expose the background, as shown in Figure 10-7. If the subject is in front of a completely black background, she can move out of the way after the flash fires. As a less-precise alternative, have the subject hold still and use a flashlight to light the subject during the exposure.

- **Hold very still**. In Figure 10-8, the photographer and a very accommodating model held perfectly still for the entire 30-second exposure. This allowed the subject to be properly exposed using only ambient light, and also exposed the starry sky. You'll never get sharp results, however—people need to breathe.

- **Move them.** With long exposures, people can move through the frame and not appear in the picture at all. Try this: set your camera for a 30-second exposure. Halfway through, step into the frame and hold still until you hear the shutter close. The picture will show you 50% transparent, as if you shot a double exposure. Allowing people to move slowly during a long exposure can give your pictures an ethereal look, as if a ghost were moving through the frame. If you look closely at the top picture in Figure 10-6, you'll see the author appears twice and is semi-transparent because he moved halfway through the shot with only ambient lights. The bottom picture in Figure 10-6 is a single 30-second exposure in which the author moved to three different places and was illuminated with a flashlight at each spot, creating the illusion of three different people.

LIGHT PAINTING

Light painting is manually adding light to a long exposure. During a long exposure (say, 30 seconds), you can walk through the frame without appearing in the final picture. This gives you the opportunity to walk around a picture and selectively add light wherever you'd like it. To help hide your movements, wear all black.

At its simplest, you might use light painting like a portrait photographer uses strobes—to improve the ambient light by filling in

Figure 10-7: Combine flash with a long exposure to illuminate people while showing the background (35mm, f/8, 1.3 sec., ISO 800).

Figure 10-8: If you don't light subjects in a long exposure, they will look blurry (24mm, f/4, 30 sec., ISO 3200).

shadows. However, light painting is also a rapidly developing art form where people create amazing pictures using night landscapes and complex, custom-build light contraptions. Though he wasn't the first light painter, Pablo Picasso showed the world light painting in 1949 when a *Life* magazine photographer Gjon Mili visited him; Picasso had been inspired when Mili showed him his photos of ice skaters with lights attached to their skates, jumping in darkness.

USING FLASHLIGHTS TO ADD LIGHT TO A SCENE

During a long exposure, you have time to trigger your camera's shutter and then run into the scene and fill in shadows with a flash or flashlight. This is the greatest part of night photography: long exposures allow you to change the lighting with a simple flashlight. During the day, adding light to a scene would require multiple flashes, light modifiers,

To watch a video on **light painting**, scan the QR code or visit:

sdp.io/LightPainting

light stands, and remote triggers. At night, a $10 flashlight can create the same effect as thousands of dollars of studio lighting equipment.

Figure 10-9 shows a picture of the whale tale fountain in New London, CT. After I took the first picture, I realized that the shape of the whale tale was lost against the black background of the sky. For the second picture, I used my LED flashlight to paint light onto the edges of the fountain, separating it from the background. Because the flashlight uses LEDs, the light appeared as a cool blue color compared to the warmer light cast by the streetlights.

You don't have to stand behind your camera while light painting. While you should stay out of the frame whenever possible, feel free to move in close to your subject while your shutter is open—when you hear the shutter click closed, you'll know your work is done. You can step into the frame to do your light painting, but if you don't want to appear in the picture, wear dark clothes, change places regularly, and avoid pointing the flashlight toward the camera.

To add just a little light to a scene, briefly wave your flashlight across it. To add more light, simply illuminate an area for longer during the exposure. It's more art than science; the amount of light you add to the scene varies depending on the brightness of your flashlight, your distance from the subject, the ambient light, and your aperture and ISO settings. It always requires a bit of trial-and-error to get right.

Note that flashlights tend to be different colors, and those colors will show up in your picture. Incandescent flashlights appear very orange, while newer LED flashlights appear very blue.

Figure 10-9: During a long exposure, use a flashlight to fill in shadows (20mm, f/8, 30 sec., ISO 100).

If you want to deliberately add color to the scene, you can buy a flashlight with colored LEDs, or you can hold colored gels over your flashlight.

To add even more light or to freeze the motion of a moving subject (such as a person), use an external flash. It doesn't need to be connected to the camera in any way; simply walk to where you want the light to come from, point it at your subject, and hit the test button to trigger the flash. To add more light, walk closer to the

Figure 10-10: Wear dark clothes and move fast to avoid appearing in the picture (58mm, f/4, 30 sec., ISO 100).

subject or fire the flash multiple times. You can also move to different locations during a single exposure to add light that seems to come from multiple sources. Bring extra batteries!

While flashes are powerful, flashlights offer much better control. If light painting was painting with ink, a flashlight would be delicate strokes with a fine brush and a flash would be throwing a bucket of paint on your subject.

USING FLASHLIGHTS POINTED AT THE CAMERA

You can draw in a long exposure by pointing a flashlight directly at the camera. For best results, turn the flashlight on by partially depressing the button just as you begin your stroke and move the flashlight constantly and smoothly. Faster strokes create thin lines, while slower strokes create thicker lines. Painting in three dimensions takes some practice; even the most accomplished artist will need to review her work and re-draw it several times over. Because the artist must be in the frame to paint the subject, it's important that she wear dark clothes and moves constantly.

As you can see in Figure 10-10, the street light caused the artist's moving (but ghostly) shape to appear while she drew the waving girl. The artist moved faster in the picture with the hearts, which used a flash to freeze the model's motion.

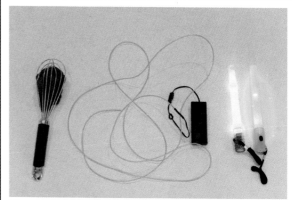

Figure 10-11: Steel wool in a whisk, glow wire, and glow sticks.

The best flashlights are small, have a high maximum brightness (look for 200 lumens), a variable brightness so you can turn it down when you don't need as much light, and a momentary-on button that you can easily turn on and off without fully clicking the button. The favorite of many light painters, including myself, is the LED Lenser P7, which you can pick up for about $35. You can certainly find cheaper flashlights that will get the job done.

CREATIVE LIGHT PAINTING TOOLS

While flashlights are the most basic tools, anything that gives off light can become a light painting brush. The sections that follow describe some common tools that the light painting community has discovered (shown in Figure 10-11), and different ways to use them. Don't limit yourself to these, though—much of the fun of light painting is experimentation. Some other tools to try include:

- A flashlight pointed into a jar of marbles, and then pointed at the camera
- A tablet computer displaying simple shapes, such as a red heart

- A smart phone with an application that changes the screen color
- Christmas lights taped to a pole or hula-hoop
- Fireflies in a jar

GLOW WIRE

As the name suggests, glow wire (also known as "electroluminescent wire" or just "el wire") is a long glowing wire. Glow wire is available in many different colors and lengths. It's inexpensive, and easiest to find on eBay. Glow wire creates a delicate, but even, light.

Swing and shake the wire through the frame to create the effect of gentle waves or fog (if your wire is blue, as shown in Figure 10-12) or soft flames (if your wire is orange or red). Using two people, have one hold either end of the wire and walk through the frame, waving it gently.

You can also tape glow wire to a pole to create straight lines or flat walls of light. Tape it around the circumference of something round like a hula hoop, and spin it to create a glowing sphere. Use it in strobe (or flashing) mode while moving it to create dashed lines.

Figure 10-12: We used glow wire to create the blue light in the foreground and flashlights to illuminate the building (22mm, f/5.6, 5 minutes, ISO 400).

STEEL WOOL

If you're considering using a sparkler in your light painting, use steel wool instead. Fine steel wool throws bright, hot, orange sparks in all directions, creating the effect of a bursting volcano.

When you light steel wool (which is most easily done with a normal lighter), you're going to be throwing burning sparks everywhere. So, don't light steel wool near anything that might catch fire. You need to protect yourself from fire, too. Wear non-flammable clothing that covers your arms, legs, hands, and feet. Cover your face, and wear goggles. Wear a hood to protect your head. To hide yourself from the picture, wear black. If you're doing it right, you'll look like a ninja. Keep a fire extinguisher nearby, and wait around at least ten minutes after you're done burning the steel wool to make sure none of the sparks start a fire.

Use a wisk to hold the steel wool while still allowing it to breathe and throw sparks. The looser you pack it, the faster it will burn. Always use 0, 00, 000, or 0000. There's not much difference between them, but don't use 1 or higher—they don't burn very well.

To get the spinning effect shown in Figure 10-13, tie the whisk to a non-flammable cord and carefully spin it. The spinning causes the sparks to fly even further than normal, so use extra caution. Always have a second person nearby ready to extinguish any sparks.

GLOW STICKS

You can use inexpensive glow sticks to simulate fire in a picture, as shown in Figure 10-14. To get the fire effect, hold the glow stick vertically, but loosely, in your hand. Move the glow stick up and down, wiggling it slightly. Move it only very slightly to the side; any sweeping motions will look odd on camera. For Figure 10-14, I moved the glow stick around the model's arms and legs.

For best results, move the glow stick over the same area multiple times. For Figure 10-14, I needed a full two minutes of continuously moving the glow stick to create a reasonable fire affect; shorter shutter speeds left too many gaps between the virtual flames.

Figure 10-13: Steel wool in a whisk, tied to a cord, and spun (19mm, f/5.6, 2 minutes, ISO 400).

FOG AND LASERS

Light only shows up on camera when it is pointed directly at the camera or when it reflects off a subject. Lasers only show up when they're either pointed directly at the camera or when they reflect off something. If you want lasers to reflect off the air, use a fog machine. Fog machines turn fog juice into a thick fog. Used alone, fog machines will fill up a room from floor to ceiling. If you want low-lying fog (like the fog you might imagine in a spooky cemetery), you will need to combine your fog machine with a chiller. The chiller routes the fog through ice, cooling it so that it sinks below warmer air. The warmer the air, the better the fog will sink.

Dry ice creates a thick, low-lying fog and does not require power, making it more portable. Smoke bombs don't work well; they give off very little smoke, and the smoke dissipates so quickly that it's difficult to photograph.

 Take a quiz!

sdp.io/Quiz10

PRACTICE

This chapter's practices help you learn to use your camera at night and to understand different lighting scenarios. Also complete the practices at the beginning of the chapter.

- Wait for a moonless night with a clear sky. Go someplace dark, away from street lights. Bring your tripod and a remote timer. Then, practice photographing stars:

  - Take a single 15-minute exposure. Then, take 30, 30-second exposures. At home, use image-stacking software to combine the 30-second exposures. Which picture turned out better?

  - Point your camera to the south, and photograph the stars for 5 minutes. Repeat with your camera facing east and north. How do the stars look different? Which direction had the most light near the horizon?

  - Take pictures of the stars at 10 seconds, 30 seconds, 2 minutes, and 10 minutes. Familiarize yourself with the length of the star trails.

- The next time your town has fireworks, photograph them. At home, create a comp of your favorite shots.

- Photograph a city's skyline at night.

- At night, set your camera to manual mode, ISO 100, f/5.6, and 30 seconds. Press the shutter button, then run in front of the camera and try drawing a person with a flashlight. Next, try writing your name—you'll need to write backwards.

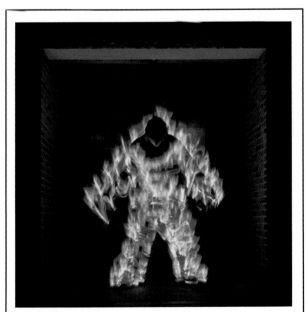

Figure 10-14: A red glow stick used to simulate fire (35mm, f/5.6, 2 minutes, ISO 200).

While most photographic techniques were originally developed using film cameras, High Dynamic Range (HDR) photography is a relatively new technique that is only possible with digital cameras and powerful software. While many people think of HDR as a way to create dramatic and artistic pictures, HDR is primarily a practical way to overcome the limitations of modern digital cameras.

HDR overcomes several photographic challenges:

- **Blown-out skies**. Normally, you can only get outdoor pictures with nicely exposed skies during the golden hours. HDR gives you perfectly exposed skies in any conditions. You can even turn a boring, overcast sky into dramatic storm clouds.

- **High contrast**. Your eyes (and brain) are great at adjusting to contrasty lighting. If you look out a window on a sunny day, you can easily see both your indoor surroundings and the outside world, even when the outside world is more than 100 times brighter. With a single photo, you could only see one or the other—if an indoor photo included a window, the window would be blown-out. With HDR, you can capture both in separate photos and process them into a single picture.

- **Noisy shadows**. Even with a professional camera at ISO 100, shadow areas show a great deal of noise. HDR exposes shadow areas as highlights in your camera, and then adjusts them in post-processing to look like shadows again—but without the noise.

HDR also provides an artistic opportunity. HDR tone-mapping accentuates the contrast in a picture, allowing you to create striking and dramatic interpretations of the original scene. Tone-mapping is a feature of HDR software that adjusts the bright and dark areas of one or more pictures to either show a greater dynamic range in a single image or to accentuate the differences between shadows and highlights.

HDR OVERVIEW

At a high level, the process of creating an HDR picture follows these steps:

1. Set your camera to aperture priority.

2. Take an autoexposed photo.

3. Take an underexposed photo by decreasing the shutter speed while keeping the aperture and ISO the same.

4. Take an overexposed photo by increasing the shutter speed while keeping the aperture and ISO the same.

5. Copy the photos to your computer.

6. Use HDR software to combine the autoexposed, underexposed, and overexposed photos into a single picture.

Figure 11-1 shows a severely backlit steam engine scene that had too much contrast to photograph normally. I took these three photos at different exposures, and then used HDR software, Photomatix Pro, to blend them into two different HDR pictures: one providing a realistic representation of what I saw (middle), and one providing a more artistic rendition (bottom).

Because of the bright lights, night photography in cities is exceptionally difficult to properly expose. Figure 11-2 shows the Brooklyn Bridge at night (taken at Dumbo Park). The first photo is two stops underexposed, leaving the brighter sky properly exposed, but completely hiding all shadow detail. I used the camera's automatic exposure for the second photo, which left the sky too bright and the bridge too dark. The third photo is two stops overexposed, showing shadow details in the bridge, but overexposing the sky and lights.

I then merged the images using Photomatix Pro, which combined the properly exposed elements of each of the photos. As I did with the train picture, I processed the photos in two ways: one showing a more realistic version of

Figure 11-1: Use HDR to combine photos with different exposures to capture highlights and shadows.

Figure 11-2: Three photos taken at different exposures and combined realistically and artistically.

To watch a video on **HDR,** scan the QR code or visit:

sdp.io/HDR

the scene than my camera could capture with a single photo (center), and one showing an artistic, dramatic version of the scene (bottom).

Besides more accurately representing what my eyes saw in the scene, the HDR pictures have far less noise in the shadows.

> **Tip:** HDR processing is notoriously bad with water. If you don't like the effect HDR processing has on part of your picture, open up both the original photo and the HDR picture in Photoshop. Then, layer parts of the original photo over the HDR picture.

Because HDR and tone-mapping emphasize contrast, they're a great way to emphasize spookiness or grittiness in a scene. Tone-mapping exaggerates contrast, so cracks, rust, and rot are highlighted. I took Figure 11-3 in an abandoned facility that really was spooky—I

couldn't wait to get out of there—but before HDR processing and tone-mapping, the pictures didn't capture the decay and absolute grossness of the bathroom.

THE HDR PROCESS

When creating HDR pictures, you'll need to take several photos at different exposures by varying the shutter speed only. Fortunately, cameras have a feature called *bracketing* that automates the process of taking pictures at different exposures. Bracketing has its roots in film; because film photographers couldn't know if they properly exposed a shot until they developed it, they would take a series of shots at different exposures just to be sure one was correct. With film, you bracket and then pick a single photo from the group. With HDR, you bracket, and then combine the best parts of each photo into a single picture.

Your pictures will always turn out sharper if you're using a tripod. However, it is possible to hand-hold HDR pictures during the day, provided you use bracketing and hold the camera steady throughout all the shots.

DETERMINING THE NUMBER OF EXPOSURES

The goal of bracketing is to capture the entire dynamic range in a scene. Often, you don't need HDR at all, and a single picture can capture the entire dynamic range. To determine whether you need HDR, take a picture and look at the histogram. Figure 11-4 shows four

Figure 11-3: Use HDR to emphasize grittiness.

histograms. If you took the picture with the first histogram, you shouldn't bother bracketing for HDR, because the scene was well-exposed with a single shot. Bracketing would be a waste of time and storage.

The second histogram shows detail in the shadow area (the left half of the histogram), while other parts of the scene are overexposed, as shown by the graph pushed against the right side of the histogram. Yet, the picture is not overexposed, because there is detail in the left half of the histogram. Here, bracketing and HDR processing would allow you to capture details in the overexposed parts of the picture without losing important details in the shadow area.

The third histogram has a significant amount of data in the left quarter of the histogram, meaning much of the photo would be lost in noisy shadows. Yet, the picture is not underexposed, because there is detail in the right quarter of the histogram. Therefore, bracketing and HDR processing would bring out the details in the shadows without overexposing the rest of the picture.

To watch a video on **manually blending multiple exposures,** scan the QR code or visit:

sdp.io/ManualHDR

The last histogram is typical of an outdoor photo where the sun is behind the subject. The sky is overexposed, as shown by the data pushed against the right side of the histogram. Yet, the subject is underexposed, as shown by the data pushed against the left side of the histogram. Bracketing and HDR processing would allow you to properly expose both the highlights and shadows in separate photos.

Refer to your camera's manual for instructions on how to enable bracketing. Typically, I set up bracketing to take three photos: -2 (two stops underexposed), 0 (properly exposed), and +2 (2 stops overexposed). Then, I examine the histogram for the underexposed and overexposed pictures. If the underexposed picture contains data in the left quarter of the histogram, or if the overexposed picture contains data pushed against the right side of the histogram, I re-shoot with five photos: -4, -2, 0, +2, and +4. If that still fails to capture the entire dynamic range, I might switch my camera to manual mode and take a few photos at +6 or -6—however, that is rarely necessary.

If your camera does not support bracketing, use exposure compensation to manually take three pictures: a properly exposed picture, a picture two-stops underexposed, and a picture two stops overexposed.

HOW TO PERFORM FIVE-STOP BRACKETING

Most newer cameras support bracketing with five shots. That's more than enough for most HDR scenes. Though the specific steps will vary for different camera models, follow these high level steps to create an HDR picture:

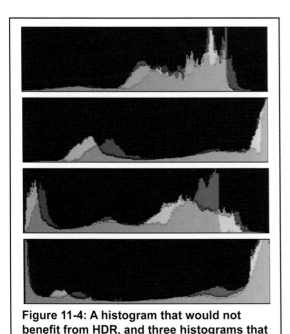

Figure 11-4: A histogram that would not benefit from HDR, and three histograms that would.

To watch a video on **dynamic range,** scan the QR code or visit:

sdp.io/DR

1. Mount your camera on a tripod and set it to aperture priority.

2. Enable bracketing for ±4 and ±2 stops, for a total of five frames.

3. Set your camera for continuous shooting.

4. Hold the shutter until your camera takes five photos: 0, -2, -4, +2, and +4.

If your camera only supports three-stop bracketing, you can still perform five-stop bracketing by taking two sets of three shots and manually adjusting the bracketing in-between:

1. Mount your camera on a tripod and set it to aperture priority.

2. Enable bracketing for ±2 stops, for a total of three frames. If you have a Fujifilm camera, you might be limited to ±1 stop.

3. Use exposure compensation to underexpose the scene by two stops. If you are bracketing ±1 stop, underexpose the scene by three stops.

4. Press the shutter until your camera takes three photos: 0, -2, and -4. If you are bracketing ±1 stop, your photos will be -1, -2, and -3.

5. Use exposure compensation to overexpose the scene by two stops.

6. Press the shutter until your camera takes three photos: 0, +2, and +4. If you are bracketing ±1 stop, your photos will be +1, +2, and +3.

If your camera supports only ±1 stop bracketing (including Fujifilm cameras) or if your camera does not support bracketing (including the Nikon D3100, D3200, and D3300), you can use exposure compensation to simulate bracketing. Take a normally exposed photo, then add -2 stops of exposure compensation and take a second photo. Then, add +2 stops of exposure

compensation and take a third photo. To perform 5-stop bracketing, repeat that process at -4 and +4 stops. If your camera doesn't support 4 stops of exposure compensation, use manual mode to specify the correct exposures.

Here's a trick that makes HDR photography easier on Canon cameras with live view: Enable live view mode and set the camera to a two-second delay. When you press the shutter, your camera will take all three shots without delay. This is especially useful when handholding HDR pictures, because you won't shake the camera while pressing or releasing the shutter.

If the scene has too much contrast to be captured with five frames, switch to manual mode, specify an ISO other than auto ISO, and manually adjust the shutter speed between frames.

Bracketing Challenges

Bracketing introduces its own challenges:

- You need more memory, because one shot requires 3-5 exposures (and sometimes more).

- Because you're trying to maximize dynamic range, should always shoot raw. This takes even more memory.

- You must plan your ISO and aperture so that your brightest exposure won't have an excessive shutter speed. If you're shooting three shots at 0, -2, and +2, and the camera autoexposes for $1/30^{th}$, the unexposed shot will be at $1/120^{th}$ and the overexposed shot will be at $1/8^{th}$. While $1/30^{th}$ might be fast enough to hand-hold the camera or to stop a slow-moving subject (like leaves on a tree or waves), shooting at $1/8^{th}$ can lead to camera shake and motion blur.

If you're shooting at night, most cameras are still limited to a maximum exposure of 30 seconds—even when bracketing. Therefore, if you need 30 seconds to expose the picture properly, you'll need to use bulb mode, along with a remote shutter with timer, to get the overexposed shots with exposures of 60-120 seconds. For more information, refer to Chapter 10, "Night Photography."

HDR SOFTWARE

While Lightroom and Photoshop provide support for combining photos into an HDR picture, they're not particularly flexible and often create flawed results. You'll find it faster and easier to use separate HDR software. While there are many different applications available, the three most common are:

- **Photomatix Pro** ($100, *sdp.io/photomatix*). The least user-friendly of the three tools, Photomatix Pro is my favorite because it works reliably and provides a great deal of control.
- **HDR Efex Pro** ($150, *sdp.io/efex*). More user-friendly than Photomatix Pro, HDR Efex Pro is fast and easy.
- **HDR Expose** ($120, *sdp.io/hdrexpose*). More expensive, and friendly, HDR tool.

Each is available as a free trial for both Windows and Mac, so try them all and pick your favorite. Any of them can produce similar results, so choose the one that you most enjoy using.

HDR PORTRAITS

If something is moving in a scene, it would be different in each of your bracketed photos, making the photos impossible to easily combine together. Unfortunately, this makes it difficult to use HDR in portraiture. To overcome this, some photographers create an HDR photograph of a background and then use Photoshop to overlay a person onto the HDR background.

To watch a video on **HDR photography for overcast skies,** scan the QR code or visit:

sdp.io/HDRovercastSky

Take a quiz!

sdp.io/Quiz11

PRACTICE

This chapter's practices help you understand your camera's dynamic range and HDR techniques.

- Photograph a still subject with dark shadows and bright highlights using HDR techniques. For example, you could take a picture of a building and include the sky. Process the picture with HDR so that both the highlights and the shadows are well exposed.
- Include part of the sun in an HDR picture. For example, photograph a building or tree with the setting sun peeking out behind it.
- Shoot a city street or skyline at night using HDR techniques. After completing the HDR processing, compare your HDR shot with the best single shot that you took. For more information about night photography, refer to Chapter 10, "Night Photography."
- Shoot a gritty scene using HDR techniques. For example, you might photograph an abandoned building, a subway station, a graffiti covered wall, or a rusted car. When you process the photos, use tone-mapping to bring out the details.
- Experiment with trial versions of Photomatix Pro, HDR Efex Pro, and HDR Expose to determine which you prefer. You might find that different tools work better for different types of photos.

Macro photography shows the most overlooked beauty around us: the tiny. With macro photography, you explore the unseen details that surround you like a child with her first magnifying glass. Macro photography is one of the few types of photography where the camera is able to see the world better than your own eyes.

Yet, macro photography is one of the more technically challenging disciplines. If you've ever tried to take a close-up picture of something, you probably discovered that the pictures came out blurry or that your camera wouldn't take a picture at all. That's what happens when you try to focus on a subject that's closer than your lens' minimum focusing distance. My favorite zoom lens won't focus closer than about 1.5 feet away when I'm zoomed all the way in. Telephoto lenses might not focus closer than 4-8 feet.

When you want to get closer, you'll need to learn about macro photography. No camera comes equipped for macro photography, even though many include the word "macro" in the description. You absolutely have to buy something. Fortunately, you don't have to spend more than $10 to get started.

This chapter covers macro photography equipment and technique. For information about photographing insects and other small animals, read this chapter first, and then read Chapter 8, "Animals."

UNDERSTANDING MINIMUM FOCUSING DISTANCE

Minimum focusing distance is typically expressed as the maximum magnification, which is baffling. Brace yourself for some math: maximum magnification is the ratio of the subject's physical size to the size of the image projected onto the digital sensor. If a lens' maximum magnification is 0.25, the size of the image projected from the lens onto the digital sensor is 0.25 times (¼) the size of the actual object. For a lens to be considered a true macro lens, it must have a maximum magnification of 1.0.

Here's what you should know: it's important to look at maximum magnification when considering a lens. Higher is better. 0.25 is pretty typical. True macro lenses are 1.0. Anything above 1.0 is going to look more like a microscope than a lens.

MACRO PHOTOGRAPHY EQUIPMENT

You can do macro photography in several different ways. In order from least to most expensive, your options are reversing rings, diopters, extension tubes, and macro lenses. Reversing rings, diopters, and extension tubes are only good for occasional use; if you're going to be taking a lot of close-up pictures, or if you hope to photograph moving subjects such as butterflies, you're going to need a true macro lens.

REVERSING RINGS

Normally, a lens' job is to make objects appear smaller. For example, when you take a picture of your cat, your lens shrinks your cat down to the size of your digital camera sensor. If you turn the lens around, it does just the opposite—it takes tiny objects and makes their image much bigger, like a film projector. That's exactly what you need when you want to get closer than 1:1 magnification.

You can't simply flip your lens around and connect the front of your lens to your camera, however. You need to be able to securely connect the front of the lens to the camera, focus the image on the image sensor, and block any stray light. You can do this in two ways:

- **With a reverse lens adapter**. This technique uses a reversing ring (also known as a reverse mount adapter ring) to mount a lens backwards to your camera body. One side of the reversing ring connects to your lens' filter threads, while the other side connects to your camera mount. A reversing ring without electronics costs about $10. Be sure to match the filter thread size to the lens you plan to reverse, and choose either a Canon or Nikon mount to match your camera body.

- **With lens stacking**. This technique connects one lens normally to your camera body, and a second lens to the front of that lens, facing it. Reversing rings attach to the filters of two lenses and allow you to connect them so that they point directly at each other. Choose a reversing ring with filter sizes matching that of the two lenses you plan to use. For best results, at least one of the lenses should be a prime—preferably in the 50mm range.

With lens stacking, one of the lenses is connected directly to your camera. Therefore, you can control that lens' aperture using your camera body. That's important for increasing the depth of field in macro photography.

To choose a higher f/stop number when using a reverse lens adapter, follow the instructions in the section titled "Using Extension Tubes that don't have Electronics" later in this chapter. There are electronic reverse lens adapters that can give you control over your lens aperture. However, they cost about $500, and if you're spending that much you should buy a dedicated macro lens.

If you like using a reverse lens adapter but want easier control over the aperture, consider buying a vintage lens with manual aperture controls. Many 35mm lenses from the 1950s through the 1990s have an aperture ring on the lens itself that you operate mechanically, rather than electronically. If you only plan to use the lens reversed, you can choose any model of lens—Canon, Nikon, and Olympus lenses will fit any body type when reversed. I suggest searching for a 50mm f/1.8 or 50mm f/1.4 lens. Your best lens bargain might include a film camera with it.

Whichever approach you take, be careful not to damage the back of your lens (which will now be the front of your lens). Lenses aren't designed to protect this back element, and its electrical contacts will be exposed.

Figure 12-1: Diopters attach like filters and allow you to focus closer.

DIOPTERS

Diopters, as shown in Figure 12-1, are magnifying glasses that attach to the front of your lens like a filter. Screw them on, and suddenly you can focus much closer to a subject.

Diopters are available in different strengths, much like reading glasses. Typical strengths vary from +1 to +10. A +1 diopter focuses at one meter, a +4 diopter focuses at ¼ meter, and a +10 diopter focuses at 1/10th meter. Diopters will prevent you from focusing on more distant subjects—the stronger the diopter, the shorter your maximum focusing distance becomes. Therefore, you should always use the lowest-power diopter you can.

Typically, you'll want to buy several different diopters, start with the smallest, and work your way up to the diopter that gives you the focusing distance you need. Fortunately, diopters are cheap, and you can get a set of four for less than $20. Like any filter, you must buy diopters in the size that matches the front element of your lens. Most lenses have the filter size written on them near the front element, such as "⌀ 77mm," which indicates the lens requires a 77mm filter. The "⌀" is the diameter symbol.

EXTENSION TUBES

While diopters attach to the front of your lens, an extension tube attaches between the lens and the camera. Extension tubes are literally just empty tubes; they have no optical elements at all. They simply move your lens farther from the sensor, increasing the size of the image circle in the same way that moving a projector farther from the wall increases the image size. Figure 12-2 shows two extension tubes connected between a lens and a camera body.

Like diopters, extension tubes prevent you from focusing on subjects in the distance—the more extension you add, the shorter your maximum focusing distance becomes. Extension tubes also reduce light to the sensor, decreasing your shutter speed and making it more difficult to focus. My unscientific experiments show that each 36mm of extension cuts the light by about half—requiring you to double your shutter speed. Therefore, you should use the least amount of extension possible to get the focusing distance that you need. Because it is different for every lens, the best way to find the right length of extension tube is trial-and-error.

To allow for different extension lengths, extension tubes come in sets with different sizes that you can mix-and-match. You can buy two different types of extension tubes:

- **Without autofocus ($10-$15).** These extension tubes don't have wiring to carry electronic messages between the camera body and lens, which causes you to lose autofocus and aperture control. Losing autofocus isn't a problem for still-life macro photography, because you will usually manually focus anyway. Losing aperture control is a problem, however, because you frequently need to choose a

Figure 12-2: Extension tubes (such as the two in this picture) connect between the lens and camera, allowing you to focus closer.

high f/stop number to get the depth-of-field you need. There's a work-around described in the next section.

- **With autofocus ($60-$180)**. These extension tubes cost more, but they allow you to autofocus (which is important for moving subjects) and they give you complete control over your aperture. Don't waste your money on the more expensive Canon or Nikon tubes; those from Kenko are the best, but many users report success with the Vivitar, CowboyStudio, and Zeikos models. They're really just hollow tubes, and the build quality won't impact your image quality.

When using extension tubes, start with the smallest in the set and work your way up to the extension that gives you the focusing distance you need. You can stack multiple extension tubes as required. Extension tubes aren't as cheap as diopters, but you can get a set of three for about $170. Generic extension tubes work as well as name-brand extension tubes.

As an alternative to extension tubes, you can use macro bellows, which cost $40-$60 for cheaper versions without electronics, and around $900 for an expensive version with electronics and a focusing rail. Like extension tubes, bellows move the lens farther from the camera body, but bellows can be expanded or contracted to different lengths like an accordion. Bellows are bulkier, more expensive, and more difficult to work with than extension tubes. However, they expand farther than would be possible with a single set of extension tubes, allowing you to focus even closer.

Extension tubes and bellows will work with any lens. 50mm is ideal for still-life subjects. If you're photographing living insects, 100-150mm will give you a better working distance, allowing you to photograph them with less disturbance. If you enjoy bird photography, it's worth investing in a set of extension tubes that

support autofocus so that you can get closer to small birds. Even with a big, professional telephoto, you can't get close enough to fill the frame with a songbird unless you use extension tubes. The longer the focal length, the more extension you will need—in other words, you'll need more extension tubes to get maximum magnification with a telephoto lens.

If you choose to use a zoom lens, avoid zooming after you connect the extension tubes; it's confusing, because you'll be able to focus closer when you are zoomed out than zoomed in.

Though macro photography often requires you to use a lens' highest f/stop number, it's helpful to use extension tubes with a lens that has a very low minimum f/stop number, such as f/2.8 or f/1.8. The extra wide aperture lets more light in, making it easier to focus. You should also consider a lens' maximum f/stop number; f/32 allows for more depth-of-field than f/22.

USING EXTENSION TUBES THAT DON'T HAVE ELECTRONICS

If you choose less expensive extension tubes that don't support autofocus, it means they don't have the electrical connections to allow the camera body to communicate with the lens. The fact that you lose autofocus isn't a problem for still life photography; you can simply manually focus. However, you won't be able to set your aperture, which means the lens will always shoot wide open at your lens' lowest f/stop number.

As you might recall from Chapter 4, "Controlling Your Camera," two of the factors that contribute to a shallow depth-of-field are moving your camera closer to your subject and using a lower f/stop number. The whole point of macro photography is to move closer to your subject. With your lens locked at the lowest f/stop number, you will now have a very, very shallow depth-of-field (perhaps thinner than a hair) that might make your pictures more blurry than sharp.

There is a work-around that allows you to select a higher f/stop number:

1. Set your camera to aperture priority mode.

2. Select the f/stop number you want to use, such as f/11 or f/22.

3. Hold down the depth-of-field preview button. The viewfinder should become dim as the aperture ring in the lens closes down to your chosen f/stop.

4. While continuing to hold down the depth-of-field preview button, disconnect your lens. You can release the depth-of-field preview button.

5. Connect your extension tubes or bellows, and then reconnect the lens.

6. You'll notice that the viewfinder is still dim, because the aperture in the lens is still small. Manually focus and take your pictures using the higher f/stop number.

If you need to change the aperture setting, remove the extension tube or bellows and repeat the process. These steps work because the aperture is contained within the lens, and it opens and closes using power provided by the camera's battery. Normally, the aperture only becomes smaller when you take a picture; while you're focusing, it stays completely open, regardless of the f/stop you have selected. However, when you press the depth-of-field preview button, the aperture ring in the lens closes down to the f/stop you specify. By disconnecting the lens from the camera's battery power with the aperture selected, the aperture is locked in place until you reconnect it to power.

Don't buy extension tubes without autofocus just because you can use this workaround. Frankly, it doesn't work that well. First, without autofocus, it will be very difficult to take a picture of a living insect. Second, even with

still-life subjects, you need to regularly adjust the aperture to get sufficient depth-of-field. Additionally, because you must focus with a small aperture, the viewfinder will be very dim, making it difficult to see your subject.

As an alternative, consider using a lens with manual aperture controls, such as the Nikon 50mm f/1.8D (about $80 used). It attaches directly to Nikon cameras. You can attach it to mirrorless cameras or Canon SLRs with the proper adapter.

MACRO LENSES

Macro lenses cost about $500-$1,000, which makes them far more expensive than using diopters or extension tubes with an existing lens. However, a true macro lens offers several benefits:

- **1:1 magnification**. This means that the image on the sensor is the same size as the subject itself. Basically, it means you can get very close to the subject, so that the image on your camera sensor is the same size as the subject itself.

- **Small minimum apertures**. Depth-of-field gets *very* small when taking macro pictures. To allow the greatest depth-of-field possible, macro lenses provide maximum f/stop numbers of f/22 or higher.

- **Restricted autofocusing**. It can take several seconds to autofocus a macro lens. To reduce that time, macro lenses often provide a switch to restrict focusing to specific ranges, such as between one and two feet, and between two feet and infinity.

- **Precision manual focusing**. Macro lenses tend to have finely adjustable focus rings that make it easier to focus on close-up subjects, but would require a great deal of spinning to focus on a distant subject.

- **Ring flash availability**. . Depending on the size of your lens, the height of your flash, and the distance to your subject, your lens might cast a shadow on your subject when using a flash mounted to your camera. A ring flash mounted to the front of the macro lens eliminates shadows and provides a more even light. Ring flashes are discussed later in this chapter.

- **Infinity focus**. When you add extension tubes or diopters to a standard lens, you lose the ability to focus on subjects in the distance. A macro lens can always focus from extreme close-up to infinity.

You can add diopters or extension tubes to a macro lens to get even closer focusing. Add too much to the macro lens, and you'll literally focus inside the lens.

When shopping for a macro lens, one aspect that you need to pay particular attention to is dust resistance. While all lenses get some dust, you don't generally notice them. However, because you tend to use macro lenses to shoot close-up subjects, the dust inside the lens can become more in focus, ruining your pictures. Before you buy a used macro lens, look for dust inside of it by looking through the lens at a light from both ends. If, and when, you get dust inside your macro lens, be prepared to spend $150-$250 to have it disassembled and professionally cleaned. While you can clean the front and rear elements yourself, disassembling a lens to clean the internal elements is a task best left to optics professionals.

GOING BEYOND 1:1

Today, there's only one lens designed to go beyond 1X (1:1) magnification: the Canon MP-E f/2.8 ($1,050). The MP-E focuses from 1X to 5X (5:1). At 5X, the subject's image on your sensor is five times larger than the subject itself. This allows you to fill the frame with even the tiniest of subjects, such as the jumping spider shown in Figure 12-3.

The MP-E lens is one of the most challenging and rewarding lenses ever made. In other words, the MP-E lens is incredibly difficult to use:

- There's no infinity focus; it won't focus on anything father than five inches away.

- Not only does it lack autofocus, but it lacks manual focus. Instead of a focusing ring, you adjust the magnification. To focus, you move your camera forward or backward (for example, by using focusing rails).

- The lens gets longer as you adjust the magnification. At 1X, it's 4 inches long, and at 5X, it's 9 inches long.

- The working distance is minimal, which scares most animals. At 1X, the front of the lens is just 5 inches from the subject. At 5X, you're two inches away.

- Light loss is extreme. At 1X, you lose two stops of light, and at 5X, you lose about 6 stops of light. In other words, if your camera would normally need a shutter speed of 1/90th, your shutter speed would need to be at about 1/25th at 1X magnification. At 5X, you would need a shutter speed of about 2.5 seconds. You will need to add a continuous light source at higher magnifications just to see your subject in the viewfinder.

- Depth-of-field is extremely shallow. You can't get an entire spider's eye in focus, even at higher f/stop numbers. This means that you will almost always need to use focus stacking, discussed later in this chapter, to combine hundreds of photos. Naturally, this makes taking pictures a very slow process.

- Diffraction reduces image quality. With conventional lenses, you can use a higher f/stop number to increase your depth-of-field.

As you move beyond 1X magnification, diffraction (a property of light) greatly reduces your image quality. Basically, at 3X magnification, anything higher than f/5.6 is unusable. At 5X magnification, you're limited to f/2.8.

Because of these challenges, and the expense, very few photographers go beyond 1X mangification. Therefore, any high-magnification pictures you make will be unique and striking.

FLASHES

As discussed in the previous section, all macro lenses have significant light loss. Additionally, the shallow depth-of-field might require you to use higher f/stop numbers, further reducing the light that reaches your sensor.

With still life, you can use a tripod and a long shutter speed. If you're photographing living

To watch a video on **macro photography,** scan the QR code or visit:

sdp.io/Macro

insects, or you want to hand-hold your camera, you can add flash to add light and allow you to use a faster shutter speed.

That's not as easy as turning on your built-in flash or connecting an external flash to your hot shoe, however. Standard flashes are designed to illuminate subjects that are farther away from the camera, and will probably not light macro subjects. Therefore, you must use either a ring flash or you can design a custom macro flash.

A ring flash, as shown in Figure 12-4, attaches directly to the front of your lens, allowing it to evenly illuminate subjects just a few inches from your camera. The ring flash must be matched to the front of the macro lens, and most lenses won't accept a ring flash.

Figure 12-3: A tiny jumping spider at 3X magnification with over 40 focus-stacked images.

To watch a video on **creating a custom macro flash,** scan the QR code or visit:

sdp.io/CustomFlash

Ring flashes show detail, but hide depth. In fact, the light tends to be downright ugly. For that reason, ring flashes are useful for people who need to precisely document small objects, such as crime scene photographers. However, they're not a good choice for those of us who wish to create more artistic photos.

Instead of a ring flash, I recommend creating a custom flash using an off-camera flash cord, a small softbox, and an inexpensive external flash. With a custom flash, you can create soft top lighting or side lighting, rather than the harsh front lighting of a ring flash. For example, to take the photo shown in Figure 12-3, I used three lights positioned directly over the spider—you can see the lights reflected in the spider's eyes. You can easily adjust your custom flash setup to create different lighting effects for different subjects. For more information and sample photos, watch the custom macro flash video.

FOCUSING RAILS

Focusing at extreme magnifications is difficult, even when your subject is still life. Of course, you can use the focusing ring on your lens to adjust your focus. However, it's often difficult to focus precisely enough—particularly if you're not working with a true macro lens.

Instead of focusing with your lens, focusing rails ($50-$250) move your camera forward and backward in tiny increments. This is particularly useful when you want to get as close as possible to your subject—simply set your lens to the minimum focusing distance, and then inch your camera forward until the subject is in focus. Focusing rails connect between your tripod head and your camera body.

My advice: don't buy focusing rails until you discover that you need them.

MACRO TECHNIQUES

The closer you get to a subject, the harder it becomes to get sharp pictures. Use these techniques to prevent your macro pictures from being shaky or blurry:

Figure 12-4: Macro lenses and ring flashes provide the ultimate in close-up capabilities.

- **Use a tripod**. All still-life macro photography should be done with a heavy tripod. The need to use a high f/ stop number (which reduces your shutter speed), combined with the need for precise focusing, makes hand-holding impractical. If your macro lens supports image stabilization, that can help, but camera shake will still be a problem close-up. If you must hand-hold your lens, such as when photographing wildlife, use a faster shutter speed than you would otherwise.

- **Remote shutter release or timer**. Vibrations are magnified when working close up. To minimize vibrations and improve sharpness, use a remote shutter release or your camera's timer to take each picture. If your camera supports it, use mirror lock-up, too.

- **Precise focusing**. As described in Chapter 4, "Controlling Your Camera," you can use precise focusing techniques when photographing still life with your camera on a tripod. Switch to live view, and then zoom in on the portion of your subject that you need to be in focus. Then, gently adjust your focus until live view shows it as sharp.

Figure 12-5: Focus stacking combines multiple photos to create one picture (shown at the bottom) with total sharpness.

To watch a video on **macro equipment,** scan the QR code or visit:

sdp.io/MacroGear

- **Steady your subject**. Even the tiniest movements are magnified in macro photography. For example, a vent in the room will move a flower enough to make a picture blurry. Steady your subjects by clipping them to solid objects. To reduce the effect of wind, shoot early in the morning, or bring flowers and insects inside when possible.

FOCUS STACKING

Sometimes, even choosing the highest possible f/stop number isn't enough to get the depth-of-field that you need, especially if you want to compose your picture with your subject at an interesting angle to the camera. One way to overcome this limitation is to use *focus stacking*, a technique that combines multiple pictures taken with different focus points. First, capture your focus-stacked pictures by following these steps:

1. Attach your camera to a tripod.

2. Choose aperture priority mode on your camera, and select a moderate aperture, such as f/8 or f/11.

3. Focus on the nearest object in the picture. Often, this will be the ground or part of a spider web rather than the nearest part of your subject.

4. Make note of the shutter speed your camera selects, and take your first picture.

5. Switch your camera to manual mode and select the same aperture and shutter speed as the first shot.

6. Focus slightly behind the front of your subject, so that the depth-of-field slightly overlaps with the first picture. Take the next picture.

7. Repeat the previous step until you have pictures covering the entire scene in the depth-of-field, including any objects behind your main subject.

Once you've captured your focus-stacked pictures, combine them using one of these applications:

- CombineZ (*sdp.io/CombineZ*) is free software for focus stacking. CombineZ does a great job; however, you'll definitely need to read the help files and spend a couple hours figuring out how to get the most from the software. If you can learn to use CombineZ well, you won't need anything else.

- Helicon Soft (*www.heliconsoft.com/*) makes the two most powerful applications for focus stacking: Helicon Focus and Helicon Remote. The free (but feature-limited) Helicon Focus Lite is also available. Helicon Focus performs the work of stacking the pictures with an intuitive user interface, and can even export the pictures to a very cool 3D model. If you run Helicon Remote and connect your camera to your computer, the application can automatically adjust your camera's focus and take the images you need to precisely create a stack of pictures.

- Adobe Photoshop CS4, CS5, CS6, or CC can perform focus stacking. First, open your images as layers in a single file (File | Scripts | Load Files Into Stack). Order the layers from front-to-back. Next, select and auto-align the layers (Edit | Auto-Align Layers). Finally, auto-blend the layers (Edit | Auto-Blend Layers) using the Stack Images option.

Figure 12-5 shows three photos out of a series of 17, showing the front, center, and rear of the flower in focus. For the first shot, I set my camera to f/16, focused my macro lens to its minimum focusing distance (a 1:1 magnification), and gradually moved the tripod-mounted camera closer to the flower until the closest petal was in focus. After I pressed the shutter, I manually moved the focus slightly farther away, taking 17 photos in all. I used Photoshop CS5 to combine the photos, and then manually touched up the final picture, shown at the bottom. As you can see, focus stacking provides sharpness front-to-back.

Compare how much of the first and third photos are shown in Figure 12-5. You can actually see far more of the edges of the flower in the third photo than in the final result. As you move focus farther away, the lens seems to zoom out—even when it is a prime lens. For this reason, as well as artifacts that focus stacking software can leave behind, leave extra room to crop when framing your picture.

PRACTICE

This chapter's practices help you understand different macro equipment and techniques.

- Using your favorite non-macro lenses, see how close you can focus on a subject. For zoom lenses, test them both zoomed in and zoomed out—the minimum focusing distance often changes while zooming.

- If you have extension tubes or diopters, see how close you can focus when using them in different combinations. Start with the shortest extension tube or the diopter with the least magnification, and see how much closer you can focus than without. Progress to using all your extension tubes and the highest magnification diopters.

To watch a video on **image stacking**, scan the QR code or visit:

sdp.io/FocusStacking

 Take a quiz!

sdp.io/quiz12

- Mount your camera to a tripod, and photograph something small, three-dimensional, and still, such as a toy car. Set your camera to aperture priority mode and ISO 100, and photograph it with a variety of different apertures. Start with the lowest f/stop number, and work your way to the highest f/stop number. How shallow is the depth-of-field with the lowest f/stop number? Was the depth-of-field with the highest f/stop number enough to get the entire subject in focus? What was the shutter speed with the highest f/stop number? Were any of your pictures shaky?

- Try taking a macro photo with your camera's built-in flash, or with an on-camera flash. How does the flash look?

- Again using a tripod and a small, three-dimension subject, use focus stacking to get the entire subject in focus. Were the results sharper than without using focus stacking? How long did it take you, in total?

Most of the world is covered in water, and much of the world's beauty is hidden beneath the surface. Whereas you might spend hours searching for a brightly-colored bird in a forest, in a tropical ocean, you'll be surrounded by living color. Underwater photography isn't just about wildlife, though. In the water, living coral reefs become your landscapes, and the sunlight filtering through the water becomes your portrait lighting.

Underwater photography is the most challenging type of photography. You must leave behind those basic elements of life that you've come to take for granted: walking, talking, gravity, stability, and even the air you breathe. Much of what you've learned about photography thus far will change, too: water bends light, changes colors, and destroys cameras.

It's an entirely different world underwater. How could you possibly resist photographing it?

EQUIPMENT

You'll need special equipment to take a camera underwater. You have a few different choices. In order from least expensive (and lowest quality) to most expensive (and highest quality), your options are:

- **Waterproof bags**. For less than $10, you can buy waterproof bags designed to house cameras of any size. These can work, but it can be difficult to push the buttons, and touch screens won't work at all. If you tear the bag on coral, or if you fail to seal it properly, you could destroy your camera.

- **Disposable waterproof cameras**. Inexpensive film cameras cost about $7 for 24 shots. Add another $10 or so for film developing and scanning, and you'll have digital images for very little investment. This is a good choice for casual vacation photos.

- **Rigid waterproof camera phone or point-and-shoot housing**. For about $100, you can buy a waterproof housing for your camera phone or point-and-shoot camera. These provide instant digital results and better quality than the disposable cameras, with the option of recording video, but you'll need to take care of the housing to protect your camera.

- **Sports cameras**. Sports cameras, such as the GoPro, cost $200-$400. These compact and durable cameras can go almost anywhere, including underwater. I wouldn't recommend buying one solely for underwater photography, but they're a great choice if you want one for other reasons.

- **Dedicated interchangeable lens underwater cameras**. The Nikonos film cameras ($150 used) and the digital Nikon AW1 ($750 new) are designed to be used underwater without any extra housing. If you want a mirrorless camera and you're serious about underwater photography, the AW1 is a perfect choice.

- **DSLR housings**. For the ultimate in control and quality, use a DSLR housing designed for your camera. They're big, heavy, and clumsy, and you'll spend $1,000 to $5,000, but they're your only option if you can't be without your DSLR for a moment. The photo on the cover of this book was taken with a 5D Mark II and an Aquatica housing.

This book focuses on underwater photography techniques, rather than equipment. For detailed information about the latest underwater gear, including sample photos and specific recommendations, read the "Underwater Photography Buying Guide" in *Tony Northrup's Photography Buying Guide* available at *sdp.io/buybg*.

TESTING THE EQUIPMENT

Before your first outing, do what's known as a "tissue test." Put a tissue in your housing instead of your camera, and take it underwater—as close to your planned dive depth as possible. When you return above land, make sure the tissue is dry. If it's wet, then the housing didn't seal correctly. You might hate wasting a dive, but you'd hate it even more if your housing failed underwater with your camera in it.

If your housing passes this test, mount the camera in the housing and spend some time practicing with the buttons on dry land. Even if you're familiar with all your camera's features, the buttons are in slightly different places on the camera housing, and you won't want to spend the time figuring things out during a dive.

PREPARING FOR THE DIVE

Before your first dive, read your housing's manual. Seriously, I hate reading manuals too, but if you setup your housing wrong, your camera is going to be soaked.

First, prepare your camera so you don't have to remove the camera from the housing during your outing. Set the ISO and shutter speeds, as discussed more thoroughly in the technique section. Make sure the battery is charged (you'll need to use live view) and the memory card is empty (you'll need to take lots of pictures). If you need it, attach a diopter to your lens.

After inserting your camera into the housing, remove all o-rings and rinse them off. If there is any sand or dirt on the o-ring, water will get through. Once the o-ring is clean, rub a bit of silicon lube on the o-ring, and slip it back into the housing. Close the housing. If your housing is translucent, visually examine the o-ring to make sure it's in place and properly sealed.

Finally, verify that all buttons and levers connect properly to your camera. If you're using a DSLR, verify that the zoom ring attachment is connected properly.

TECHNIQUE

If you've ever taken landscape pictures on a hazy day, you'll notice that objects in the distance become faded and gray. That effect is far more exaggerated underwater—anything more than a couple of feet away will almost completely disappear. All you can do is minimize the amount of water between you and the subject by getting get very, very close—within a foot.

I took the picture in Figure 13-1 more than a decade ago with an underwater film camera. The snorkeler is only a foot or two in front of me, which is why you can see the blue in his flippers and the yellow in his float. The dolphin in the background is perhaps ten feet farther away, but it's blurry and all color except blue is completely washed out.

SWIMMING

Several non-photography skills separate the good and great underwater photographers:

- **Swimming and diving**. You need to be able to get at the same level as the fish

Figure 13-1: To get sharp pictures, stay close to your subject (shot on film).

you're photographing. Therefore, you must know how to dive efficiently. You also need to know how to move through the water swiftly; ideally, you will swim alongside fish, rather than coming at them from the top, front, or bottom. Especially with larger aquatic housings, simply holding the camera can make swimming more difficult. Avoid kicking at the surface of the water, as this will scare fish. Also avoid kicking near sand, as the sand will obscure your view. Avoiding coral takes some practice, too, especially when the surf is up.

- **Marine biology.** Many of the most amazing subjects, such as sharks and octopus, hide in caves. Knowledge of their habits and habitats will allow you to find the animals and photograph them without disturbing them. If you don't have this knowledge, a SCUBA or snorkeling guide can help.

- **Local geography and weather.** It takes years to find the locations most rich with life and when the water will be clear enough for photography. I always hire a knowledgeable guide.

FRAMING

Most housings allow you to frame your picture using either the optical viewfinder or the LCD screen. I find it much easier to use the LCD screen, however. When you factor in your goggles and the housing, your eye will always be at least several inches from the optical viewfinder. Also, it's hard to keep the optical viewfinder steady, especially near the surface of the water.

Finally, because you need to get as close as possible to your subjects, you often need to hold the camera at arm's length. If you need to hold your camera at an odd angle, you might not even be able to see the viewfinder. In these circumstances, you'll need to shoot blind (a technique that gets better with practice, especially if you review your shots after). Use a

wide-angle lens, take lots of pictures, and hope some of them include your subject—you can crop the photos down once you're dry.

If you're shooting with a wide-angle lens, try to include the surface of the water in shots, as shown in Figure 13-2 The sunlight streaming through the surface creates a beautiful effect, and it gives the viewer a sense of depth. When snorkeling, this will require you to hold the camera low and angle it parallel to the surface or slightly upward. To get more depth when snorkeling, take a deep breath, dive underwater, and then take your pictures. If you have a problem diving low enough, let some air out of your lungs to reduce your buoyancy. When you surface, exhale in a rapid burst to blow the water out of your snorkel.

If you have trouble coordinating the snorkeling and camera, consider skin diving. With skin diving, you wear flippers and a mask, but skip the snorkel. The snorkel isn't useful below the surface, anyway, and if you spend most of your time diving, the snorkel just complicates your breathing.

Even if you can't angle the camera upwards enough to include the surface of the water, holding the camera more parallel to the ground shows more of the underwater landscape, providing a foreground, middleground, and background—critical elements for an

Figure 13-2: Include the surface of the water in your shots by swimming low and pointing the camera back up (21mm, f/14, 1/320th, ISO 800).

interesting picture. This perspective also allows you to show the eyes of wildlife, as Figure 13-3 illustrates.

If you switch between shooting over and under the water, or you want a shot with the lens half submerged, you'll discover that water drops on the housing will ruin your pictures. To reduce the presence of water drops, apply Rain-X (typically used for car windshields) to the outside of the housing in front of the lens. Use a smaller aperture to maximize depth-of-field for over/under shots, because the water will make one or the other seem out of focus.

Tip: If you're really committed to getting the perfect over/under shot, use a neutral density filter to balance the brightness above the water.

FOCUSING

The downside to using the LCD screen is that, with some cameras, focusing is slower. To help this, place the focusing point on a well-lit, high contrast part of the subject. Some strobes have built-in focusing lights that always stay on, and that extra light can really improve your camera's focusing speed.

Nonetheless, because both you and your subjects are constantly moving, focus will almost always be a bit off. Using a higher f/stop number and a wide-angle lens will increase your depth-of-field, making focusing less critical. If

you're using a wide-angle lens and your subject is roughly the same distance from you, don't bother focusing between each shot. The focus will be close enough, and taking the time to refocus would make you miss too many shots.

LIGHTING

Throughout this book, I've reminded you to take pictures in the morning and evening. Well, good news—you now have a way to kill those afternoon hours. When you're underwater, you need all the light you can get. So, the best times are when the sun is bright and directly overhead.

Sunlight penetrates the top few feet of the water, so you can always snorkel without strobes. In fact, you're generally okay using natural lighting to about 40 or 50 feet—sometimes deeper if it's a sunny day and the water is clear.

If you go any deeper than 50 feet, or if you plan to shoot under ledges or in caves, you'd better bring a pair of strobes attached to the left and right sides of your camera. Two strobes provide more even lighting, just as they do above ground. Strobes are heavy and bulky, though. Combined with the weight of your underwater housing, you need help just getting your gear on and off the boat.

Unlike shooting on the surface, using a single strobe underwater causes *backscatter*, which reflects light off of particles directly back to the camera. Backscatter can ruin pictures taken with a single strobe positioned above the camera. Even with two strobes, try to do without them if the water is murky.

CAMERA SETTINGS

When shooting underwater, start by keeping your camera in shutter priority (Tv or S) with a shutter speed of 1/200th. That should be enough

Figure 13-3: Hold the camera parallel to the surface to show the eyes of wildlife (35mm, f/8, 1/45th, ISO 400).

to freeze the motion of fish and to prevent the inevitable camera shake caused by the constantly moving water.

Start by setting your ISO speed to 400. The higher the ISO, the more noise there will be in your picture. However, getting enough light is always a challenge underwater. If you're using strobes, higher ISO speeds will increase the exposure of the background and reduce the electrical draw on your strobes—shortening recycling time. If your shutter speed is too low at ISO 400, if you want more depth-of-field, or if you want your strobes to recycle faster, double the ISO. If your shutter speed is faster than 1/500th, lower the ISO speed to ISO 400 or ISO 200 to reduce noise.

Auto white balance should work with your camera, but pictures will still have a very strong blue-green tint. You can also try setting the white balance to cloudy skies. For best results, however, bring a laminated white or gray card and use it to set your color temperature while underwater. If you shoot raw, you can simply take a picture of the card, and use it to set the color temperature for all your pictures; Adobe Lightroom makes it simple to apply a single setting to all your pictures at once. You'll almost certainly need to do some adjusting on the computer to get the color and contrast right, however. Underwater pictures always require some editing.

Even if you typically shoot JPG, switch to raw for your underwater photography. The white balance will almost certainly be way off, the exposure will be all over the place, and contrast will be low. Shooting raw allows you to adjust those elements of the picture above land, so you can focus on your environment while you're underwater.

UNDERWATER PORTRAITS

Water brings striking qualities to portraits. As the light shines through the ripples on the surface, the light becomes ethereal and casts complex, constantly changing shadows. As shown in Figure 13-4, being submerged adds a dream-like movement to hair and fabric that simply isn't possible above the surface.

Underwater portraits have become more common, especially with the "Trash the Dress" movement, in which brides don their wedding dresses after the ceremony and dive into a pool or lake. If getting a good picture of someone in a studio is a challenge, imagine dealing with the different way light passes through water, the constant motion, the difficulty most people have posing in water, and not being able to breathe. Nonetheless, the most difficult shots are always the most rewarding, and that applies for underwater portraiture as well.

You'll need very clear water to keep the picture contrasty. If you're shooting in a natural body of water, you'll need to plan the shoot around the weather to choose a morning with no wind. A better idea is to use a pool. Even pools aren't always clear, so be sure that the pool is well-maintained with clear water. Direct sunlight is best for shooting in a pool.

Pesky models often want to breathe on a regular basis, so you'll need to shoot in bursts between dives. Take this opportunity to review the pictures and show some to the model. Posing underwater is very unnatural, and it's important for models to see interim pictures so they can bend and twist the right way.

Figure 13-4: Water adds a flowing motion to clothes and hair (20mm, f/4.5, 1/90th, ISO 400).

To watch a video on **editing underwater photos,** scan the QR code or visit:

sdp.io/EditingUnderwater

Take a quiz!

sdp.io/Quiz13

Air bubbles present a challenge. If a model exhales underwater, the bubbles cover her face and often take a few seconds to move to the surface. If the model needs to remove the air from her lungs to dive deep, she should do it before she enters the water. All but the most graceful dives will cover the model in bubbles, so entering the water smoothly and slowly is generally the best idea.

Wedding dresses are a perfect choice for an underwater shoot, because the lacy fabric flows with the water, achieving a grace not possible on the surface. Reds and yellows really pop against the cool underwater colors, too, as shown by the chapter cover. Makeup is a challenge, but a makeup artist can apply waterproof cosmetics that can hold up well when submerged. Alternatively, you can apply makeup digitally in post-processing.

The walls of a pool do not make a great backdrop. However, you have three better alternatives:

- **The surface of the water**. As shown by the book cover, the surface of the water provides a dynamic backdrop and allows you to use the sun for backlighting. As the photographer, you'll need to dive four or five feet underwater and then turn to face the surface. The model will need to dive one to two feet underwater.

- **The floor of the pool**. Pool floors reflect the ever-changing pattern of light caused by

sunlight shining through surface ripples. For best results, you want several feet between yourself and the model, and several feet between the model and the pool floor. Therefore, your model will need to dive deep, and then turn around to face you.

- **Fabric**. Just as you would in a studio, you can use fabric backdrops to cover the floor or walls of a pool. Bring far more fabric than you think you might need; the wide-angle lenses typically used for underwater photography show a great deal more background than traditional portrait lenses. Also bring weights to hold the fabric in place so that it does not float away.

If someone isn't a great swimmer, put a fabric backdrop over the steps of a pool, have the model lie next to the steps, and submerge his face just below the surface of the water. Having the model hold still makes the photographer's job much easier, too. It also allows you to get closer to the model's face, reducing the contrast-killing water between the lens and the model.

While you might be able to use bright sunlight streaming through the surface of the water, you can also add your own light. On-camera underwater strobes add front lighting, and you can use a boom to position standard strobes above the surface of the water. Be exceptionally careful when dealing with high-voltage lights near water, however.

Underwater portraits require significant post-processing. Skin tones tend to look very blue, and water seems to highlight blemishes and birthmarks. Bubbles often appear in awkward places, such as over someone's forehead. If you use a wide-angle lens underwater, be prepared to repair some of the distortion in Photoshop. Body parts near the edges of the frame will become extremely lengthened. You can use this for creative effect, but most people won't be pleased with clown feet and artificially thickened thighs.

PRACTICE

This chapter's practices help you become more comfortable in the water, use your camera in its underwater housing, and understand how light behaves underwater.

■ Go to your local pool and practice diving from the surface and swimming 4-10 feet underwater. To simulate the experience of holding a camera underwater, practice swimming without using your hands. Roll over to face the surface and pull your body upright as if to take a picture horizontally.

■ With your camera, practice diving 4-10 feet underwater and shooting horizontally so that you capture both the floor of the pool and the surface of the water in the picture.

■ Get your SCUBA certification. Even if you don't plan to use your camera with SCUBA, the lessons you learn about handling yourself underwater will make underwater photography much easier.

■ If you can swim outdoors, pay attention to the way the water passes through the surface. Notice how quickly the light disappears as you get deeper.

■ Practice your underwater portraiture by bringing a friend who is a strong swimmer into the pool to be your model. After you both get comfortable in the water, add fun outfits and props. Vary your positions so that you are above, below, and beside the model.

AFTERWORD

First, congratulations on finishing this book! A reader and teacher, Jared Frazin, suggested I repeat three things I most want you to remember:

■ Patience, practice, and persistence pay off.

■ Make pictures; don't take pictures.

■ Capture what you feel, not what you see.

I'd hate to waste the rest of this page, so here are some more thoughts. Skills are learned through study and practice. Talent is something you're born with. Photography is a skill, not a talent. Any passionate person can be an amazing photographer, but none of us start that way.

Like almost everything in life, photography rewards energy. The more passionate you are, the more energy you have. Studying photography and preparing for a shot won't always be as fun as watching TV or browsing the web, but it's far more rewarding. When you feel like you've run out of energy, push yourself a little farther. That builds constitution. Constitution is humanity's most important trait.

The best way to learn is to teach others. We provide one opportunity at our private readers' group (*sdp.io/fb*). Answering questions and giving people feedback on their pictures every day will make you a better photographer.

Most important, teach children photography. Children learn in a different way than adults; the lessons become part of who they are. The world needs more people who find light amazing, who notice every animal around them, and who can isolate beauty in an ugly scene.

I know this book isn't perfect. If you find a mistake, or you think of a way we can improve the book, please email me at *tony@northrup.org* and I'll fix it in the next update. If we've helped you make better pictures, it would really help us if you suggest the book to your friends. Five-star reviews on Amazon and iBooks mean the world to us, too.

Index/Glossary

Dutch angle (pp. 21-22). A compositional technique involving rotating the camera to create an image that seems for fun and candid.

dynamic range (pp. 66-69, 85, 103-104, 179, 193, 207-213). The difference between the darkest part of a picture and the brightest part of a picture. Most cameras have a dynamic range of 8-12 stops, but the human eye has a dynamic range of about 20 stops.

exposure (pp. 65-73). The camera settings that determine the digital camera sensor's sensitivity and how much light it will capture. The exposure consists of the aperture (such as f/5.6), the shutter speed (such as 1/60th), the ISO (such as ISO 200), and how much flash was added to the scene.

exposure compensation (pp. 65-67). A camera setting that increases or decreases the exposure to produce a brighter or darker picture. Use exposure compensation when your camera's *auto-exposure* produces a picture that is too dark or too bright.

extender (p. 162, 169). Also known as a teleconverter. An extender is an optical attachment connected between the lens and camera body that increases the lens' effective focal length. A 1.4x extender zooms in an additional 1.4 times, making a 300mm f/4 lens effectively 420mm f/5.6. For detailed information, refer to the Photography Buying Guide at *http://sdp.io/buybg*.

feminine pose (pp. 110-111). The subject tilts their head towards the higher shoulder.

fill flash (pp. 5-6, 39-41, 48, 98-99, 132, 145). A secondary source of light used to reduce shadows caused by the *main light*.

film. A non-reusable memory card for use in vintage cameras. Requires developing and scanning before your friends can comment on the pictures.

flaring (p. 36). The introduction of lens flare, which are roughly circular shaped lights in the picture caused by bright light reflecting off of internal lens elements.

flash (pp. 5, 39-48, 120-125). A bright light, typically built into the camera or attached to the top of the camera, which fires at the exact moment you take your picture to add lighting. *Strobes* are similar to flashes, but people tend to use the term strobe to mean external flashes.

flyaways. Stray hairs that stand out from the head.

focal length (pp. 58-63). A lens' zoom. Wide-angle lenses have a short focal length, such as 24mm, and show you a great deal of the scene. Telephoto lenses have a long focal length, such as 200mm, and show you a small portion of a scene.

focal plane. The two-dimensional plane at the lens' focus distance. Anything in front of or behind the focal plane will be slightly out of focus. See *depth-of-field*.

focus and recompose (pp. 51-52). A technique for controlling the focal point of a picture with almost any camera. Place the focal point in the center of the picture, and then partially depress the shutter button. Recompose the picture so that the focal point is off-center, and fully depress the shutter button to take the picture.

full-frame. A DSLR with a sensor the same size as 35mm film. You can use standard 35mm lenses with a full-frame DSLR and not lose any of the picture. Refer to the Photography Buying Guide at *http://sdp.io/buybg*.

grid (pp. 123-124). Grids, also known as honeycombs, narrow a beam of light, reducing the amount of light that spills.

hair light (pp. 120-121). A narrow beam of light that shines on a subject's hair. Hair lights are most commonly used with dark-haired subjects to add shape and texture to the hair and to separate the hair from the background.

High Dynamic Range (HDR) (pp. 207-213). A photographic process that combines multiple photos of a single subject taken at different exposures. HDR allows you to capture more detail in highlight and shadow areas than would be possible with a single exposure.

honeycomb. See *grid*.

image stabilization (pp. 61-63). A camera or lens feature that compensates for shaky hands. With image stabilization, you can hand-hold pictures two, three, or even four stops longer than normal. Also refer to the Photography Buying Guide at *http://sdp. io/buybg*.

ISO (pp. 63-65, 82-83, 89, 146, 151, 156). ISO, refers to the International Organization for Standardization. Photographers refer to a camera's sensitivity simply as "ISO," pronounced *eye-so* (really).

main light (pp. 32-33, 120-121). Also known as the *key light*, this is the primary source of light in your picture.

manual mode (pp. 55-75). A mode that disables your camera's autoexposure system, requiring you to specify the aperture and shutter speed.

masculine pose (pp. 110-111). The subject holds his or her head straight or tilts it towards the lower shoulder, giving them a more powerful stance.

megapixel. A million *pixels* that make up a picture. Refer to the Photography Buying Guide at *http://sdp.io/buybg*.

metering (pp. 65-73). The process of determining the correct exposure for a photo by measuring the brightness of a scene.

middle gray or middle grey (pp. 65-67). Also known as 18% gray, a neutral shade half-way between black and white.

monolight (pp. 120-125). Large, powerful lights that plug into the wall. Monolights can be independently adjusted. Monolights allow you to easily attach softboxes, beauty dishes, and other modifiers.

monopod (pp. 145, 150-151). A camera support, like a tripod, but with a single leg.

negative space (p. 25). Everything in an image not consumed by the subject.

noise. Incorrectly colored pixels that make your picture look less clear and vibrant. See *ISO*.

pixel. Picture elements, or more simply, colored dots that make up a picture.

RAW (pp. 72-73). A file format that captures every piece of information recorded by your digital camera's sensor. RAW files consume far more space than JPG files; however, they can produce higher quality images, especially if you need to adjust the white balance or exposure on your computer.

recycling or recycle time (pp. 89-90, 146, 156, 231). The time it takes for a flash or strobe to recovery between shots.

reflector (pp. 44-45, 97-102). Can refer to either a circular dish that attaches directly to a strobe or a large reflective panel used to bounce light.

rim light (pp. 98-99, 107). A secondary source of light shining from behind the subject that highlights the edge of a subject and filters through hair. Rim lights are useful for showing the shape of a subject and separating it from the background. See also *backlighting*.

rule of thirds (pp. 13-14). A compositional guideline to position the subject, and key elements of the picture, one-third of the way through the frame.

short lighting (p. 42, 122). A lighting technique characterized by having the main light directed to the side of the model's face farthest from the camera. Short lighting illuminates less of the visible part of the face than *broad lighting*.

shutter speed (pp. 60-63). The length of time the shutter stays open, exposing the camera's digital sensor to light through the lens.

snoot (p.121, 127). Snoots create a small tunnel of light. Snoots are most often used as hair lights, though they can be used any time you need to create a small spot of light.

soft boxes (pp. 43, 80-81, 102, 106, 115, 121-125). Soft boxes do a much better job of diffusing and softening light than umbrellas. The bigger the soft box, the softer the light will be.

spot metering (pp. 66-69, 153). A camera exposure mode that chooses the exposure by using the brightness at a very small area in either the center or focus point of the picture.

stop (pp. 71-72). A measurement of light levels. One stop doubles or halves the amount of light.

strobe. Another name for a *flash* or *monolight*—a bright light that fires at the exact moment you take your picture to add lighting.

teleconverter. See *extender.*

tripod (pp. 63, 145, 150-151, 189-205)**.** A camera support with three legs. Tripods produce sharper pictures by eliminating camera shake caused by hand-holding pictures.

vignetting (p. 5). A darkening at the corners of a picture, often caused by filters or poor quality lenses.

warm. Colors in the orange and red portion of the spectrum. See *color temperature.*

wide-open. Setting the aperture to its widest setting—the lowest f/stop number possible.

white balance. See *color temperature.*

zoom lens. A lens that uses moving optical elements to change the *focal length.*